NEIGHBORHOOD WATCH

Although racism has plagued the American justice system since the nation's colonial beginnings, private White Americans are taking matters into their own hands. From racist 911 calls and hoaxes to grassroots voter suppression and vigilante "self-defense," concerted efforts are made every day by private citizens to exclude Black Americans from schools, neighborhoods, and positions of power. *Neighborhood Watch* examines the specific ways people police America's color line to protect "White spaces." The book charts how these actions too often result in harassment, arrest, injury, or death, yet typically go unchecked. Instead, these actions are promoted and encouraged by legislatures looking to expand racially discriminatory laws, a police system designed to respond with force to any frivolous report of Black "mischief," and a Supreme Court that has abdicated its role in rejecting police abuse. To combat these realities, *Neighborhood Watch* offers preliminary recommendations for reform, including changes to the "maximum policing" state, increased accountability for civilians who abuse emergency response systems, and proposals to demilitarize the color line.

Shawn E. Fields is a legal scholar, civil rights attorney, and criminal justice reform advocate. He has represented dozens of clients challenging unconstitutional criminal detentions, and currently teaches Criminal Procedure and Criminal Law at Campbell University School of Law. He previously opened the first refugee rights law office in East Africa, representing over 500 refugees in status determination hearings. Shawn lives in Raleigh, North Carolina, with his wife and their two children.

Neighborhood Watch

POLICING WHITE SPACES IN AMERICA

SHAWN E. FIELDS
Campbell University School of Law

CAMBRIDGE
UNIVERSITY PRESS

CAMBRIDGE
UNIVERSITY PRESS

University Printing House, Cambridge CB2 8BS, United Kingdom

One Liberty Plaza, 20th Floor, New York, NY 10006, USA

477 Williamstown Road, Port Melbourne, VIC 3207, Australia

314–321, 3rd Floor, Plot 3, Splendor Forum, Jasola District Centre,
New Delhi – 110025, India

103 Penang Road, #05–06/07, Visioncrest Commercial, Singapore 238467

Cambridge University Press is part of the University of Cambridge.

It furthers the University's mission by disseminating knowledge in the pursuit of
education, learning, and research at the highest international levels of excellence.

www.cambridge.org
Information on this title: www.cambridge.org/9781108840064
DOI: 10.1017/9781108878661

First published 2022

A catalogue record for this publication is available from the British Library.

ISBN 978-1-108-84006-4 Hardback
ISBN 978-1-108-79350-6 Paperback

Cambridge University Press has no responsibility for the persistence or accuracy of
URLs for external or third-party internet websites referred to in this publication
and does not guarantee that any content on such websites is, or will remain,
accurate or appropriate.

For Noël
The love of my life

Contents

Acknowledgments

This book has been a labor of love many years in the making, and it simply would not exist without the support and encouragement of countless individuals and institutions. There are too many selfless, wonderful people in my life to thank for making this book a reality, but a few deserve special mention here. My research assistant, MaryAnne Hamilton, who worked tirelessly on this project and prodded me gently to the finish line. My editor, Matt Gallaway, a man with clarity of vision and who appears to never sleep. Institutional support from Campbell Law School, and from Deans Rich Leonard and Sarah Ludington, who gave this junior faculty member room to run. Professor Roger Manus, whose decades of work on behalf of civil rights and racial justice continue to inspire me. The dozens and dozens of people who have offered wisdom and guidance along the way, including Tuneen Chisolm, Bobbi Jo Boyd, Tony Ghiotto, Marcus Gadson, Lucas Osborn, Arleen Myers, Sara Acosta, Tracey Maclin, Ken Simons, Don Dripps, Jordan Barry, Dov Fox, Mila Sohoni, Joseph Blocher, and participants in the SEALS New Scholar Panels, including Mitch Crusto, Missy Lonegrass, Cynthia Alkon, Pat Metze, and Raff Donelson. My wife, coparent, partner, and confidante, Noël Harlow, whose patience, love, and support made this book possible. My children, Jordan and Sage, who inspire me to be my best self. My parents, Roger and Brenda Fields, who have always believed in me, no matter what.

A Note on Language

Any discussion on race is fraught with questions about labels, language, and word choice. Common discussions in newsrooms across the country in the wake of 2020's "Summer of Racial Reckoning" centered around whether to capitalize "black" and "white" as racial designations, when and whether to use the terms "people of color" or "African Americans" in lieu of another designation, and what objectives are promoted or frustrated in doing so. For purposes of this book, I have chosen to capitalize both "Black" and "White" and, with rare exception as dictated by context, to use the terms "Black" and "White" rather than "person of color," "African American," "Caucasian American," or any other label. Several considerations drive these decisions.

First, capitalizing "Black" and "White" recognizes a form of collective ownership of these artificially created groupings. Race is a social construct, and the terms "black" and "white" to refer to skin color obviously refer not to facts of color or characteristics of biology, but to historically significant and highly artificial sorting. In other words, "racial identities were not discovered but created, and the capital letter conferred to these designations" helps to highlight "the artificiality of race."[1] In one sense, then, the capital letter forces society to "take responsibility" for these artificial, dangerous, and absurd designations – to do otherwise would allow "black" and "white" to "disguise themselves as common nouns and adjectives."[2]

Another reason, and perhaps the one most important to this book, is that "Black" and "White" people are perceived as such by others, must respond to those perceptions and reactions accordingly, and thus have some collective shared experience not just as a person but as a "Black" or "White" person. Here, it makes sense to deal with each designation separately. As New York University Professor Kwame Anthony Appiah observes, "a good reason to capitalize the racial designation 'black' is precisely that black is not a natural category, but a social one – a collective

---

[1] Sally Haslanger, *A Social Constructionist Analysis of Race,* in Revisiting Race in a Genomic Age 56–57 (2008).
[2] Kwame Anthony Appiah, *The Case for Capitalizing the B in Black,* The Atlantic (June 18, 2020), https://www.theatlantic.com/ideas/archive/2020/06/time-to-capitalize-blackand-white/613159/.

identity – with a particular history."[3] While the "Black experience" is not monolithic and generalizing to any degree creates certain risks, the particular experience of Black people as *Black people* in this country, and to some degree the world, justifies this capital designation.

What is that collective identity, that shared experience? For the purpose of this book, I speak narrowly about the shared experience in America of Black people being perceived primarily – if not only – as "Black" by those around them and being forced to respond to those often negative, dismissive, fearful, and violent perceptions. The capital letter then refers to the collective primacy of "race" and "Black" as the dominant perceived feature driving much of the interaction between "Black America" and "White America." As detailed in these pages, when a neighbor spots an unfamiliar Black person walking down a residential neighborhood at night or a police officer pulls over a Black driver, they do not see *a person* – they see a *Black person*. The overriding importance of that socially and historically constructed racial designation, shared collectively by millions in this country, justifies the capital "B."

It is for this reason that I do not use the term "African American," which refers most accurately to Black citizens of the United States of America. While it may be important to refer specifically to this group in some contexts, "African American" is underinclusive in the racial fear context. For the racially fearful, it does not matter whether the Black person they see is from California, Canada, or Cameroon. All that matters is skin color. Indeed, "the NYPD officers who shot Amadou Diallo, a Guinean immigrant, did not care whether their victim's foods, languages, music, and religious traditions were similar to those of most African Americans," and neither did they care about his citizenship status. All that mattered was that he was Black.

I also largely avoid the term "people of color," because that term tends either to be overinclusive or at least overly generalizes the unique experiences of different marginalized groups in this nation's history. This book explores the specific fear-based prejudice faced by Black people in America as a result of a uniquely Black, centuries-long history of pernicious mythmaking. For four centuries, Black people in this country have been derisively and inaccurately labeled as inherently violent, "bestial," and prone to criminality, and have endured unique horrors that shaped and perpetuated these stereotypes. Slavery, Jim Crow, convict leasing, segregation, redlining, and mass incarceration all affected solely or primarily Black individuals, and the implicit biases driving today's racially fearful policing of the "White space" spring from this unique experience. In contrast, the horrors inflicted on Native American communities, while no less deserving of recognition or reprobation, have not lent themselves to the same sort of contemporary response in Native American-White interactions. Likewise, Latinx and Asian American and Pacific Islander communities have borne the brunt of their own unique experiences with racism

---

[3]   *Id.*

and continue to suffer the indignities, insecurities, and physical violence that is the product of these histories. But those histories also are unique and different from the historical and contemporary experience of Black people, which is the focus of this book.

That leaves perhaps the most controversial choice made in this book: to capitalize "White." Some who view capitalizing "Black" as a reclaiming of power and dignity stripped away over centuries view capitalizing "White" as an unjust and undeserved conferral of equality that "should be awarded only after white supremacy has been rolled back."[4] I find more problematic another common justification for not capitalizing "white": that Black people describe and think of themselves as Black but "people in the white majority don't think of themselves in that way."[5]

Whether that is true or not – a dubious proposition – this "white majority" argument encapsulates so much of the problem driving this book. To those in dominant, powerful societal demographic groups – White people, men, etc. – they are afforded the luxury of not thinking of themselves as a particular identity different from others. Indeed, to not capitalize "white" in some ways strikes me as a supremacist act in that it casts Whiteness as normal, neutral, standard, and thus non-Whiteness as different, abnormal, out of place. It is this sense that Black people in America are different and out of place – physically, metaphorically, psychologically – that allows so much of the implicit racial fear discussed in these pages to flourish. Thus, at least in this book, it is important to discuss the relationships between and the actions of "White" people as White people towards "Black" people as Black people. Both view each other through this prism and behave accordingly, even if one group may have the greater luxury not to be reminded of their own skin color and its marginalized place in America.

---

[4] *Id.; see also* Anne Price, *Spell it with a Capital "B"*, Insight Center for Community Economic Development (October 1, 2019), https://insightcced.medium.com/spell-it-with-a-capital-b-9eab112d759a.

[5] Luke Visconti, *Why Capitalizing the "B" in Black Still Matters for Cultural Competence and Accurate Representation*, DiversityInc. (August 18, 2020), https://www.diversityinc.com/why-the-b-in-black-is-capitalized-at-diversityinc/.

Introduction

A Personal Protection Agency

Christian Cooper loves birdwatching. He became fascinated with birds at the age of ten after building a feeder as a 4-H project and watching the various species visit his backyard.[6] In college, Christian served as president of the Harvard Ornithological Society.[7] He currently serves on the Board of Directors of New York City Audubon.[8] He has appeared in birdwatching documentaries,[9] often while exploring an area of New York's Central Park known as "The Ramble," a wild 36-acre woodland that is home to more than 230 species of birds.[10] Christian Cooper also happens to be Black.

On Memorial Day 2020, Christian was birdwatching in the Ramble when he happened upon a woman walking her dog off-leash. City regulations require dogs to be leashed in the Ramble, both to protect the years-long restoration project creating the sanctuary and to minimize disruptions to wildlife, including birds.[11] Avid birdwatchers report regular violations of this rule and often record off-leash dogs to support enforcement.[12] Christian recorded the dog he saw that day. What happened next made national headlines.

In a video later posted to social media by Christian's sister, Christian asked the dog's owner, Amy Cooper (no relation to Christian), to leash the dog.[13] She refused

6 Sarah Maslin Nir, *The Bird Watcher, That Incident and His Feelings on the Woman's Fate*, NEW YORK TIMES (May 27, 2020), www.nytimes.com/2020/05/27/nyregion/amy-cooper-christian-central-park-video.html.

7 Royce Dunmore, *Christian Cooper: Everything to Know About Man Who Exposed Central Park "Karen,"* NEWSONE (May 26, 2020), https://newsone.com/3948383/christian-cooper-everything-to-know-exposed-central-park-karen/.

8 Nir, *supra* note 6.

9 *See, e.g., Documentary Footage Shows Christian Cooper Talking about Birdwatching in Central Park*, MIAMI HERALD (May 28, 2020, 9:17 a.m.), https://www.miamiherald.com/news/nation-world/national/article243050646.html.

10 *The Ramble*, CENTRAL PARK CONSERVANCY, www.centralparknyc.org/attractions/the-ramble.

11 *Id.*

12 Allie Yang, *Christian Cooper Accepts Apology from Woman at Center of Central Park Confrontation*, ABC NEWS (May 28, 2020). abcnews.go.com/US/christian-cooper-accepts-apology-woman-center-central-park/story?id=70926679.

13 Melody Cooper (@melodyMcooper), Twitter (May 25, 2020, 1:03 p.m.), https://twitter.com/melodyMcooper/status/1264965252866641920. This summary, and all quotations from the confrontation, are drawn from this video.

and demanded that Christian stop recording her. When he declined to do so, Amy Cooper looked directly into the camera and said, "I'm going to call the police and tell them an African American man is threatening me." She then called 911 and frantically told the dispatcher at least three times that an "African American man" was threatening her and her dog. The resolution of the confrontation was initially unclear; by the time police arrived, both individuals were gone.[14]

This incident highlights a troubling yet all too common aspect of life in twenty-first century America. Despite the increasingly pluralistic and diverse makeup of the country and undeniable racial progress over the last century, Black people in America remain subject to suspicion, derision, sanction, threats, arrests, and violence simply for "existing while Black." Specifically, Black persons in public who fail to conform to stereotype and dare to cross into a White space – be it a predominantly White neighborhood, profession, or hobby – do so at their own peril. Formal segregation ended more than fifty years ago, but the vestiges of this apartheid persist in the continued rejection of Black people in White spaces. And increasingly, the enforcers of this de facto color line are private citizens armed with a cell phone, a grudge, and (often) a gun.

The "Birdwatching While Black" incident fits within a larger phenomenon covered by the media in recent years and well known to most Americans: White people calling 911 on Black people for "Living While Black." Often captured in trendy hashtags on social media like #BarbecuingWhileBlack, #SleepingWhileBlack, or #GolfingWhileBlack, these stories illustrate the myriad ways Black bodies are policed by private White actors while engaging in mundane, everyday activities that arouse contempt, suspicion, and fear solely because of the skin color of the person trying to exist in public. Christian Cooper's experience highlights many of the themes defining this phenomenon and explored in this book: the automatic and unconscious fear White people have of Black people in public, the "Black tax" excised on those attempting to enter previously "White only" ground, and the ever-present threat of violence that follows, in the form of an armed police officer primed to meet the "outsider" with force or a vigilante private citizen standing his ground in the name of self-defense.

Christian Cooper was keenly aware of his outsider status and the threat his mere presence might communicate to those around him. In an interview with the *New York Times*, Cooper noted that birdwatching is a hobby predominantly enjoyed by older White men and that his presence in this space often arouses undue attention and suspicion. As a Black man "shuffling the undergrowth [in a park] after a rare bird, with a metal object, the binoculars, in hand," Cooper acknowledged that observers were more likely to think he was armed and engaged in criminal activity than a White man doing the same thing.[15] Cooper even changed

[14] Yang, *supra* note 12.
[15] Nir, *supra* note 6.

his appearance to protect himself from these racist associations and the threats that accompany them, declining to wear contacts "[b]ecause people react differently to a black man who wears little round nerdy eyeglasses than to one who doesn't."[16] This hyperawareness extends to other Black birdwatchers, including professional nature photographer Dudley Edmonson, author of *The Black and Brown Faces in America's Wild Places*. While birdwatching, Professor Edmonson has been accused of being drunk or on drugs and of taking photos of people's homes to come back later and rob them, "things that I'm guessing in their minds fits more the description of what an African American male would be doing, as opposed to . . . watching birds."[17] Fellow Black birdwatcher Drew Lanham, also the victim of threats and intimidation while in nature, explained, "[I]t's almost like watching with one eye in the binocular and one eye outside of that field of view trying to understand where you are."[18]

These birdwatchers communicate unease with what Yale sociology professor Elijah Anderson has called "the White space," an overwhelmingly White physical and sociocultural space in which Black presence and participation is informally off-limits.[19] The "anonymous Black person" in the White American psyche is synonymous with criminal or deviant behavior more closely associated with the "urban ghetto."[20] When a White person is confronted with an anonymous Black person in the White space – be it a gentrified neighborhood, a high-end department store, or a birdwatching adventure – the unconscious, automatic sense that the Black person is out of place drives an assumption that he or she must be there only for a reason associated with the "iconic ghetto" – crime, violence, deviance. This sense gives way to suspicion, which gives way to the formal social control mechanism of a 911 call. Or worse.

Three months before Amy Cooper called the police, White father and son Greg and Travis McMichael pursued twenty-five-year-old Ahmaud Arbery, who was out for a jog in his rural Georgia town, in their pickup truck.[21] That Arbery, a Black man, was running for exercise did not conform to the McMichael's "iconic ghetto" image of young Black men, who in their mind were, more often than not, engaged in criminal behavior. While a third man videotaped, the McMichaels jumped out of their truck, confronted Arbery with a rifle, and after a brief tussle shot him dead. When questioned about the killing, the men told police they suspected Arbery of

[16] CBS News, *"That Act Was Unmistakably Racist": Christian Cooper Speaks out After Viral Encounter with White Dog-Walker*, CBS NEWS (June 9, 2020), www.cbsnews.com/news/amy-cooper-christian-cooper-speaks-out-that-act-was-unmistakably-racist/.

[17] Eric Levenson, *The Realities of Being a Black Birdwatcher*, CNN (May 27, 2020, 8:52 p.m.), https://www.cnn.com/2020/05/27/us/birdwatching-black-christian-cooper/index.html.

[18] *Id.*

[19] Elijah Anderson, *The White Space*, 1 SOC. RACE & ETHNICITY 10, 15 (2015).

[20] Elijah Anderson, *Black Americans Are Asserting Their Rights in "White Spaces." That's When Whites Call 911*, VOX (August 10, 2018), https://www.vox.com/the-big-idea/2018/8/10/17672412/911-police-black-white-racism-sociology.

[21] Elliott C. McLaughlin, *What We Know About Ahmaud Arbery's Killing*, CNN (May 12, 2020), https://www.cnn.com/2020/05/11/us/ahmaud-arbery-mcmichael-what-we-know/index.html.

planning to steal equipment from homes under construction in the neighborhood.[22] Like Professor Edmonson, who was falsely accused of casing homes to rob later while he was birdwatching, Ahmaud Arbery was simply trying to exist in public when he was targeted for "I guess . . . what an African American male would be doing."

Greg and Travis McMichael were arrested on May 7, 2020, seventy-four days after killing Arbery, seventy-three days after a district attorney handling the matter concluded that the McMichaels were making a valid citizen's arrest and had every right to chase "a burglary suspect," sixty-nine days after a second prosecutor concluded the McMichaels could not be arrested because they acted in self-defense under Georgia's "Stand Your Ground" law, fifty-one days after a third prosecutor recused himself without making any arrests, and two days after cell phone video clearly showing Ahmaud Arbery's murder went viral on the internet. On November 24, 2021, all three men involved in Arbery's death were convicted of murder.

Why do people remain so quick to whip out their cell phones or unholster their sidearms when confronted with Black people in the White space? Certainly, a segment of the US population continues to harbor express, conscious racist beliefs and acts accordingly. From the "Unite the Right" rally in Charlottesville in 2017 to the emergence of the Proud Boys in 2020, the rise in visible, vocal White supremacy in recent years confirms as much. But the private policing of Black movements is too pervasive to be explained by White nationalist views alone. Rather, the reflexive distrustful response to Black people in White spaces stems from a deep, unconscious emotion baked into the psyche of the American experience: racial fear. Fear, internalized from four centuries of messaging about dark skin as synonymous with brutality, violence, vice. Fear, from four centuries of laws, norms, and unwritten codes rejecting the "other," always coded as non-White.

Amy Cooper weaponized that fear in the most explicit terms, threatening her target that she would tell police an "African American" was attacking her before leading with that unnecessary descriptor two more times on her 911 call. What Christian Cooper experienced is the role reversal so many Black people experience every day: being threatened unjustly with police violence because their skin threatened others around them. Indeed, while Amy Cooper insisted in later media interviews that she is "not a racist," she acknowledged she called the police that day because she views them as a cost-free personal "protection agency," a "luxury" that "so many people in this country [who look like Christian Cooper] . . . don't have."[23]

[22]   Elliott C. McLaughlin, *Ahmaud Arbery Was Killed Doing What He Loved, and a South Georgia Community Demands Justice*, CNN (May 2, 2020), https://www.cnn.com/2020/05/07/us/ahmaud-arbery-shooting-demands-justice/index.html.

[23]   Jasmine Aguilera, *White Woman Who Called Police on a Black Man at Central Park Apologizes, Says "I'm Not a Racist,"* TIME (May 26, 2020), https://time.com/5842442/amy-cooper-dog-central-park/.

One may ask why we should care so much about Christian Cooper and the petty indignities of a 911 call. After all, other than an uncomfortable encounter with a fellow citizen, Christian Cooper came to no harm. In fact, both he and Amy Cooper had vanished by the time police arrived. No harm, no foul, right?

The events that transpired twelve hours later prove otherwise.

On Memorial Day 2020, George Floyd allegedly passed a counterfeit twenty-dollar bill at a convenience store in the Powderhorn Park neighborhood of Minneapolis, Minnesota. Another 911 call, another armed response, another cell phone video. Only this video documented a real-time modern-day lynching, as an officer pressed his knee into the neck of a motionless and handcuffed Floyd for nine minutes and twenty-nine seconds while three other officers stood by and watched.[24] His dead body lay on the ground for several more minutes while officers busied themselves scattering the crowd of horrified onlookers.[25] All for passing a bad twenty.

Calling 911 and summoning armed government agents to confront people is in many ways "the epitome of escalation."[26] When those agents are called to enforce the color line, "these callers aren't expecting cops to treat black folks politely, but instead to remind them that the consequences for making white people angry or uncomfortable could be harassment, unfair prosecution or death."[27] Not all racially motivated, frivolous 911 calls end in violent tragedy. But each such call is its own tragedy, another opportunity for distrust in police to harden, for the color line to crystallize, and for the indignity of the Black tax to be exacted against innocent Black people trying to live in the White space.

This book explores the private weaponization of racial fear that drives modern-day enforcement of these Black and White spaces. More than any express hatred of African Americans or desire to return to formal segregation, private White actors today react to deeply ingrained, systemic, and often unconscious racial fear of Black people who appear "out of place" in their public environment. They weaponize this racial fear in a variety of ways, including by abusing 911 to enforce formal social control via armed government agents, by trafficking in racial fear to whitewash their own misdeeds through "racial hoaxes," and by exacting vigilante justice through extrajudicial killing under the guise of self-defense and standing one's ground. Each of these approaches perverts and exploits the weapon of choice – the criminal justice system – with violent repercussions for the Black targets of this subformal apartheid.

[24] Evan Hill et al., *How George Floyd Was Killed in Police Custody*, NY TIMES (May 31, 2020), https://www.nytimes.com/2020/05/31/us/george-floyd-investigation.html.

[25] Haley Willis et al., *New Footage Shows Delayed Medical Response to George Floyd*, NY TIMES (August 11, 2020), https://www.nytimes.com/2020/08/11/us/george-floyd-body-cam-full-video.html.

[26] Jason Johnson, *From Starbucks to Hashtags: We Need to Talk About Why White Americans Call the Police on Black People*, THE ROOT (April 16, 2018), https://www.theroot.com/from-starbucks-to-hashtags-we-need-to-talk-about-why-w-1825284087.

[27] Stacey Patton & Anthony Paul Farley, *There's No Cost to White People Who Call 911 About Black People. There Should Be*, WASH. POST (May 16, 2018), https://www.washingtonpost.com/news/post everything/wp/2018/05/16/theres-no-cost-to-white-people-who-call-911-about-black-people-there-should-be/.

More often than not, private actors employing these methods enjoy the express or implicit support of government officials at all levels, from local police departments to state legislatures to the United States Supreme Court.

A note on structure. Chapter 1, "Cycles of Racial Fear," explores the long, disgraceful history of powerful Americans inciting panic about Black people in public and the role of that incitement as the preeminent driving force behind physical and psychological White spaces. This "Negrophobia" began with the arrival of the first slave ships to the American continent in 1619 and the concerted effort of slave owners to instill fear of the "heathenish, brutish" enslaved Africans forced into human bondage. From the creation of the first slave patrols to police Black movements and control Black slaves as a "dangerous kinde of people"[28] to the rise of racial terror lynching to protect White women from the sexual appetites of "Black brutes," formal control of Black bodies in White spaces has always been driven and justified by irrational, pernicious racial fear based on stereotypes. Jim Crow apartheid rested on that foundation of fear, and its formal dismantling gave way to the fear of drug-crazed "superpredators" upon which the racist War on Drugs and consequent mass incarceration cemented the "iconic ghetto" image of the poor, opportunistic, criminal Black person.

This is not ancient history. It is the explanation for White America's current pervasive, fearful enforcement of Black and White spaces. The logical and inescapable consequence of this unbroken history of racial fear is that White people in America (and to a lesser extent, all people in America) collectively and implicitly fear Black people in public. Compelling, overwhelming research about people's automatic associations and unconscious neurological bias reinforced by this historical narrative confirm that both private citizens and government actors harbor deeply ingrained beliefs about the nefarious, violent, libidinous, criminal tendencies of darker-skinned individuals. This racial fear is indelibly woven into the fabric of American identity. It is a part of America's soul.

Because these fears are so deeply imbedded within White people, they also are largely unchangeable. This conclusion may sound pessimistic. It is. But it also has been confirmed by recent research on implicit bias and racial sensitivity trainings and other corporate band-aid remedies for the open wound of racism.[29] Four centuries of racist ideals cannot be eliminated with a TED talk, a highly publicized company retraining course, or even a more robust police academy bias awareness initiative. These sanitized approaches to antiracism represent a drop in the bucket in a vast ocean of racist currents and may even prove counterproductive in the short

[28] From the Barbados Slave Code of 1661. Quoted in Maalik Stansbury, *Barbados Slave Codes*, STMU HISTORY MEDIA (October 19, 2016), https://stmuhistorymedia.org/barbados-slave-codes/.

[29] See, e.g., Katie Herzog, *Is Starbucks Implementing Flawed Science in Their Anti-Bias Training?*, THE STRANGER (April 17, 2018), https://www.thestranger.com/slog/2018/04/17/26052277/is-starbucks-implementing-flawed-science-in-their-anti-bias-training; Jessica Nordell, *Is This How Discrimination Ends?*, ATLANTIC (May 7, 2017), https://www.theatlantic.com/science/archive/2017/05/unconscious-bias-training/525405/.

term. And to the extent these institutional bias retraining efforts are effective, they are limited to a target audience and "cannot systematically retrain the biased brains of civilians who irrationally feel threatened in their daily lives."[30]

That is not to suggest we should simply throw up our hands and admit defeat. Antiracism work is necessary. But it is generational. And the sooner we acknowledge the hard truth – that reflexive, flinching racial fear dictates more than we would like to admit, and that it is not going anywhere anytime soon – the sooner we can craft workable solutions to combat the weaponization of America's criminal justice system for racially fearful ends.

And herein lies a primary claim of this book: Criminal justice reform, including police reform, should focus less on improving the quality of interactions between police and the communities they serve and more on decreasing the quantity of such interactions. If unconscious racial fear is so pervasive, unchanging, and dangerous, lawmakers and police departments should make every effort to minimize unnecessary adversarial contacts with communities of color, at least those contacts initiated by a threadbare accusation of Living While Black. Likewise, legislators and courts should deter private citizens from acting on their frivolous racial anxieties and punish those who baselessly pick up the phone or fire their weapon in fearful defense of the White space.

In reality, however, the opposite is true. Chapter 2, "White Caller Crime,"[31] highlights how racially fearful White citizens abuse 911 to enforce the color line, with impunity and with the tacit support and encouragement of police and courts. This highly effective method of racial antagonism represents a growing phenomenon of utilizing law enforcement to exert formal social control over Black people in White spaces. Whether playing golf at a country club, sleeping in an Ivy League dormitory, or moving into a Manhattan apartment in an upper-income building, Black people who fail to fulfill the "iconic ghetto" stereotype arouse automatic suspicion and panicked, breathless calls for help.

And police are all too willing to oblige. Police departments across the country require dispatchers and armed officers to respond to virtually all 911 calls, no matter how frivolous or racially motivated. These policies not only deploy scarce law enforcement resources inefficiently; they also create countless unnecessary contacts between police and communities of color, contacts fraught with centuries of mutual distrust and suspicion. Police approaches to these encounters exacerbate that tension. Having practiced proactive "smart policing" (a euphemism for racial profiling) for decades, many of the nation's largest police departments have so overpoliced poor, Black communities that they have internalized their self-created implicit bias about the inherent criminality of Black targets. When police respond to 911 calls

---

[30] Shawn E. Fields, *Weaponized Racial Fear*, 93 TUL. L. REV. 931, 937 (2019).

[31] I first encountered this term in Chan Tov McNamarah 's article, *White Caller Crime: Racialized Police Communication and Existing While Black*, 24 MICH. J. RACE & L. 335 (2019). McNamarah provides a brief history of the term and its use in his author's acknowledgement footnote. *Id.* at 335.

about "suspicious" Black people, they bring this tainted view of the world, leading to increased rates of harassment, intimidation, use of force, and arrest of innocent Black targets of such calls. In this sense, the "weapon" of racial fear is an effective one.

This fearful enforcement of the color line finds official sanction in another government institution: the United States Supreme Court. In "Just a Hunch," Chapter 3 explores how, rather than restricting the ability of police to target civilians without probable cause backed by solid evidence, the Court's unilateral assault on Fourth Amendment protections has given law enforcement near carte blanche to target, detain, and search nearly anyone for any reason. What case law calls "reasonable suspicion" is in reality any suspicion whatsoever, often nothing more than a person appearing out of place. Far too often that person out of place is a Black person in a White space. And while the Court at least restricts police from relying explicitly on race, it allows police to launder their racist responses to color line violations through manufactured suspicions about the person's behavior – his or her nervousness, lack of nervousness, eye contact, lack of eye contact, willingness to help police, unwillingness to help police.

This formless nonstandard provides cover not only for bad police behavior but also for White caller criminals. While the Fourth Amendment does not apply to the actions of these private citizens, the Supreme Court has held that an anonymous 911 call reporting criminal or suspicious behavior, by itself, is sufficient to create reasonable suspicion. That reasonable suspicion then gives police the lawful right to confront, forcefully detain, and search the body of the suspect. Thus, permissive court standards work hand in glove with aggressive police practices to hone the private 911 abuser's weapon of choice, giving implicit government sanction to this form of racist social control.

Of course, not all racially fearful citizens wait for police to arrive. As in the tragic case of Ahmaud Arbery, and Trayvon Martin nearly a decade before, some trigger-happy citizens take the law into their own hands when confronted with a Black person in the White space. Chapter 4, "Defending White Space," examines the unjustified use of lethal force by racially fearful private citizens against Black people in the name of self-defense. As with the private 911 abuser, these private vigilantes find formal government protection for their actions, as an increasing number of states broaden the once-narrow concept of self-defense to encompass a range of aggressive violent tactics, including chasing and gunning down "suspicious" people in public places.

A chorus of scholars and empirical researchers have demonstrated the disproportionate impact of relaxed self-defense standards, including "Stand Your Ground" laws, on communities of color. Far more homicides are committed in Stand Your Ground jurisdictions,[32] and a disproportionate percentage of those homicide victims

---

[32]   Chandler B. McClellan & Erdal Tekin find a 6.8 percent increase in the homicide rate in states that pass Stand Your Ground laws. Chandler B. McClellan & Erdal Tekin, *Stand Your Ground Laws,*

are Black. Far more killings of Black targets by White shooters are deemed justified than killings of White targets by Black shooters. And most telling, when controlling for all other variables, the homicides most likely to be deemed justified by prosecutors and juries are those involving a White vigilante killing a Black victim in a predominantly White neighborhood – regardless of whether the deceased was armed, committing a crime, or even running away.[33]

These findings are shocking but not surprising. If White people all harbor pernicious racial bias and that bias is triggered most quickly when faced with a Black body out of place in a White residential neighborhood, an irrationally fearful defensive response is to be expected. Nationwide relaxation of gun control laws provides the lubricant for these defensive reactions to turn more violent more quickly. And those racially fearful citizens on the street are the same people inhabiting jury rooms. What is surprising, however, is the willful failure of state legislatures to acknowledge this fact in their zeal to protect an ever-widening range of lethal conduct from prosecution. By permitting armed private citizens to shoot and kill one another in more places and for less provocation, states have declared open season on Black people.

Chapter 5 explores the blurred line between private and public violence, exploring the absolute nature of so-called "qualified" immunity and situating this new Wild West within the context of what Justice Sonia Sotomayor calls the "shoot first, think later culture" of policing.[34] The increased permissiveness with which private citizens can kill each other parallels almost perfectly the increased permissiveness with which courts have allowed police officers to kill those same citizens. Much as the concept of self-defense has been broadened in the private homicide context, the concept of when it is "objectively reasonable" for an officer to use force has been so broadened by the Supreme Court that neither "objective" nor "reasonable" retains much of its original meaning. And even in the rare case where a court finds that an officer used excessive force, the Supreme Court's unilateral expansion of the qualified immunity doctrine has shielded virtually all police brutality from the reach of the law. This near absolute immunity for police to shoot first and think later not only provides a potent weapon for White caller criminals seeking an armed response, but

---

Homicides, and Injuries 20 (Nat'l Bureau of Econ. Rsch., Working Paper No. 18187, 2012); *see also* Marc Levy et al., *Stand Your Ground: Policy and Trends in Firearm-Related Justifiable Homicide in the US*, 230 J. Am. Coll. Surgeons 161 (2020). John K. Roman, Urban Inst., Race, Justifiable Homicide, and Stand Your Ground Laws: Analysis of FBI Supplementary Homicide Report Data 7 (July 2013); C. Cheng & M. Hoekstra, *Does Strengthening Self-Defense Law Deter Crime or Escalate Violence? Evidence from Expansions to Castle Doctrine*, 48 J. Hum. Res. 821 (2013).

[33]   Roman, *supra* note 32; Daniel A. Lathrop & Anna Flagg, *Killings of Black Men by Whites Are Far More Likely to Be Ruled "Justifiable,"* The Marshall Project (August 14, 2017), www.themarshallproject.org/2017/08/14/killings-of-black-men-by-whites-are-far-more-likely-to-be-ruled-justifiable.

[34]   *Mullenix v. Luna*, 577 U.S. 7, 26 (2015) (Sotomayor, J., dissenting).

also helps explain why "society as a whole" has crept ever closer to sanctioning private vigilante justice.

In "Permanent Fear," Chapter 6 revisits a central premise of this book: that the implicit bias at play underneath this racially fearful violence is largely unchangeable in the short term. This reminder sets the stage for Chapters 7 and 8, which offer proposed solutions for walking back the militarization of the color line. In Chapter 7, "Rethinking Maximum Policing," I focus on changes police departments, legislatures, and courts can make to reduce the quantity of unnecessary police contacts with civilians, especially contacts with Black people started by a frivolous private complaint. I also offer model legislation to address the rise in racially motivated 911 abuse. Chapter 8, "Resisting a 'Shoot First, Think Later' Culture," proposes systemic changes to reduce private and public vigilante justice.

If the Summer of Racial Reckoning which began on Memorial Day 2020 is to lead to lasting change, if society indeed is as serious about racial justice as its #BlackLivesMatter hashtags indicate, then we must start with stepping back from this violent, militarized policing and self-policing. We must work not only to deter frivolous 911 abuse and unnecessary police response, but also to resist "shoot first, think later" culture, by repealing Stand Your Ground laws, narrowing the definition of affirmative self-defense, redefining objectively reasonable police use of force, and ending qualified immunity. Anything less will only ensure another generation of violent enforcement of America's Black and White spaces.

1

Cycles of Racial Fear

For the first 350 years of America's history, race relations were defined by overt, de jure segregation built on violence against and fear of Black persons.[35] During this period, enforcement of Black and White public spaces was not only obvious but intentional, codified in law throughout the country. Even after the end of formal segregation following the passage of the Fair Housing Act in 1968, de facto enforcement of Black and White spaces continued through facially neutral but racially motivated housing, drug, education, and criminal justice policies. Even as race relations evolved through periods of human bondage, racial apartheid, and mass incarceration, a singular constant was proffered to justify these abuses: fear.

A perverse cycle defines the history of fear-based racial segregation in America. Step one in this cycle begins with the creation of inhumane and unsustainable conditions for the Black underclass by the dominant White social caste. Step two involves the natural and justified resistance to this treatment by the Black underclass. That resistance – whether it be expressed as escape from bondage, civil protest against Jim Crow, or assertion of constitutional rights in encounters with police – is then turned against the resistors. This reframing becomes step three: White social leaders mischaracterize resistance as evidence of lawless, violent, criminal behavior, using the lie to stoke racial fear and justify further oppression.

Formal segregation may have faded from law and the prevalence of conscious hatred of "savage" Black persons diminished, but irrational fear of Black persons in public life has become so collectively ingrained that the fact of this fear-based segregation is impossible to deny. This chapter sketches the major cycles of racial fear in American history – from slavery and Jim Crow to mass incarceration and fear of the "iconic ghetto" – to highlight how fearful interpretations of Black movements in public spaces have become a loathsome part of the American psyche. Whether this fear-based enforcement of Black and White spaces is de jure, de facto, or unconscious makes little practical difference.

---

[35] Kenneth W. Mack, *Rethinking Civil Rights Lawyering and Politics in the Era Before Brown*, 115 YALE L.J. 256, 271 (2005) (discussing the history of *de jure* segregation prior to 1954).

1.1 "REBELLIOUS NEGROES"

From 1619 until at least 1865, southern American society and the entire American economy depended on chattel slavery, a labor system defined by violence and forced subjugation.[36] While all forms of slavery are abhorrent assaults on human dignity, historians have convincingly argued that American chattel bondage represented "the most cruel form of slavery in history."[37] Unlike slavery practices elsewhere at the time, including in the Gold Coast and other regions of west Africa, slavery in America was defined by the denial of legal or practical personhood to enslaved persons, horrific and often lethal working conditions, forced separation of families, and an unmatched brutality; these were the tools with which the slavery-industrial complex maintained itself.[38]

As with any system of forced oppression, the oppressed resisted. Enslaved persons resisted in three primary ways: escape, sabotage, and rebellion.[39] Escape and sabotage caused economic strain, but the specter of rebellion struck fear in the hearts of slave owners and the wider White social caste. "Whites – even those who never owned a slave – lived with the fear that [the existing] racial order might be turned upside down."[40] Many Whites lived in a continual "crisis of fear" that surged from one rumor of rebellion or insurrection to another.[41]

That fear led directly to the development of Slave Codes and slave patrols. For most of the seventeenth century, slave owners and overseers were responsible for controlling slaves on their plantations; runaways were captured and returned, in exchange for a fee, by private slave catchers.[42] But "fear of would-be rebellious slaves fueled the creation of slave patrols in the colonial era."[43] Beginning in 1661, Slave Codes shifted responsibility for the social control of slaves from slave owners to the deputizing of private vigilantes, a shift that culminated in the emergence of slave patrols in the early eighteenth century.[44]

The preambles of patrol laws frequently mentioned the fear of rebellion as a motivator for the laws. These Slave Code preambles show something more than reasonable fear. They show a conscious distorting of Black enslaved persons' actions; attempts to escape bondage are rendered as instinctual, "brutish," "heathenish," or

[36] *See United States v. Nelson*, 277 F.3d 164, 189–90 (2d Cir. 2002) (discussing the history of chattel slavery and accompanying violence in the United States); *see also* Stephen Kantrowitz, *America's Long History of Racial Fear*, WE'RE HISTORY (June 24, 2015), http://werehistory.org/racial-fear/ (connecting the violence of slavery to contemporary racially fearful violence).
[37] Howard Zinn, A PEOPLE'S HISTORY OF THE UNITED STATES 286 (1987).
[38] *Id.*
[39] Philip L. Reichel, *Southern Slave Patrols as a Transitional Police Type*, 7 AM. J. POLICE 51, 55 (1988).
[40] Kantrowitz, *supra* note 36.
[41] JOHN HOPE FRANKLIN, *The Militant South 1800–1861* 73 (1968); Reichel, *supra* note 39, at 64.
[42] Seth W. Stoughton, *The Blurred Blue Line: Reform in an Era of Public & Private Policing*, 44 AM. J. CRIM. 117, 123 (2017); *see also* SALLY E. HADDEN, SLAVE PATROLS: LAW & VIOLENCE IN VIRGINIA & THE CAROLINAS 14–19 (2001).
[43] Hadden, *supra* note 42 at 7.
[44] Stoughton, *supra* note 42 at 124.

"dangerous" behavior.[45] For example, the Preamble to Charleston, South Carolina's 1704 Slave Code, the "Act for the Better ordering and governing of Negroes," revealed the motivating impulse behind the law's enactment: Slaves were a "heathenish brutish" and "dangerous kinde of people" who had to be controlled.[46] Other codes referenced the "barbarous" and "irregular" behavior of enslaved persons.[47]

These images of an inherently violent race were used to further justify the enslavement of Black people. In turn, slavery reified perceptions of Blacks as subhuman, enshrining in law the slave's status as property rather than person.[48] The perception of Black persons as innately criminal fed, and was fed by, slave-holders' pervasive fears of slave revolt, expressed in laws that made almost any Black activity punishable by law. Slave Codes were justified, sometimes explicitly in the laws themselves, by characterization of Blacks as less than human, "naturally prone and inclined" to bestial behavior.[49]

The patrols were charged with keeping enslaved persons in their place, literally and metaphorically; their primary activities included enforcing curfews and ensuring Black people had the proper passes to authorize their presence wherever they were. Slave Codes controlled where slaves could go, what they could do, how they dressed and acted. They stripped slaves of civil rights; barred them from marrying, testifying in court, owning property of their own, or seeking an education; and mandated their continued enslavement.[50] Slaves were forbidden from carrying weapons in most jurisdictions and curfews were universal.

The treatment of slaves in law represented a peculiar contradiction: subjection to the law implicitly recognized the personhood of slaves – only human beings are subject to human laws – even as it explicitly marked them as subhuman.[51] Thus,

---

[45] Deborah A. Rosen, *Slavery, Race, & Outlawry: The Concept of the Outlaw in Nineteenth-Century Abolitionist Rhetoric*, 58 AM. J. LEGAL HIST. 126, 128–29 (2018).

[46] Barbados Slave Code, *supra* note 8.

[47] For instance, South Carolina's 1740 Patrol Act decries the "many late horrible and barbarous massacres ... Actually committed and many more designed, on the white inhabitants of this Province, by negro slaves." Reichel, *supra* note 39, at 55. Georgia's 1757 patrol act calls for the "prevention of an Cabals, Insurrections or other Irregularities amongst [slaves]." *Id.* at 56.

[48] Rosen, *supra* note 1145, at 130.

[49] *Id.* at 129.

[50] Most codes at least discouraged manumission; a few outright barred it. Slave Codes were extensive and specific; between 1689 and 1865, Virginia passed 130 separate slave statutes. Otis S. Johnson, *Two Worlds: A Historical Perspective on the Dichotomous Relations between Police & Black & White Communities*, 42 HUM. RTS. 6, 7 (2016). *See also* Victor E. Kappeler, A *Brief History of Slavery & the Origins of American Policing*, EASTERN KENTUCKY UNIVERSITY POLICE STUDIES ONLINE (January 7, 2014), https://plsonline.eku.edu/insidelook/brief-history-slavery-and-origins-american-policing.

[51] Rosen, *supra* note 45, at 130. The laws that permitted such treatment justified it by characterizing Black people as less than human, "either by collectively representing slaves as savage by nature or by specifically portraying fugitive slaves as people who had chosen to live in a lawless condition ... outside of the civilized community." *Id.* at 129. These depictions referred to slaves being "naturally prone and inclined" to bestial behavior. *Id.* In other words, slaves – and especially runaway

slaves were punished more severely than Whites for many crimes, especially those that affected the well-being of Whites.

Patrols all accomplished these duties through the same activities: nightly riding of a defined "beat" to look for Blacks who were out of place, often with broad powers to "police" public spaces, including slave quarters.[52] This policing of public space fell to all White society. Generally, all Whites, including slaveowning women, were required by law to participate in slave patrols.[53] Enforcement of the codes – and thus control of Black persons and their bodies – was a paramount civic duty.

Slave insurrection panic intersected with civic duty in other alarming ways. Slave codes in Virginia and the Carolinas initially required all White men to bring their weapons to church services, where Whites feared they were most vulnerable to surprise attacks.[54] Eventually, because of the growing fear of Black insurrection, all White persons – men and women – were required by law to own and carry firearms.[55] And ministers in Virginia were required to read the entirety of that state's Slave Code twice a year to their congregations or pay a fine of 600 pounds of tobacco (approximately $37,000 in 2020).[56]

In this very real sense, slavery – and the Slave Codes required to enforce it – was more than an economic system. It was also "a gigantic police system."[57] And that police system was based inherently on a system of private, fear-based racial segregation. As Sally Hadden wrote in her book *Slave Patrols*, "Bondsmen could easily be distinguished by their race and thus became easy and immediate targets of racial brutality. As a result, the new American innovation in law enforcement during the eighteenth and nineteenth centuries was the creation of racially focused law enforcement groups in the American South."[58]

Indeed, as discussed in greater detail in Chapter 3, a direct line can be drawn from southern slave patrols to the creation, maintenance, and tactics of modern police forces. The irrational racial fear created by America's "original sin" is indelibly woven into the fabric of contemporary American policing. Modern-day municipal policing in the United States evolved initially from these slave patrols, the legacy of which undeniably echoes through contemporary police practice and structure. Then, as now, these law enforcement units had a common charge: to control the "dangerous classes."[59] Then, as now, the overlap between the perceived "dangerous classes" and Black persons was substantial. In short, this early system of slave control,

---

slaves – were not human beings, but beasts whose threat to human society must be contained, violently if necessary.

[52] Franklin, *supra* note 41, at 72; Hadden, *supra* note 42, at 24; Reichel, *supra* note 39, at 61–62.

[53] Hadden, *supra* note 42, at 22; Reichel, *supra* note 39, at 60.

[54] Hadden, *supra* note 42, at 23.

[55] *Id.* at 28.

[56] *Id.*

[57] Carl T. Bogus, *The Hidden History of the Second Amendment*, 31 U.C. Davis L. Rev. 309, 335 (1998) (quoting H. M. Henry).

[58] Hadden, *supra* note 42, at 75.

[59] Gene Grabiner, *Who Polices the Police?*, 43 Soc. Just. 58, 58 (2016); Reichel, *supra* note 39, at 54.

known for its "brutality and ruthlessness," institutionalized destructive and lasting messages to the White populace about Black people's dangerousness and inherent criminality.[60] To be Black was to be dangerous. To be Black was to be violent. To be Black – especially in public – was to be criminal.

1.2 "BLACK BRUTES"

That those messages survived slavery is no accident. In the aftermath of the Civil War, Southern Whites faced a changed world. The end of slavery meant the end not only of a way of life but of an infrastructure that reserved economic and political power to Whites – particularly wealthy, slaveowning Whites.[61] Emancipation, followed by the rapid expansion of rights for Blacks, via a stream of Reconstruction Era legislation and the passage of three constitutional amendments in just twelve years (1865–77), represented an existential challenge to White supremacy. It also presented a real economic challenge for the Southern states, which desperately needed a workforce to rebuild a landscape devastated by war.[62]

But even with the world "turned upside down," White supremacists sought to restore the previous order, enforcing racial superiority through de jure segregation, Jim Crow laws, and symbolic domestic terrorism. As with the efforts to subordinate Black slaves, the "struggle" to maintain formal dominance required significant effort. Part of that effort involved sowing intense fear of newly freed Black persons as violent criminals to justify official action reinforcing the nation's caste system, thus repeating, and reinforcing, the cycle of racial fear.

Neither Slave Codes nor slave patrols disappeared after the Civil War. They merely morphed into new forms of Black control. The Slave Codes became the Black Codes of Reconstruction, and then reappeared as Jim Crow laws.[63] The slave patrols evolved into two separate institutions: the law enforcement function was redirected toward southern police forces and the more violently repressive impulses found expression in the Ku Klux Klan.[64] Both institutions promoted the myth of Black violence and criminality to instill White fear and justify a similar mission: the social control of Black people.

---

[60] Danyelle Solomon, *The Intersection of Policing and Race*, CTR. AM. PROGRESS (September 1, 2016), https://www.americanprogress.org/issuesrace/rports/2016/09/01/143357/theintersection-of-policing-and-race/.

[61] Even poor Whites, who lacked the political power of the slaveholding class, saw freed Blacks as economic competition, as positions once reserved to Whites were opened up to Blacks. Calvin John Smiley & David Fakunle, *From "Brute" to "Thug": The Demonization and Criminalization of Unarmed Black Male Victims in America*, 26 J. HUM. BEHAV. SOC. ENV'T 350, 353 (2016).

[62] Teri A. McMurtry-Chubb, *The Codification of Racism: Blacks, Criminal Sentencing, and the Legacy of Slavery in Georgia*, 31 T. MARSHALL L. REV. 139, 140 (2005).

[63] K. B. Turner, David Giacopassi, & Margaret Vandiver, *Ignoring the Past: Coverage of Slavery & Slave Patrols in Criminal Justice Texts*, 17 J. CRIM. JUST. EDUC. 181, 184 (2006); Hadden, *supra* note 42 at 23.

[64] Hadden, *supra* note 42, at 220.

Economic fear also found a target in newly freed Blacks, who were seen as displacing Whites, and morphed into something much darker: "The widespread anxiety among White men that they would not be able to provide for their wives and children easily transformed into concerns that they would not be able to protect their wives and children."[65] Lawmakers and groups like the Ku Klux Klan took advantage of the fear to create power structures that preserved their status and revitalized White supremacy. Economic anxiety was refocused on controlling Blacks, through law if possible and through lynching if necessary.

One of the great victories of White supremacy in this era was the effective propagation of the false claim that Whites faced an "epidemic of Black men raping White women."[66] Despite overwhelming evidence that no such threat existed, the fantasy that predatory Black men routinely victimized White women became the justification for lynching. During a 1921 debate on the floor of the US House of Representatives, for instance, Rep. James Buchanan of Texas denounced a proposed anti-lynching bill, decrying:

> the damnable doctrine of social equality which excites the criminal sensualities of the criminal element of the Negro race and directly incites the diabolical crime of rape upon White women. Lynching follows as swift as lightning, and all the statutes of the State and the Nation cannot stop it.[67]

Rep. Thomas Upton Sisson of Mississippi also opposed the bill; White southern men, he said, "are going to protect our girls and womenfolk from these black brutes. When these black fiends keep their hands off the throats of the women of the South then lynching will stop."[68]

In the mid-nineteenth and early twentieth centuries, lynching – "America's signature act of racial terror"[69] – was public spectacle; lynchings were festive events attended by hundreds, including women and children, who cheered on lynch mobs and scrambled for souvenirs, including bloody ropes, torn and bloodied clothing,

---

[65] Joshua D. Rothman, *The Charleston Massacre and the Rape Myth of Reconstruction*, WE'RE HISTORY (June 22, 2015), http://werehistory.org/charleston-rape-myth/. Historians have argued that the Black brute myth also expressed White men's displaced sexual anxieties, provided cover for White men's own interracial sexual practices, and served as a mechanism for keeping White women fearful and vulnerable, and thus under male control, just as women's rights movements were first emerging in the South. Barbara Holden-Smith, *Lynching, Federalism, and the Intersection of Race and Gender in the Progressive Era*, 8 YALE J.L. & FEMINISM 31, 48–49 (1996). Ida B. Wells argued, in her 1892 antilynching pamphlet *Southern Horrors*, that the focus on Black men's supposedly insatiable sexuality functioned to draw attention away from White men's rape of Black women. *See* Crystal N. Feimster, *Ida B. Wells and the Lynching of Black Women*, N.Y. TIMES (April 28, 2018), https://www.nytimes.com/2018/04/28/opinion/sunday/ida-b-wells-lynching-black-women.html.

[66] Kantrowitz, *supra* note 36.

[67] Quoted in Rothman, *supra* note 65.

[68] *Id.*

[69] *Id.*

and, horrifyingly, victims' body parts.[70] Historians have long argued that racial terror lynchings were carried out in response to rape allegations. But recent research on America's history of racial terror lynching confirms the contemporaneous analysis of anti-lynching activist (and pioneering investigative journalist) Ida B. Wells, who found that far fewer than half of all lynchings were "justified" by rape claims.[71] In fact, Blacks were lynched for any number of offenses; the list of documented motivations for lynching represents "a bizarre mixture of what now seem to be innocuous breaches of the social code and serious violations of the criminal law,"[72] informally codifying social norms delineating acceptable Black and White behavior in Black and White spaces.

Yet public defenders of lynching argued for its power to deter one offense above all others: the rape of White women. Freed of the restraints of slavery, White supremacists claimed, Black men resorted to rape to satisfy their desire for White women. The only way to restrain the "Black brute" was with the fear of lynching: "it was practically axiomatic in the minds of White southerners that such extralegal mob violence was necessary to clamp down on Black predators with designs on the bodies of White women."[73]

The "Black brute" stereotype caricatures Black men, portraying them as "innately savage, animalistic, destructive, and criminal ... hideous, terrifying predators who target helpless victims, especially White women."[74] This description of the "Black brute" tracks with other stereotypical characterizations of Black men, including the Mandingo or "Black buck" and the Nat, all of which focus on the physicality and unrestrained sexual appetites of Black men.[75] These images built on a pervasive cultural image of Blacks as "only narrowly removed from the animal kingdom," perpetuated from Europeans' first contacts with Africa.[76] That animality, Europeans

[70] Holden-Smith, *supra* note 65, 37. *See also* Equal Justice Initiative, LYNCHING IN AMERICA: CONFRONTING THE LEGACY OF RACIAL TERROR 37 (3d ed., 2017), https://lynchinginamerica.eji.org/report/.

[71] Ida B. Wells Barnett, *Lynching and the Excuse for It*, 53 THE INDEPENDENT 1133 (1901), available from the Northern Illinois University Digital Library at https://digital.lib.niu.edu/islandora/object/niu-gildedage%3A24185. *See also* Ida B. Wells-Barnett, *The Red Record: Tabulated Statistics and Alleged Causes of Lynching in the United States* (1895), https://www.gutenberg.org/files/14977/14977-h/14977-h.htm. For modern research supporting Wells's findings, *see* Holden-Smith, *supra* note 65, at 38.

[72] Holden-Smith, *supra* note 65, at 37.

[73] Rothman, *supra* note 65.

[74] David Pilgrim, *The Brute Caricature*, JIM CROW MUSEUM OF RACIAL MEMORABILIA (2012), https://www.ferris.edu/jimcrow/brute/.

[75] The Mandingo trope focuses on "the strength, breeding ability, and agility of muscular young black men." National Museum of African American History & Culture, *Widespread and Pervasive Stereotypes of African Americans*, https://nmaahc.si.edu/blog-post/popular-and-pervasive-stereotypes-african-americans. The Nat was an "angry, crazed, revengeful brute with a bloodthirsty hatred for whites." The name refers to slave rebellion leader Nat Turner. David Pilgrim, *The Nat Caricature*, JIM CROW MUSEUM OF RACIAL MEMORABILIA (2012), https://www.ferris.edu/HTMLS/news/jimcrow/nat/homepage.htm.

[76] N. Jeremi Duru, *The Central Park Five, the Scottsboro Boys, and the Myth of the Bestial Black Man*, 35 CARDOZO L. REV. 1315, 1321 (2004).

believed, was expressed in extraordinary sexual potency and ingrained criminality. Black people were widely understood "to be born and bred Villains" prone to "All sorts of Baseness."[77]

The myth of Black bestiality, and especially Black rapaciousness, was a staple of cultural production as well, featuring in melodramatic novels, plays, and songs. It was the centerpiece of D. W. Griffith's *The Birth of the Nation*, which so galvanized viewers that it led to the founding of the second Ku Klux Klan (the first having been dismantled in the 1870s after state laws forbade gatherings in mask or costume). During slavery, the Black brute and the Nat fueled slaveowners' most heated fantasies of slave revolt; after Emancipation, the Black brute, in combining Black men's propensity for violence with their insatiable sexual appetites, captured Whites' deepest fears about freed Blacks.

Endemic belief in the innate criminality and violence of Blacks, as captured in the myth of the Black brute, provided a solution to both the economic and the psychic problems. The 13th Amendment to the Constitution ended slavery, but it also provided a loophole: "Neither slavery nor involuntary servitude, *except as punishment for a crime whereof the party shall have been duly convicted*, shall exist within the United States, or any place subject to its jurisdiction."[78] Southern states, like Georgia, quickly set about exploiting that loophole to recapture their lost workforce; legislatures created new criminal codes that largely imported the antebellum Slave Codes into criminal law. The laws were, explicitly or implicitly, targeted to Blacks; they assigned hard labor as the penalty for a long list of crimes widely perceived as "'Black' crimes."[79] Convict leasing quickly replaced slavery as a source of both labor and state revenues, and postbellum criminal codes "increasingly gave the state more control over the bodies of its convicts . . . [and] replicated the master/slave relationship."[80] The only difference was that the innate criminality of the slave was now explicitly encoded in law – before the Civil War, being a slave made a person a de facto criminal; after, being a criminal made a person a de facto slave.

This move from defining Black people as criminal to making Black people into criminals was supported by popular science, which offered rational support for Black brute imagery.[81] New narratives of Black criminality were supported by claims based in eugenics and sociology, many of them predating Emancipation. For instance, an

---

[77] *Id.* at 1322.

[78] U.S. Const. Amend. XIII § 1 (emphasis added).

[79] McMurtry-Chubb, *supra* note 62, at 142–43.

[80] *Id.* at 143. Ava DuVernay's powerful documentary, *13th* (Netflix 2016), traces the consequences of this process in the nation's current regime of mass incarceration.

[81] Khalil Gibran Muhammad, in THE CONDEMNATION OF BLACKNESS (2010), offers a comprehensive account of how nineteenth- and early twentieth-century social scientists bolstered the myth of Black criminality and then used it to justify denying rights to Blacks, justifying "white oppression . . . as 'the corner-stone of our republican edifice.'" Ta-Nehisi Coates, *The Black Family in the Age of Mass Incarceration*, section IV, THE ATLANTIC, October 2015, https://www.theatlantic.com/magazine/archive/2015/10/the-Black-family-in-the-age-of-mass-incarceration/403246/.

1839 morphological study concluded that Blacks were an entirely different species from Whites.[82] Josiah C. Nott, who would later become Dean of Harvard University's school of science, made a similar argument in an 1844 paper.[83] Postbellum "scientists" drew on this foundation to warn the masses that freedom had given "'loose reins to the animal.'"[84] These theories combined with social Darwinism and other theories of heredity to characterize Blacks as carrying an inescapable genetic heritage of criminality.[85] The warnings were all the more potent because of their claims to scientific objectivity.[86] Apparently indisputable statistics showing a Black crime wave – a crime wave generated by Southern criminal codes that essentially criminalized being Black – gave even more authority to pseudoscientific notions about heritable criminality and Blackness.[87]

The myth of the innately criminal Black brute provided cover for a brutal campaign to ensure the continuation of White supremacy. The Ku Klux Klan, Southern politicians, and others played on heightened public fear of free Black men, using that fear to create support for legal and extralegal measures to keep Blacks in their place. While historians, sociologists, and others have identified a host of underlying forces in the rise of lynching after the Civil War, from perceived ineffectiveness of judicial structures to the cultural constructions of chivalry and pure White womanhood to psychosexual issues, a consistent theme emerges from all these accounts: "lynchings emanated from and reflected extreme racial hatred."[88]

This myth of the "Black bogeyman," the Black man as a violent and crazed sexual criminal, endures. During the Civil Rights Movement of the 1950s and 1960s, White supremacists argued that segregation was necessary to keep Black predators from raping White women and leading to the "mongrelization" of the White race. And on June 17, 2015, Dylann Roof entered an African American church in Charleston, South Carolina, and shouted at the prayer group inside, "You rape our women and you're taking over our country."[89] He then opened fire and killed nine people.

---

[82] Anderson Bellegarde François, *Et in Arcadia Ego: Buck v. Davis, Black Thugs, and the Supreme Court's Race Jurisprudence*, 15 Ohio St. J. Crim. L. 229, 237 (2017).

[83] *Id.*

[84] *Id.* at 238 (quoting Eugene R. Corson, *The Future of the Colored Race in the United States from an Ethnic and Medical Standpoint, a Lecture Delivered before the Georgia Medical Society* (June 6, 1877), in Equal Protection and The African American Constitutional Experience: A Documentary History 149 (Robert P. Green, Jr. ed., 2000)).

[85] *Id.* at 239.

[86] *Id.*

[87] *Id.*

[88] Daniel P. Mears, Patricia Y. Warren, Ashley N. Arnio, Eric A. Stewart, & Miltonette O. Craig, *A Legacy of Lynchings: Perceived Black Criminal Threat Among Whites*, 53 Law & Soc'y Rev. 487, 489 (2019).

[89] The statement was widely reported, but for comment and analysis, *see* Kantrowitz, *supra* note 36; Rothman, *supra* note 65.

1.3 "SUPERPREDATORS"

The post-Civil War era of Jim Crow and racial terror lynching were the first step in the twentieth century's cycle of racial fear: humiliation and subordination by the dominant social caste. The Civil Rights Movement of the 1950s and 1960s represented the second step: natural and justifiable resistance to injustice. This resistance primarily, though not exclusively, took the form of nonviolent civil disobedience. Even when supremacists turned firehoses on children in Birmingham, loosed attack dogs on marchers in Selma, and threw a bomb into a church, killing four young girls, Martin Luther King Jr. prevailed upon activists to employ nonviolence. Almost a decade before these defining moments, on December 15, 1956, Dr. King explained to a crowd, "[W]e must rise up and protest courageously wherever we find segregation. Yes, we must do it nonviolently. We cannot afford to use violence in the struggle."[90] Dr. King recognized that even justified violence would be used by the dominant White social caste to again paint Blacks as inherently criminal.

This third step took shape in the immediate aftermath of Dr. King's assassination in 1968, when a wave of civil unrest later known as the Holy Week Uprising swept across the United States. As expected, this unrest deeply affected White Americans' perceptions of Black communities, "setting the stage for the backlash against the racial justice victories of the 1960s."[91]

Enter Richard Nixon. His "law and order" campaign for president in 1968 kicked off with a notorious television ad, "The First Civil Right," a clear dog-whistle reference to the great civil rights victories of the decade. In the ad, images of protestors, the rubble of riots, and militarized police officers flash over ominous music as Nixon declares, "Let us recognize that the first civil right of every American is to be free from domestic violence. So I pledge to you, we shall have order in the United States."[92] This race-baiting platform worked, and it paved the way for President Nixon to target Black Americans as dangerous drug users requiring stiff criminal sanctions.[93]

---

[90] Martin Luther King Jr., Desegregation and the Future, Address Delivered at the Annual Luncheon of the National Committee for Rural Schools (December 15, 1956), https://king institute.stanford.edu/king-papers/documents/desegregation-and-future-address-delivered-annual-luncheon-national-committee.

[91] V. Noah Gimbel, *There Are No Children Here: D.C. Youth in the Criminal Justice System*, 104 GEO. L. J. 1307, 1314 n.28 (2016).

[92] *The First Civil Right* (Nixon–Agnew Victory Committee, 1968). Video is available at Museum of the Moving Image, 1968 Nixon vs. Humphrey vs. Wallace, THE LIVING ROOM CANDIDATE: PRESIDENTIAL CAMPAIGN COMMERCIALS 1952–2012, at http://www.livingroomcandidate.org/commercials/1968/the-first-civil-right.

[93] Tali Mendelberg, THE RACE CARD: CAMPAIGN STRATEGY, IMPLICIT MESSAGES, AND THE NORM OF EQUALITY 135 (2001) ("Law and order for Nixon boiled down to the 'damn Negroes,' but he could not say this in his [campaign] ad ... He intended to convey racial meaning implicitly. He wanted to appeal to racial stereotypes, fears, and resentments, yet conform to the norm of racial equality.").

Although President Nixon would not declare "drug abuse" to be "public enemy number one" until 1971, ushering in the unofficial War on Drugs,[94] Nixon campaign advisor John Ehrlichman later acknowledged:

> The Nixon campaign in 1968, and the Nixon White House after that, had two enemies: the antiwar left and black people. . . . We knew we couldn't make it illegal to be either against the war or black, but by getting the public to associate the hippies with marijuana and blacks with heroin, and criminalizing both heavily, we could disrupt those communities. We could arrest their leaders, raid their homes, break up their meetings, and vilify them night after night on the evening news. Did we know we were lying about the drugs? Of course we did.[95]

Throughout the Nixon presidency, the administration orchestrated public drug raids almost exclusively targeting communities of color, buttressing both Nixon's self-cultivated "watchdog" reputation and the "Black bogeyman" myth; this time, the bogeyman took the form of a violent, drug-crazed inner-city criminal.[96]

But the most severe effects of the War on Drugs were not felt until the Reagan administration, when draconian legislation targeted communities of color for shockingly disparate sentencing treatment. The Sentencing Reform Act, passed by Congress in 1986, established twenty-nine new mandatory minimum sentences for drug offenses, including minor drug use and possession offenses.[97] The Act also created a 100-to-1 sentencing disparity for trafficking or possessing crack cocaine compared to penalties for trafficking or possessing powder cocaine.[98]

This disparity had racist origins; it targeted African Americans, who were more likely to use cheaper crack cocaine than White Americans, who were more likely to use more expensive powder cocaine.[99] As Nixon had, President Reagan sought public support for his disparate sentencing laws by deliberately misleading the public about the nature of crack cocaine, incorrectly asserting that it was more potent, more harmful, and more addictive than powder cocaine.[100] The "Black

---

[94]   Frontline, *Thirty Years of America's Drug War: A Chronology*, PBS, http://www.pbs.org/wgbh/pages/frontline/shows/drugs/cron/.

[95]   Quoted in Dan Baum, *Legalize It All: How to Win the War on Drugs*, HARPER'S, April 2016, https://harpers.org/archive/2016/04/legalize-it-all/.

[96]   *See* Shima Baradaran, *Drugs and Violence*, 88 S. CAL. L.R. 227, 246–47 (2015) (describing Nixon's racially charged declaration of the War on Drugs).

[97]   *See id.* at 247–49 ("President Nixon's war on drugs culminated in President Ronald Reagan's own war. . . . During President Reagan's tenure in office, two major anti-drug laws were passed," including one "mandating minimum sentences"); Sentencing Reform Act, 18 U.S.C. § 3582 *et seq.*

[98]   *Dorsey v. United States*, 567 U.S. 260, 266 (2012) ("The 1986 Drug Act . . . treated crack cocaine crimes as far more serious. It applied its 5-year minimum to . . . only 5 grams of crack (as compared to 500 grams of powder) . . . thus producing a 100-to-1 crack-to-powder ratio.")

[99]   *See* Naomi Murakawa, *The Racial Antecedents to Federal Sentencing Guidelines: How Congress Judged the Judges from Brown to Booker*, 11 ROGER WILLIAMS L. REV. 473, 480 (2006).

[100] *See* Baum, *supra* note 95; *see also* U.S.S.C. Pub. Hrg. Trans. (June 1, 2011) ("[T]here is no scientific reason for the sentencing disparity. We know that crack and powder cocaine are pharmacologically indistinguishable. . . . ongoing research . . . has eroded the myth that crack cocaine is more addictive

bogeyman" myth was reborn in the shape of "crack whores" and "crack babies" hollowing out American cities and "welfare queens" bilking honest taxpayers to feed their addictions.[101] By 1986, *Time* magazine had declared crack cocaine the issue of the year.[102] The 100-to-1 mandatory minimum sentencing disparities became law later that year.[103]

Republican administrations were not alone in peddling the trope of the Black criminal underclass. The Clinton administration doubled down on the War on Drugs with its own harsh, disparate sentencing policies. In 1996, then-First Lady Hillary Rodham Clinton defended zero-tolerance and "three strikes" policies with the claim that an entire generation of "superpredator" children, born without conscience or empathy, needed to be brought "to heel."[104]

Coined by Princeton political science professor John DiIulio in a 1995 article, the term *superpredator* referred to "severely morally impoverished" juvenile offenders "perfectly capable of committing the most heinous acts for the most trivial reasons."[105] DiIulio's description was widely understood to refer to Black and Latino youths; it also echoed the language of Richard Nixon's Southern strategy, which exploited fear of rising crime as a cover for racism. The superpredator proved to be another myth – statistics show that juvenile crime decreased in the mid-1990s[106] – but a durable one. The concept was used by legislators to justify a host of "tough on crime" laws at the state and federal levels, including laws that allowed life sentences for juvenile offenders. Nearly two-thirds of juveniles sentenced under these laws were Black.[107]

than powder cocaine; [or] that crack cocaine users are, because of their choice of drug use, more violent than powder cocaine users.").

[101] Kathleen R. Sandy, *The Discrimination Inherent in America's Drug War: Hidden Racism Revealed by Examining the Hysteria Over Crack*, 54 Ala. L. Rev. 665, 683–85 (2003) (describing media coverage of drug use in the 1980s and 1990s as having "an overwhelmingly racist tinge, focusing on 'the crack whores, the welfare queens, and the crack baby' – characters all given a Black face").

[102] Jacob V. Lamar Jr., *Crack: A Cheap and Deadly Cocaine Is a Fast-Spreading Menace*, Time (June 2, 1986), http://content.time.com/time/magazine/article/0,9171,961485,00.html.

[103] *See Dorsey*, 567 U.S. at 288.

[104] Hillary Clinton, Campaign Speech at Keene State University, January 25, 1996, https://www.c-span .org/video/?69606-1/hillary-clinton-campaign-speech.

[105] John DiIulio, *The Coming of the Super-Predators*, Wash. Examiner (November 27, 1995) https://www .washingtonexaminer.com/weekly-standard/the-coming-of-the-super-predators. Reprinted in the Chi. Tribune (December 15, 1995), https://www.chicagotribune.com/news/ct-xpm-1995-12-15- 9512150046-story.html.

[106] Kirsten West Savali, *For the Record: "Superpredators" Is Absolutely a Racist Term*, The Root (September 30, 2016), https://www.theroot.com/for-the-record-superpredators-is-absolutely-a-racist- t-1790857020. One commenter suggests another reason for the decline in juvenile crime: DiIulio's superpredator, Kevin Drum suggests, was "a portrait of a lead-poisoned teenager raised in an already violent environment." According to Drum, juvenile crime declined in the mid-1990s as a delayed effect of the banning of lead paint and leaded gasoline in the previous decade. Kevin Drum, *A Very Brief History of Super-Predators*, Mother Jones (March 3, 2016), https://www.motherjones.com /kevin-drum/2016/03/very-brief-history-super-predators/.

[107] Priyanka Boghani, *They Were Sentenced as "Superpredators." Who Were They Really?*, PBS: Frontline (May 2, 2017), https://www.pbs.org/wgbh/frontline/article/they-were-sentenced-as- superpredators-who-were-they-really/.

Together with the War on Drugs and welfare reforms that disproportionately affected Black communities, the concept of the superpredator led, more or less directly, to today's mass incarceration.[108] Mandatory minimum sentences and disparate sentencing treatment for drug offenses committed predominantly by African Americans sparked an explosion in the United States prison population. The state and federal prison population nearly tripled in the twelve years immediately following passage of the Sentencing Reform Act.[109] In 1974, the state and federal prison population stood at 218,466.[110] By 2014, that total had risen to 1,508,636, a nearly 600 percent increase.[111] Today, imprisonment for drug offenses has grown more than 1,000 percent since 1974, with the disproportionate brunt of this epidemic of incarceration borne by communities of color.[112]

The effects of this "new Jim Crow" are far-reaching and catastrophic.[113] "The War on Drugs foreseeably and unnecessarily blighted the lives of hundreds of thousands of young, disadvantaged Americans, especially black Americans, and undermined decades of effort to improve the life chances of members of the urban black underclass."[114] It perpetuated institutional poverty by removing significant portions of the population from the workforce and by marking millions of Black men and women with the scarlet letter of a felony drug conviction, making them all but unemployable. Psychologically, the fact that Black and Brown Americans comprise nearly three-fifths of the United States prison population reinforces the unfounded, irrational fear that people of color are predisposed to crime.[115]

---

[108]   *Id. See also* Savali, *supra* note 106; Coates, *supra* note 81.

[109]   *Criminal Justice Facts*, THE SENTENCING PROJECT, http://www.sentencingproject.org/criminal-justice-facts/ (interactive graph showing prison population in 1984 at 443,398, and 1996 prison population at 1,137,722).

[110]   Lauren Carroll, *How the War on Drugs Affected Incarceration Rates*, POLITIFACT (July 10, 2016), https://www.politifact.com/truth-o-meter/statements/2016/jul/10/cory-booker/how-war-drugs-affected-incarceration-rates.

[111]   *Id.*

[112]   *Id.* ("About 58 percent of all sentenced inmates in 2013 were Black or Hispanic, yet the two groups make up just about 30 percent of the total [United States] population. . . . [A 2014 study] found that white people are more likely than black people to sell drugs and about as likely to consume them. Even so, black people are 3.6 times more likely than white people to be arrested for selling drugs and 2.5 times more [likely to be arrested] for drug possession.").

[113]   *See generally* MICHELLE ALEXANDER, THE NEW JIM CROW: MASS INCARCERATION IN THE AGE OF COLORBLINDNESS (2012).

[114]   Michael Tonry, *Race and the War on Drugs*, 4 U. CHI. LEGAL F. 25, 27 (1994).

[115]   Tasha Hill, *Inmates' Need for Federally Funded Lawyers: How the Prison Litigation Reform Act, Case, and Iqbal Combine With Implicit Bias to Eviscerate Civil Rights*, 62 UCLA L. REV. 175, 218 (2015) ("Overinclusion of minority groups in the prison population may make it even more difficult for (overwhelmingly White) judges to overcome their implicit biases against both inmates and people of color.").

1.4 THE "ICONIC GHETTO"

The current incarnation of racial fear has taken hold within this context. An entire generation of White Americans has come to expect a "ghettoization" of Black people, portrayed in the news media and entertainment outlets as poor, urban, and prone to drug use or other criminal activity.[116] When people of color fail to fulfill that stereotype, whether by shopping at an upscale clothing store,[117] attending a prestigious university,[118] or walking through a neighborhood that "isn't Oakland,"[119] deeply ingrained and automatic apprehensions of the "Black bogeyman" once again rise to the surface.

Yale sociology Professor Elijah Anderson attributes these apprehensions to White confusion over Blacks occupying "the White space" in public life, areas that were traditionally "off limits" to people of color.[120] By not conforming to the idea of the "iconic ghetto"[121] in which Black people are supposed to remain, completely innocent people of color having a barbecue,[122] attending a pool party,[123] or checking out of a home rental[124] elicit suspicion from a fearful White majority: "[F]or many Whites, the anonymous Black person in public is always implicitly associated with the urban ghetto."[125] When a White person sees a Black person in the "White space," the sight sparks an unconscious idea, passed down over generations, from slavery to Jim Crow to mass incarceration to the present day, that the Black individual is out of

---

[116] *See* Anderson, *supra* notes 19, 20.

[117] Rachel Siegel, *Nordstrom Rack Apologizes After Calling the Police on Three Black Teens Who Were Shopping for Prom*, WASH. POST (May 9, 2018), https://www.washingtonpost.com/news/business/wp/2018/05/08/nordstrom-rack-called-the-police-on-three-Black-teens-who-were-shopping-for-prom/?utm_term=.ee62d9b59b80.

[118] Cleve R. Wootson Jr., *A Black Yale Student Fell Asleep in Her Dorm's Common Room. A White Student Called Police.*, WASH. POST (May 11, 2018), https://www.washingtonpost.com/news/grade-point/wp/2018/05/10/a-Black-yale-student-fell-asleep-in-her-dorms-common-room-a-White-student-called-police/?utm_term=.905bfb8e4990.

[119] *See* Rachael Herron, *I Used to Be a 911 Dispatcher. I Had to Respond to Racist Calls Every Day*, VOX (October 31, 2018), https://www.vox.com/first-person/2018/5/30/17406092/racial-profiling-911-bbq-becky-living-while-black-babysitting-while-black.

[120] Anderson, *supra* note 20.

[121] *Id.* ("In this sociological context, the urban ghetto is presumed to be, descriptively, 'the place where the black people live.' But it's also, stereotypically, a den of iniquity, a fearsome, impoverished place of social backwardness where black people perpetrate all manner of violence and crime against one another.").

[122] Gianluca Mezzofiore, *A White Woman Called Police on Black People Barbecuing. This is How the Community Responded*, CNN (May 22, 2018), https://www.cnn.com/2018/05/22/us/White-woman-Black-people-oakland-bbq-trnd/index.html.

[123] Sarah Mervosh, *A Black Man Wore Socks in the Pool. After Calling Police on Him, a Manager Got Fired.*, N.Y. TIMES (July 9, 2018), https://www.nytimes.com/2018/07/09/us/memphis-pool-manager-fired-socks.html.

[124] Daniel Victor, *A Woman Said She Saw Burglars. They Were Just Black Airbnb Guests.*, N.Y. TIMES (May 8, 2018), https://www.nytimes.com/2018/05/08/us/airbnb-Black-women-police.html.

[125] Anderson, *supra* note 20.

place and must only be there for a reason associated with the iconic ghetto – crime, violence, or opportunistic gain.

This tension is exacerbated by today's complex sociological landscape. Black Americans appear more often in places of privilege, power, and prestige in the increasingly diverse twenty-first-century meritocracy. Federal reforms aimed at keeping the promise of the civil rights movement, combined with historic racial integration and a prolonged period of economic expansion, helped lead to the growth of the Black middle class, which is now the largest it has been in American history.[126] Black Americans in the last half century occupied "professional positions in which they have rarely appeared before, including as doctors, lawyers, professors, corporate executives, and major elected officials."[127] Social reforms followed, marked by increases in Black membership at exclusive country clubs, private schools, and predominantly White churches.

But this progress, following nearly four hundred years of explicit racial stereotyping, has unnerved many White Americans. As one researcher observed, the "lag between the rapidity of Black progress and White acceptance of that progress" may be responsible for the impulse of many White Americans to view innocent behavior in "White spaces" as suspicious or criminal.[128] Thus, while members of the Black middle class may become "increasingly more accomplished," Professor Anderson reminds us that "in terms of phenotype and skin color, most are virtually indistinguishable from those who reside in the local ghetto, and they are profiled for this reason."[129] This "Black tax" reflects the essence of what popular culture today refers to as "existing while Black." While a White student sleeping in a Yale dormitory enjoys the benefit of being perceived as a student first and White second (if at all), a Black student engaged in the same behavior is viewed first and primarily as Black, a status that supersedes any other status as a successful, law-abiding citizen. At least in the White space, Blackness comes first, along with the undeserved baggage and suspicions associated with it.

Demographic sorting exacerbates this tension. Despite broad cosmopolitan integration, racial segregation persists in most parts of the country. Wider society is still replete with "overwhelmingly White neighborhoods, restaurants, schools, universities, workplaces, churches and other associations, courthouses, and cemeteries," reinforcing a normative sensibility that White is presumed and Black is unexpected and suspicious.[130] This fear of Black people where they "don't belong" is the defining feature of the current wave of American racial fear. "In times past, before the civil rights revolution, the color line was more clearly marked. Both White and Black people knew their so-called place, and for the most part, observed it. When people

---

[126] *Id.*
[127] Anderson, *supra* note 19, at 11.
[128] Anderson, *supra* note 20.
[129] Anderson, *supra* note 19, at 11.
[130] *Id.* at 10.

crossed that line – Black people, anyway – they faced legal penalties or extra-judicial violence."[131] Today, the line is much fuzzier, the boundaries of White space and Black space less defined and easier to cross. Lacking traditional formal delineations of what behavior is permitted where and by whom, racially fearful Americans struggle to figure out who belongs where. Increasingly, they turn to police to enforce an invisible color line, complaining about such "suspicious" behavior as working out at a gym[132] or waiting for a friend in a coffee shop.[133] This "White fragility"[134] triggers a range of defensive reactions, including frivolous 911 calls, fraudulent reports of crimes committed by "unidentified Black males," declarations that Black Americans should "go back where they came from," and violent confrontation of Black people peacefully existing in "White space." These reactions further reinforce the idea of the iconic ghetto, "shaping the conception of the anonymous Black person" four hundred years in the making.[135]

Collectively, private weaponization of racial fear through 911 abuse, racial hoaxes, and stand-your-ground vigilantism illustrates how Black persons remain subject to arbitrary social expectations, and how violating those expectations is punishable by private and public shows of force. Decades after the collapse of legal segregation, these trends also show that spaces like clothing stores, coffee shops, neighborhoods, and universities remain strongly controlled along racial lines: "White people need to put the Black interlopers in their place, literally and figuratively. Black people must have their behavior corrected, and they must be directed back to 'their' neighborhoods and designated social spaces."[136]

1.5 ANCIENT HISTORY?

Undoubtedly, some will read this chapter and wonder what "ancient history" like slave codes and lynching has to do with American life in 2022. In the wake of George Floyd's murder and the national reckoning about confederate monuments, some politicians decried the attempt to connect an isolated incident in Minnesota to a long-forgotten history that, most believe, ended with the Civil War in 1865. A familiar refrain began echoing in certain segments of society. Black Americans

---

[131] Anderson, *supra* note 20.
[132] Rachel Siegel, *LA Fitness Employees Called 911 on Two Black Men They Say Didn't Pay. They Had.*, WASH. POST (April 20, 2018), https://www.washingtonpost.com/news/business/wp/2018/04/20/la-fitness-employees-called-911-on-two-Black-men-they-said-didnt-pay-they-had/?.
[133] Rachel Siegel, *Two Black Men Arrested at Starbucks Settle With Philadelphia for $1 Each*, WASH. POST (May 3, 2018), https://www.washingtonpost.com/news/business/wp/2018/05/02/african-american-men-arrested-at-starbucks-reach-1-settlement-with-the-city-secure-promise-for-200000-grant-program-for-young-entrepreneurs/?.
[134] *See generally* ROBIN DiANGELO, WHITE FRAGILITY: WHY IT'S SO HARD FOR WHITE PEOPLE TO TALK ABOUT RACISM 9–18 (2018) (asserting that racially segregated White people, lacking consistent connection with people of color, respond defensively when confronted with an uncomfortable situation).
[135] Anderson, *supra* note 20.
[136] *Id.*

were unfairly trying to "dig up the past" to justify their current plight instead of dealing with the present. Suddenly, "everything is about race." For some, the idealized notion of a "post-racial" United States resurfaced. America had elected, and reelected, an African American president, so surely it had made enough racial progress as a society to move past the "race issue." Obsessing over centuries of irrelevant history only makes matters worse, or so the argument goes.

A few responses are in order.

First, America has never fully reckoned with its history of chattel slavery and postbellum domestic terror. Most public school history curricula devote a single day to the 250-year history of slavery, showing the iconic transatlantic slave ship drawings, defining the three-fifths compromise, and reading the Emancipation Proclamation. Rarely do students learn about the brutal domestic slave trade of the early nineteenth century or the fact that enslaved persons literally created the economic boom that propelled America onto the world stage. Neither do schools discuss the 4,743 Black Americans murdered through racial terror lynching after the Civil War, focusing instead on a truncated discussion of segregation punctuated by pictures of "Colored Only" signs above water fountains. This sanitized discussion of Jim Crow gives way to a sanitized discussion of the Civil Rights Movement, told mostly through uplifting but incomplete biographies of Rosa Parks and Martin Luther King Jr. This persistent failure to confront America's ugly history of racial fear contributes, at least in part, to a continued ignorance of the connections between slave patrols and police departments, between Black brute tropes and racial hoaxes, between criminality myths and stand-your-ground "self-defense" killings of Black persons peacefully existing in White spaces.

Second, the parallels between America's history of racial fear and its current climate are increasingly, and terrifyingly, obvious. Dylann Roof expressly invoked the Black brute myth to justify gunning down nine Black Americans at church a hundred years after that pernicious trope was born. But he was a twenty-one-year-old lone wolf with vague White supremacist beliefs apparently driven by Barack Obama's mere existence in the White House. What of the man who launched his entire political career with a racist "birther" conspiracy theory that the first Black person to occupy the ultimate White space did not belong because he was an illegitimate other? This effort to foment racial fear, successful enough to garner nearly 63 million votes in 2016, drew on America's long history of racial fear and the national impulse to enforce Black and White spaces.

Indeed, President Trump's reelection strategy in 2020, a fifth of the way through the twenty-first century, appeared at times more suited to a campaign for the "last president of the Confederacy." By vowing to protect "at all costs" monuments of confederate generals whose historical significance is entirely premised on their leading thousands of young Americans to slaughter in a treasonous attempt to maintain chattel slavery, the president directly tethered himself to this history of racial fear. Leaving no doubt about the continued relevance of this "ancient history," the president expressly and repeatedly borrowed from the race-baiting Nixon campaign, declaring himself the "law and order president," calling peaceful protestors "THUGS" and threatening state-sanctioned violence against them, unilaterally rejecting his military leaders' plans to remove Confederate names from military bases, praising the extrajudicial killing of a Black Lives Matter protester by federal agents, and declaring the phrase "Black Lives Matter" a "symbol of hate."

Third, as discussed in greater detail in Chapter 6, this long history of racial fear is relevant in a pervasive and largely invisible way. Generations of explicit messaging through law, police practices, entertainment, and media, warning of the existence of a dangerous Black criminal underclass, have embedded themselves into the nation's collective unconscious, creating deep and largely immovable implicit biases about dark-skinned individuals. This reality helps explain why so many White people take aggressive private enforcement action against Black people doing mundane things in White spaces. It also supports a central thesis of this book, that criminal justice reform should begin not with a largely futile attempt to change the quality of interactions between Black people and police, but with a decrease in the number of such interactions.

Personally, though, when I am accused of unnecessarily dredging up America's ugly racist past, I think about John Hartfield. I first learned about Mr. Hartfield when I visited the Legacy Museum in Montgomery, Alabama, an incredibly curated museum exhibiting the history of slavery, Jim Crow, and mass incarceration in America. Mr. Hartfield was a Black man who lived in Ellsville, Mississippi, in the early part of the twentieth century. In 1915, he was forced to flee because the local chapter of the Ku Klux Klan caught wind that he was dating a White woman, Ms. Ruth Meeks. He stayed away for four years, living in East St. Louis. By 1919, the lure of home proved too much. He returned to Mississippi and reunited with his girlfriend, taking a position as a hotel porter.[137]

Mr. Hartfield's return immediately became known to the Klan, who spread false rumors that Ms. Meeks was underage and that she had been raped by Mr. Hartfield. A lynch mob was organized, and these terrorists tracked Mr. Hartfield for weeks. After several unsuccessful informal outings, Sheriff Allen Boutwell raised donations to fund a hunting party with bloodhounds. Mr. Hartfield was eventually apprehended attempting to board a train. Sheriff's deputies took him into custody and then released him to a lynch mob. Rather than killing Mr. Hartfield immediately, the terrorists decided to make a spectacle of his murder. Major newspapers across the South, including the *Jackson Daily News* and the *New Orleans States*, ran articles under the headline, "John Hartfield will be lynched by Ellisville mob at 5:00 this afternoon." The article stated, "Officers have agreed to turn him over to the people of the city at 4 o'clock this afternoon where it is expected he will be burned." The terrorists delayed the lynching by a day because the response to the newspaper article

---

[137] Equal Justice Institute, *A Lynching Survivor Returns*, EJI (September 18, 2015), https://eji.org/news/lynching-survivor-mamie-lang-kirkland-returns-to-mississippi/.

was so overwhelming that crowds of people from all over the region descended onto Ellisville. During the wait, a White doctor was engaged to treat Mr. Hartfield's wounds to ensure he lived long enough to be murdered.

By 5:00 p.m. on June 26, 1919, a cheering crowd of more than 10,000 people gathered in a "carnival-like" atmosphere. John Hartfield was hung from a tall sweet-gum tree, where he asphyxiated for several minutes before dying. Once his death was declared official, the crowd riddled his body with bullets, firing approximately 20,000 rounds at him. When he was brought to the ground, his corpse was chopped into pieces and sold as souvenirs. The rest of his body was burned. Commemorative postcards of the lynching with graphic photos of Mr. Hartfield's body were sold nationwide for twenty cents.[138]

When asked why he did not intervene, Gov. Theodore Bilbo claimed he was powerless to stop the mob, but then declared that Mr. Hartfield's death sent a much-needed reminder: "This is a White man's country, with a White man's civilization and any dream on the part of the Negro race to share social and political equality will be shattered in the end."[139]

I think of John Hartfield because a few hours after visiting the Legacy Museum I set out to conduct further research on him. I temporarily forgot his first name and typed in the name "James Hartfield." Rather than being redirected to a 1919 lynching, I learned about the murder of unarmed Black man James Hartsfield at the hands of police nearly one hundred years after John Hartfield's murder.

At approximately 4:15 a.m. on October 7, 2017, Lyft driver James Hartsfield was parked outside a Little Rock, Arkansas, nightclub waiting to pick up a passenger when Officer Brittany Gunn approached his vehicle.[140] Dashcam video shows Officer Gunn opening and entering the front passenger side door of Hartsfield's car without warning, startling Hartsfield, and prompting him to put the car into drive. It appears from the footage that Hartsfield may have believed he was being carjacked, but that will forever remain speculation. Immediately upon opening the door, Officer Gunn fired five shots, killing Hartsfield immediately and causing the car to slam into a nearby wall, endangering onlookers.

The entire episode took eight seconds. Officers rushed to check on Gunn, who had been thrown from the moving vehicle. Eight minutes elapsed before anyone checked on Hartsfield.[141] Police later claimed, without evidence, that Gunn

[138] *Id.; see also* Donna Ladd, EDITOR'S NOTE: *No More "Lynching Logic" to Excuse Brutality Against Black People*, JACKSON FREE PRESS (September 2, 2020), https://www.jacksonfreepress.com/news/2020/sep/02/editors-note-no-more-lynching-logic-excuse-brutali/.

[139] Michael Eli Dokosi, *100 years ago, John Hartfield was hanged, shot, roasted for dating a white lady and his body parts shared to spectators*, FACE 2 FACE AFRICA (November 20, 2019) https://face2face africa.com/article/100-years-ago-john-hartfield-was-hanged-shot-roasted-for-dating-a-white-lady-and-his-body-parts-shared-to-spectators.

[140] David Lippman, *James Hartsfield's Family Sues City of Little Rock and Police Officer Who Killed Him*, THV11 (May 13, 2019), https://www.thv11.com/article/news/crime/james-hartsfields-family-sues-city-of-little-rock-and-police-officer-who-killed-him/91-c40c5841-fb89-4d2e-a760-43071a45e9b6.

[141] *Id.*

suspected Hartsfield of drinking liquor in his car, though no alcoholic containers were found in the vehicle, autopsy reports indicated no alcohol in his body, and friends and acquaintances confirmed that Hartsfield did not drink at all. Gunn also told prosecutors Hartsfield had violently resisted her, though dashcam footage seems to show otherwise. Prosecutors eventually cleared Gunn of any wrongdoing, finding her unprovoked killing of an unarmed Black man sitting alone in a White neighborhood to be both "justified" and "necessary."[142]

That my internet search for information about a 1919 lynching led me to a 2017 modern-day lynching of a nearly identically named Black man floored me. Of course, the experiences of John Hartfield and James Hartsfield are not directly comparable; few incidents match the grotesque inhumanity of John Hartfield's Mississippi lynching. But modern racism is often, though not always, more subtle. This racism expresses itself less in overt White supremacy and more often in violent attempts to patrol the color line – through race-conscious community watch programs, paper-thin "reasonable suspicion" calculations by law enforcement in "high crime areas," aggressive pursuits of Black people in the name of self-defense, and the pervasive unconscious racial bias informing and infecting these actions. The balance of this book considers these modern-day attempts to enforce the public color line.

And as to Messrs. Hartfield and Hartsfield, their vastly different experiences were identical in one important respect: both ended in the unjustified killing of a Black man existing in a White space, with the express blessing of the government.

---

[142]   *Id.*

2

White Caller Crime

DISPATCHER:	*911, what's the address of your emergency?*
CALLER:	*[Provides address.] There's a woman pushing a shopping cart in front of my house.*
DISPATCHER:	*I'm sorry, I'm not getting it. What's the problem?*
CALLER:	*You need to get out here now.*
DISPATCHER:	*Um. I'm sorry, I don't understand what you're reporting.*
CALLER:	*She's black.*
DISPATCHER:	*Sir, I'm still not seeing the problem. Is she being loud? Is the noise of the cart disturbing your peace?*
CALLER:	*Where do you live?*
DISPATCHER:	*Oakland.*
CALLER:	*You wouldn't understand, then. This isn't Oakland. We don't have people like her in this neighborhood. Just send someone out to get rid of her. I'm not talking to you anymore. [Click.]*[143]

When former 911 dispatcher Rachel Herron received this call from an "affluent and very white" northern California neighborhood, she knew exactly what was happening.[144] She "had to respond to racist calls every day."[145] But when she recounted this particular racist phone call to a reporter in 2018, Ms. Herron noted that the caller's bias was not the most troubling part of the encounter: "The worst thing about it? I had to send someone out."[146] Accurately summarizing 911 dispatcher policies across the country, Ms. Herron explained that "[d]ispatchers usually don't get to choose which calls lead to the dispatching of emergency personnel and which don't." Instead, she observed, if "a person wants to make a report, they get to

---

[143] Adapted from Rachael Herron, *I Used to Be a 911 Dispatcher. I Had to Respond to Racist Calls Every Day*, Vox (October 31, 2018, 12:08 p.m.), https://www.vox.com/first-person/2018/5/30/17406092/racial-profiling-911-bbq-becky-living-while-black-babysitting-while-black (last updated October 31, 2018) (emphasis omitted).

[144] *Id.*

[145] *Id.*

[146] *Id.*

make a report. You can think of police as being like lawsuits. Anyone can make one about anything, no matter how stupid."[147]

This analogy is only partly correct. Yes, millions of frivolous 911 calls flood police lines each year, much like the thousands of frivolous lawsuits clogging court dockets each year. But unlike frivolous litigants, who face significant threat of sanction for abusing the court system, virtually no risk of punishment exists for 911 abusers – even those clearly motivated by racial animus. Instead, these "white caller criminals"[148] operate with near absolute impunity, as state and local governments show little ability to overcome the logistical challenges of apprehending these individuals or desire to do so at all. As a result, calling 911 to summon armed government agents to confront a Black person in the White space has become one of the most effective and expedient methods of enforcing society's public color line, one that is costless for the caller. It is also one of the most dangerous.

2.1 "THE TYRANNY OF 911"

The majority of police contacts with the public are what criminologists refer to as "reactive police contacts," meaning contacts "initiated by individuals seeking help from the police."[149] These reactive police contacts most often – though not always – begin with a 911 call. Callers to 911 play a critical role in the criminal justice system, "because they initiate . . . formal [police] interventions [in] situations that may have otherwise gone largely undetected by police." In this sense, "reporters serve as gatekeepers for neighborhood policing and the experience of formal social control for many individuals contacted by the police."[150] This "formal social control" of innocent public conduct through police protection has become an unfortunate by-product of the nation's 911 call system. But it was not always like that.

When police departments first began developing 911 emergency call systems in the 1970s, they were lauded for taking a "professional" approach to "reduc[ing] response time to an absolute minimum" when a civilian needed help.[151] But as early as 1990, officers began complaining about "the tyranny of 911," referring to the sheer amount of

---

[147]   *Id.*

[148]   The phrase "white caller crime" appears to have been popularized in a 2018 article in The Root magazine by Michael Harriot. *See* Michael Harriot, *"White Caller Crime": The Worst Wypipo Police Calls of All Time*, THE ROOT (May 15, 2018), https://www.theroot.com/white-caller-crime-the-worst-wypipo-police-calls-of-1826023382. It has since been used in the title of at least one academic article reflecting on the "phenomenon" of White persons calling 911 to report innocent behavior by Black persons. *See* McNamarah, *supra* note 31. While I neither agree with nor subscribe to all ideas articulated by Messrs. Harriot and McNamarah, I borrow this phrase with gratitude.

[149]   Charles C. Lanfear et al., *Formal Social Control in Changing Neighborhoods: Racial Implications of Neighborhood Context on Reactive Policing*, 17 CITY & CMTY. 1075, 1093 (2018).

[150]   *Id.* at 1075.

[151]   David C. Anderson, *Editorial, The 'Tyranny' of 911*, N.Y. TIMES (September 17, 1990), at A22.

time police spent responding to an endless stream of calls.[152] One of the great benefits of having a number the public could easily remember in an emergency also became a significant hindrance, as frivolous calls flooded the lines. As one report explained, "When the 911 phone system was established, it gave citizens a fast, easy way to reach police in an emergency. But it also created a logistical challenge for law enforcement: Police departments got so many calls, 911 can be as much a burden as a boon."[153]

This burden is immense in scope. Drawing from records maintained by separate regional call centers, the National Emergency Number Association (NENA) estimates that approximately 240 million 911 calls are placed nationally each year.[154] Misuse and abuse of 911 accounts for a shockingly high percentage of these calls. While no national statistics exist, individual states estimate that as many as 70 percent of all calls to 911 could be labeled as frivolous.[155]

Police agencies and organizations studying 911 usage distinguish between two types of inappropriate calls: unintentional and intentional. Unintentional calls are labeled "misuses" of the system, while intentional inappropriate calls are deemed "abuses" of the system.[156] Unintentional calls occur when a person inadvertently dials 911, either through a "phantom wireless 911 call," 911 misdial, or 911 hang-up.[157] Intentional calls, or abuses of 911, generally fall into one of four categories: nonemergency calls, exaggerated emergency calls, lonely complaint calls, and prank calls.[158] Racially fearful complaints alleging criminal behavior fall into either the nonemergency or exaggerated emergency category, depending on the circumstances.

While little reliable data exists defining the scope of race-based abusive calls to 911, several of the nation's largest and most overworked law enforcement jurisdictions report that half or more of all intentional 911 calls are for nonemergencies.[159] For example, one study found that "[m]ore than half of the calls to the San Diego County Sheriff's Department's 911 line are frivolous ones that tie up phone lines and

---

[152] Staff, *Police Take Different Approaches to "The Tyranny of 911,"* NPR Cities Project (June 28, 2013, 5:28 p.m.), https://www.npr.org/2013/06/28/196588465/police-take-different-approaches-to-the-tyranny-of-911.

[153] *Id.*

[154] NENA, *9–1-1 Statistics,* https://www.nena.org/general/custom.asp?page=911statistics.

[155] Rana Sampson, ASU Center for Problem Oriented Policing, *Misuse and Abuse of 911* 1 (2002), https://popcenter.asu.edu/content/misuse-and-abuse-911-0.

[156] *Id.*

[157] *Id.*

[158] *Id.*

[159] *See, e.g.,* M. Alex Johnson, *911 Systems Choking on Non-Emergency Calls,* MSNBC.com (August 5, 2008, 6:30 p.m.), http://www.nbcnews.com/id/26040857/ns/us_news-crime_and_courts/t/systems-choking-non-emergency-calls/ (reporting that 45 percent of 911 calls across California were frivolous, and as many as 80 percent in Sacramento); Kenneth Ma, *Frivolous 911 Calls Drain Sheriff's Resources,* San Diego Union-Trib. (February 19, 2001, 12:00 a.m.), https://www.sandiegouniontribune.com/sdut-frivolous-911-calls-drain-sheriffs-resources-2001feb19-story.html (reporting that about 65 percent of the calls to the San Diego County Sheriff's Department's 911 line were frivolous, and that only 20 percent reported real emergencies).

keep the department from handling life-threatening emergencies."[160] These frivolous calls ranged from questions about the weather at Disneyland to reports of
broken toilets.[161] In Sacramento, officials estimate that, year over year, as many as
80 percent of all 911 calls are frivolous.[162] Florida dispatchers have expressed similar
frustration. Palm Beach County dispatchers reported handling as many as 400,000
nonemergency calls per year, while the Broward Sheriff's Department estimated
that half of its 2.5 million annual calls are frivolous.[163]

Occasionally, particularly humorous or egregious 911 call transcripts make
national news, such as when a Texas man called 911 to order a cab, a Florida
man called 911 to complain that a Subway employee failed to put mayonnaise on
his sandwich, or a Tennessee man called to complain that his stepfather wanted
him to do the laundry.[164] But "police officials and system administrators warn that
911 systems are being choked with clueless, frivolous, even prank, calls."[165] A Knox
County, Tennessee, 911 dispatcher put it plainly: "You've got a true emergency
with somebody out there – that there's a shooting or something – then those
officers are not able to respond to that emergency call, because they're taking
care" of 911 abusers.[166]

2.2 NO DISCRETION

In the three decades since 911 abuse first became a problem, many departments
around the country have adopted innovative approaches to make police responses
more efficient. "[S]ome cities have adopted 311, a non-emergency, easy-to-remember
number for police assistance and other public services."[167] Miami, Florida, uses
public service aides – uniformed but unarmed quasi-mediators dispatched to handle
certain 911 calls that appear to be nonemergencies.[168] But the vast majority of police
departments around the country still require a uniformed, armed police officer to
respond to any 911 call describing a purported criminal "event" in progress, no
matter how trivial or clearly lawful the event sounds.[169]

Even before the 911 call is routed to an officer, dispatchers have a surprising lack of
discretion in screening calls. Ms. Herron explained that, throughout her seventeen

[160] Ma, *supra* note 159.
[161] *Id.*
[162] Johnson, *supra* note 159.
[163] Robert Nolin, *Drunken Dialing, Mental Confusion, Can Prompt Frivolous 911 Calls,* PALM BEACH
       POST (September 13, 2010, 12:01 a.m.), https://www.palmbeachpost.com/article/20100913/NEWS/
       812027192.
[164] Johnson, *supra* note 159.
[165] *Id.*
[166] *Id.*
[167] *Police Take Different Approaches to "The Tyranny of 911," supra* note 152.
[168] *Id.*
[169] *See, e.g.,* Herron, *supra* note 143; *id.* (discussing the effect of an overload of 911 calls on police
       response).

years of experience, all calls had to be routed to officers.[170] Her experience mirrors that of the vast majority of 911 call centers in the country.[171] Dispatchers have virtually no discretion to decide whether to ignore a clearly frivolous call or decline to dispatch armed government agents to respond.[172] Many dispatchers do have discretion in how they "code," or prioritize, calls. Many dispatch centers use a priority system that reserves Priority 1 for clear, imminent threats to life and property, and assigns lower priority designations to less serious threats.[173] But this priority system still requires dispatchers to route all calls – even Priority 3 or lower calls – to officers for response.[174] In Eugene, Oregon, for example, police department guidelines list nine priority codes but expressly require officers to respond to all calls regardless of the code.[175] Likewise, in Grant Park, Illinois, police department guidelines state that officers will respond to all calls – even those coded as non-emergency "routine" calls – unless every police officer is already "dispatched on priority 1, 2, or 3 calls."[176]

In many areas, including major metropolitan areas with overworked police forces, officers may not have an opportunity to respond to Priority 3 calls simply because of the scarcity of law enforcement resources.[177] But nothing prevents idle officers from responding to lower-priority calls, even calls motivated by race. And in many cases, they do:

DISPATCHER: *Oakland Police . . .*

CALLER: *Yeah, I'd like to report that someone is illegally using a charcoal grill in a nondesignated area in Lake Merritt Park near Cleveland Cascade. I'd like it dealt with immediately so that coals don't burn more children and we have to pay more taxes.*

DISPATCHER: *Ok, person using the grill, I need a description. What race are they?*

CALLER: *African American.*[178]

---

[170] See Herron, *supra* note 143.

[171] See, e.g., Johnson, *supra* note 159 ("Because police have to respond to almost every call in case it's a real emergency, people have figured out that a quick call to 911 guarantees action.")

[172] See *id.*; Herron, *supra* note 143.

[173] See Herron, *supra* note 143 ("[A] Priority 3 call . . . essentially means 'not important' . . ."). Different dispatch systems use different priority levels and codes. Shawn Messinger et al., *The Distribution of Emergency Police Dispatch Call Incident Types and Priority Levels Within the Police Priority Dispatch System*, ANNALS EMERGENCY DISPATCH & RESPONSE, no. 2, Aug. 2013, at 12, 14–17 (analyzing nationwide data on how calls are coded and routed).

[174] See, e.g., Ed Gilgor, *Is Your 911 Call a Priority?*, GRANT PARK NEIGHBORHOOD ASS'N, http://grantpark .org/info/16029 (describing four priority levels for which an officer could be dispatched in Atlanta, Georgia, including nonemergency "routine" calls).

[175] Eugene, Or., Police Dep't, *Police Call Priority Definitions*, https://www.eugene-or.gov/ DocumentCenter/View/530/Police-Call-Priority-Definitions.

[176] See Gilgor, *supra* note 174.

[177] Cf. *id.* (insisting that even minor disturbances warrant a 911 call and police response).

[178] For the full recording of this call, and of the follow-up call, see Hilary Hanson, *Listen to Full 911 Audio of "BBQ Becky" Calling Cops on Black Men Grilling*, HUFFPOST (September 2, 2018, 1:56 p.m.), https://www.huffpost.com/entry/bbq-becky-911-calls-grill_n_5b8c0f07c4b0162f4724a74c.

When Jennifer Schulte placed this 911 call on April 29, 2018, the dispatcher initially coded it low priority and assured her that an officer would eventually come and investigate. The call was calm and lasted less than two minutes. But when no officer appeared, Ms. Schulte called again. Released audio of the second 911 call revealed an enraged Jennifer Schulte demanding to know when police would respond to this alleged municipal infraction:

CALLER:	*I called about two hours ago about someone illegally grilling. When are the police going to come?[inaudible yelling]*
DISPATCHER:	*Why is there yelling over a barbecue? I don't understand.*
CALLER:	*I need the police to come right away!*
DISPATCHER:	*Why are you in an argument with these people? Can you walk away? Can you get away from them? Do you live in the park or something?*
CALLER:	*I would like a police officer to come as soon as possible!*
DISPATCHER:	*How are we going to find you? What race are you? You're going to have to tell me what race you are, how old you are, and what you're wearing. They'll never be able to find you.*
CALLER:	*[describes clothing]*
DISPATCHER:	*What is your race?*
CALLER:	*My race doesn't matter!*
DISPATCHER:	*Have you ever been to John George [a nearby mental health facility]?*
CALLER:	*No! Where are the police? I don't see them! Where are they?*[179]

This infamous incident, dubbed "BBQing While Black," helped spark a nationwide conversation about 911 abuse and the private policing of "White space." Locally, activists in Oakland held a "BBQing While Black" community awareness event in the same park where the incident took place, with a revival of the event in 2019; the plan is to make the event an annual occurrence.[180]

Lost in the shuffle of breathless "BBQ Becky" coverage was the fact that multiple armed police officers responded to Ms. Schulte's racially fearful 911 calls and questioned the Black targets of the calls, as well as Ms. Schulte. Ultimately, no arrests were made or tickets issued. But the fact that officers responded at all – after the first dispatcher properly coded the call low priority and the second dispatcher rightly questioned Ms. Schulte's frenetic demands for police protection "over a barbecue"[181] – illustrates how easily fragile White citizens can enforce public color lines through 911 abuse.

[179]   *Id.*

[180]   Marisa Kendall, *Oakland's Second "BBQing While Black" Party Draws Big Crowds*, THE MERCURY NEWS (July 21, 2019, 5:06 p.m.), https://www.mercurynews.com/2019/07/21/oaklands-second-bbqing-while-black-party-draws-big-crowds/.

[181]   Simone Aponte, *2 Investigates Obtains "BBQ Becky's" Viral 911 Calls*, KTVU (September 2, 2018), https://www.ktvu.com/news/2-investigates-obtains-bbq-beckys-viral-911-calls.

2.3 #LIVINGWHILEBLACK

The automatic response of dispatchers and police officers to millions of non-emergency calls each year highlights the woefully inefficient allocation of resources plaguing police departments and emergency response organizations across the country. But when civilians make frivolous calls for racially motivated reasons, the consequences extend far beyond overtaxing an overworked system.

In many ways, "calling the police is [the epitome of escalation."[182] When White callers dial 911 to report that Black people are engaged in nuisance-based behavior, they are engaging in a "formal social control process" with "distinct interracial dynamics."[183] Indeed, "[c]alls for service to the police initiate a process that is often marked by the cumulative bias and structural racism" prevalent in all walks of modern American life,[184] perhaps no more so than in the criminal justice system. At every step in the process following the formal social control of a citizen report to the police, Black individuals experience disproportionate adverse effects, in the treatment they receive from police, in the rate at which they are subjected to stop-and-frisk and other invasive searches, in the rate at which they are arrested, and in the rate at which force is used against them, including lethal force. When a Black person is the target of 911 abuse, "the worst-case scenario is that the police will show up with guns blazing. Even in the best-case scenario, Black folks will probably have to deal with the trauma of having been placed in mortal fear," a mortal fear reinforced by centuries of state-sanctioned violence.[185]

Scholars and commentators have long noted that White callers summoning armed officers to police innocent Black behavior is more than frivolous: "these callers aren't expecting cops to treat black folks politely, but instead to remind them that the consequences for making white people angry or uncomfortable could be harassment, unfair prosecution or death."[186] Or as another commentator explained, "Calling 911 on Black people for innocent conduct is the continuation of a racist American tradition with deep historical roots: Private citizens and police using feckless interpretations of the law to convert blackness into criminal trespass."[187]

Racially motivated abuse of 911 systems is not new, nor is it clear that the practice is necessarily on the rise. But the ubiquity of cell phone video cameras and the rise in social media posting about racially charged incidents drew attention to the issue beginning in early 2018. In a thirty-day period in April and May 2018, over a dozen stories about White individuals calling 911 to report Black people for engaging in entirely innocent conduct in a traditionally "White space" garnered national

---

[182] Jason Johnson, *From Starbucks to Hashtags: We Need to Talk About Why White Americans Call the Police on Black People*, THE ROOT (April 16, 2018, 12:59 p.m.), https://www.theroot.com/from-starbucks-to-hashtags-we-need-to-talk-about-why-w-1825284087.

[183] Lanfear et al., *supra* note 149, at 1075.

[184] *Id.* at 1076.

[185] Patton & Farley, *supra* note 27.

[186] *Id.*; *see also* Johnson, *supra* note 182 ("[C]alling the police on black people for noncrimes is a step away from asking for a tax-funded beatdown, if not an execution.").

[187] Patton & Farley, *supra* note 27.

attention. During this period, national media airwaves were saturated with news coverage about White people demanding police investigate Black individuals for sitting quietly in a Starbucks,[188] barbecuing in a park,[189] playing golf "too slow,"[190] working out at a gym,[191] moving into a new apartment,[192] flying on a plane,[193] shopping for a prom outfit,[194] buying a money order to pay rent,[195] checking out of an AirBnB rental,[196] and taking a nap in a Yale dormitory.[197]

The response to these frivolous calls, by dispatchers and by police, varied in each case, but in one very important respect, the response was the same – in every instance, the dispatchers notified the police, and armed police officers personally showed up to investigate. No matter how patently frivolous the call, no matter how wasteful the use of scarce law enforcement resources, officers responded to the calls. These incidents highlight both the ubiquity of the use of 911 by White individuals to protect White spaces and the consistency with which these efforts are supported by law enforcement responses.

[188] Phil McCausland, *Protests Follow Outrage After Two Black Men Arrested at Philly Starbucks*, NBC News (April 15, 2018, 4:05 p.m.), https://www.nbcnews.com/news/us-news/protests-follow-outrage-after-two-black-men-arrested-philly-starbucks-n866141.

[189] *See supra* notes 178–181.

[190] Tony Marco & Lauren DelValle, *A Group of Black Women Say a Golf Course Called the Cops on Them for Playing Too Slow*, CNN (April 25, 2018, 5:21 p.m.), https://www.cnn.com/2018/04/25/us/black-women-golfers-pennsylvania-trnd/index.html.

[191] Jeff Goldman, *L.A. Fitness Fires 3 Workers After Black Men Get Kicked Out of N.J. Gym*, NJ.com (April 18, 2018), https://www.nj.com/hudson/2018/04/3_la_fitness_employees_fired_after_kicking_2_men_o.html; Mark Boyle & Mitzi Morris, *Charlotte Man Says He Was Racially Profiled at Gym*, WCNC (May 2, 2018, 8:50 p.m.), https://www.wcnc.com/article/news/charlotte-man-says-he-was-racially-profiled-at-gym/275-548235962.

[192] Eli Rosenberg, *A Black Former White House Staffer Was Moving into a New Apartment. Someone Reported a Burglary*, Wash. Post (May 1, 2018, 10:12 p.m.), https://www.washingtonpost.com/news/post-nation/wp/2018/05/01/a-black-former-white-house-staffer-was-moving-into-a-new-apartment-someone-reported-a-burglary/.

[193] Rachel Herron, *Woman Humiliated After Flight Attendant Calls Cops on Her for "Flying While Fat and Black,"* BET (April 30, 2018), https://www.bet.com/news/national/2018/04/30/black-woman-has-cops-called-on-her-on-american-airlines-flight.html.

[194] Matthew Haag, *Nordstrom Rack Apologizes to Black Teenagers Falsely Accused of Stealing*, N.Y. Times (May 8, 2018), https://www.nytimes.com/2018/05/08/business/nordstrom-black-men-profiling-shopping.html.

[195] Tia Berger, *Man's Girlfriend Brought to Tears After Being Accused of Fraud While Buying Money Order With Cash*, Atlanta Black Star (May 9, 2018), https://atlantablackstar.com/2018/05/09/mans-girlfriend-brought-tears-accused-fraud-buying-money-order-cash/.

[196] Daniel Victor, *A Woman Said She Saw Burglars. They Were Just Black Airbnb Guests*, N.Y. Times (May 8, 2018), https://www.nytimes.com/2018/05/08/us/airbnb-black-women-police.html.

[197] Britton O'Daly, *Black Student Reported to YPD for Napping in Dormitory Common Room*, Yale Daily News (May 8, 2018, 10:52 p.m.), https://yaledailynews.com/blog/2018/05/08/black-student-reported-to-ypd-for-napping-in-dormitory-common-room/. This list is far from exhaustive. For more examples, *see* Brandon E. Patterson, *11 More Things You Can't Do While Black*, Mother Jones (May 9, 2018), https://www.motherjones.com/crime-justice/2018/05/11-more-things-you-cannot-do-while-black-starbucks-nordstrom-rack-1/. Patterson was updating a 2014 story. *See* Lauren Williams, *21 Things You Can't Do While Black*, Mother Jones (February 12, 2014), https://www.motherjones.com/politics/2014/02/21-things-you-cant-do-while-black/.

These incidents also showcase the various ways racial fear finds expression in the White mind. In some cases, the unconscious intuition driving fear stems from a dark-skinned individual existing in an area historically or statistically reserved for White folks. In others, fear stems from Black persons inhabiting spaces of power or privilege traditionally reserved for the dominant White class, such as a private golf course, a wealthy Manhattan neighborhood, or an Ivy League dormitory. In others, the fear appears to stem from an apprehension that otherwise innocent or trivial conduct – such as using charcoal in a park or filling water cups with soda in a restaurant – is an inevitable precursor to more serious criminality, requiring an immediate armed response to snuff out the minor infraction before it escalates.

2.4 GENTRIFICATION: THE COLOR LINE'S BATTLEGROUND

Donisha Prendergast is a stylish Jamaican actress and filmmaker with slender features and long, flowing dreadlocks. She also happens to be the granddaughter of Bob Marley. In April 2018, she and two other filmmaker friends, Kelly Fyffe-Marshall and Komi-Oluwa Olafimihan, rented an Airbnb in a predominantly white neighborhood in Rialto, California, a small suburban desert town west of San Bernardino. On April 30, the friends checked out of the house and began loading their luggage into the car when they noticed an elderly White neighbor staring at them while she picked up her phone. She was calling 911.[198]

On the call, the neighbor can be heard telling police, "I walked out here and uh, just to check the mail and I see these strange people coming and going back and forth. You know, with luggage and I didn't recognize them." When the dispatcher asked what she thought made them strange, the neighbor responded, "Um, because they had luggage in their hand and they weren't really looking at me. You know, they just kind of avoided me or they didn't wave, you know, like neighbors."

DISPATCHER:	*OK, he's a black male. And what color shirt is he wearing?*
CALLER:	*Um, I'm not sure. . . . It's a black station wagon. . . .*
DISPATCHER:	*OK, that black station wagon – does it look new or old?*
CALLER:	*It's a newer model black station wagon, parked almost in front of the house.*
DISPATCHER:	*Tinted windows?*
CALLER:	*Yeah, tinted windows, uh huh.*
DISPATCHER:	*OK, is it just him, is he the only person you see going in and out of that house?*
CALLER:	*Yeah, yeah.*
DISPATCHER:	*Is he bringing anything out other than just luggage? Do you see him carrying anything else out?*

---

[198] *See* Victor, *supra* note 196, for full narrative.

CALLER: *I haven't seen like a TV or something. No, I haven't seen anything like that. I just saw luggage.*

DISPATCHER: *Now, with the luggage – is he, do you think he's going to the car and unloading it, or do you think he's just putting the luggage inside the car?*

CALLER: *He's just putting the luggage inside the car. He's inside the house now. . . .*

CALLER: *Yeah, I see another man coming out of the house who's also black. No, it's a woman . . . it's a woman, it's a black woman. . . . She's got a phone in her hand and she's got a long braid, or long hair like in a ponytail. . . .*

DISPATCHER: *Tell me when they're in the car, getting ready to leave, OK?*

CALLER: *Now there's a white woman.*

DISPATCHER: *Coming out of the car?*

CALLER: *Coming out of the house. And she has blond hair. . . . The white woman, a white female, she's going back inside the house now. OK, maybe everything's OK. It's just hard to tell.*

DISPATCHER: *It's OK, we'll double check. Maybe the white female is somebody that lives there?*[199]

When Prendergast saw the neighbor on the phone she joked with her friends that she was "probably calling the police." Less than one minute later, four police cruisers arrived with lights flashing. Video of the incident taken by Fyffe-Marshall, along with partial body camera footage released by the Rialto Police Department, shows that at one point seven police cars and a police helicopter were on the scene in response to the 911 call. The neighborhood appeared to be locked down, and police records of the incident indicate that questioning lasted forty-five minutes; the sergeant in charge ordered the filmmakers detained because he had never heard of Airbnb and assumed the individuals were lying. The three innocent renters were eventually released.[200]

In response to outrage over the incident, Rialto Mayor Pro Tem Ed Scott defended the caller, stating that "residents in this community want to be able to call for service and want police officers to arrive when we see something suspicious."[201] The owner of the Airbnb rental went further, saying the renters

[199]   Marissa Wenzke, *Neighbor's 911 Call About "Suspicious" Airbnb Guests Is Released by City of Rialto After Accusations of Racial Profiling,* KTLA5 (May 23, 2018, 7:50 p.m.), https://ktla.com/news/nationworld/911-call-falsely-reporting-airbnb-guests-as-burglars-released-by-city-of-rialto-after-accusations-of-racial-profiling/.

[200]   Dog Criss & Amir Vera, *Three Black People Checked Out of Their Airbnb Rental. Then Someone Called the Police on Them,* CNN (May 10, 2018), https://www.cnn.com/2018/05/07/us/airbnb-police-called-trnd/index.html; N'dea Yancey-Bragg, *Bob Marley's Granddaughter Plans to Sue California Police After Alleged Racial Profiling,* USA Today (May 9, 2018), https://www.usatoday.com/story/news/nation-now/2018/05/09/bob-marley-granddaughter-airbnb-racial-profiling-lawsuit/595420002/.

[201]   Wenzke, *supra* note 199.

were "strange people [in a] strange vehicle in a suburban neighborhood, and they're not friendly. She called the police, and I don't blame her."[202] In a separate interview, she resisted Prendergast's interpretation of the incident: "They're making it sound like it's racially motivated, and it has nothing to do with that."[203]

These defenses are belied by the call transcript. The caller worries about the "very curious" and "very strange" behavior of the Black individuals on her street, but as soon as she sees a White person on the property she posits that "maybe everything's OK." The caller later admitted not knowing any of the individuals, White or Black, but claimed the Black individuals simply "didn't behave like neighbors." In reality, what Mayor Scott defended as a citizen speaking up about seeing "something suspicious" in her neighborhood was a citizen speaking up about seeing someone Black in her White neighborhood – a neighborhood known for its "four and five bedroom homes ... upper-middle income ... family friendly atmosphere," and 3.5 percent Black population.[204]

This "Airbnbing While Black" incident also illustrates another factor driving the complicated, fearful enforcement of White and Black spaces: the rapidly changing demographics of Rialto, California. The city of Rialto has traditionally reflected the racial and ethnic diversity of much of southern California. The 2000 census reported a racial makeup that was 39 percent White and 22 percent Black, with slightly over half of all residents identifying as Hispanic or Latino. But by 2018, when the Airbnb incident occurred, 61 percent of the city identified as White and only 12 percent identified as Black.[205] This rapid whitening of the community coincided with significant increases in median incomes and in the city's population generally. In a word, Rialto is gentrifying.

Few words spark more debate among urban planners than *gentrification*. By one account, gentrification represents the revitalization of poor, dilapidated neighborhoods via financial investment, a rebirth of urban areas leading to improved housing, more attractive business opportunities, and safer streets. By another account, gentrification is little more than the usurpation of neighborhoods by wealthy White

---

[202] Associated Press, *Airbnb Owners Blames Her Black Guests' "Lack of Good Nature" as Reason for Her Neighbor Calling the Police*, Los Angeles Sentinel (May 10, 2018), https://lasentinel .net/airbnb-owner-blames-her-black-guests-lack-of-good-nature-as-reason-for-her-neighbor-calling-the-police.html.

[203] *Id.*

[204] News outlets reported that the 911 call and incident took place on the 2600 block of West Loma Vista Drive in Rialto. *See* Brian Whitehead, *Rialto city leaders to meet with Airbnb CEO in wake of controversy involving Bob Marley's granddaughter*, SUN (May 15, 2018), https://www.sbsun.com/2018/ 05/15/rialto-city-leaders-to-meet-with-airbnb-ceo-in-wake-of-controversy-involving-bob-marleys-granddaughter/. This residential area overlaps with the Verdemont/Devore, Locust/Casa Grande, and Sierra Heights neighborhoods, which Neighborhood Scout describes as "wealthy ... among the 15% highest income neighborhoods in America" and majority White. Neighborhood Scout, https:// www.neighborhoodscout.com/ca/fontana/locust-ave.

[205] United States Census Bureau, *Quick Facts: Rialto city, California*, https://www.census.gov/quick facts/rialtocitycalifornia.

investors at the expense of disadvantaged people of color who inevitably are pushed further to the margins of society as they are displaced from their neighborhoods – a modern form of colonization.

Regardless of whether gentrification is better represented as renewal or colonization, the process indisputably involves significant social upheaval marked by dislocations and relocations of significant, once racially heterogeneous communities – and usually, the replacement of those communities with White communities. A 2018 study from the University of Southern California found that gentrifying neighborhoods overwhelmingly become more White over time, and that the socioeconomic ascent marked by gentrification "actually perpetuat[es] existing racial inequality within and between neighborhoods."[206] The study found that a significant percentage of the "ascending" neighborhoods that were formerly majority Black became majority White as a result of concerted gentrification efforts.[207]

The social upheaval that marks rapid gentrification, including the arrival of new residents to a formerly static community, can contribute to diminished social cohesion and increased distrust. One study examining the impacts of reactive policing on racially heterogeneous urban neighborhoods found that "rapid neighborhood change – such as gentrification – can lead to social disorganization by dismantling social cohesion and impacting residents' response to criminal behavior." The lack of familiarity with one's neighbors in rapidly changing neighborhoods can "reduce trust between neighbors [and] lead to diminished levels of social control and increased reliance on state authorities [like police] to solve social problems." In other words, as residents become less comfortable dealing directly with their neighbors, they may rely more heavily on police to resolve minor complaints and enforce social norms. This is particularly true in gentrifying neighborhoods filled with "newcomers unfamiliar with neighborhood legacies, prior police contact, or crime control norms in the area." Lacking local knowledge of connections, these new residents "may apply stricter standards to deviant behavior, leading to more calls to the police for infractions that would have been ignored in the past."[208]

These problems are only exacerbated by race. Changing racial demographics define much of this country's urban gentrification, with White residents claiming ownership in formerly Black spaces and redefining the norms for acceptable social behavior. Coupled with a lack of cross-cultural competency and implicit racial fear, this dynamic may lead White residents to defer to state-sanctioned armed agents to resolve even minor perceived violations of social norms. In Seattle, for example, increased ethnic and racial heterogeneity is "among the strongest community

---

[206] Press Release, University of Southern California, Gentrification Draws More Whites to Minority Neighborhoods (May 1, 2018), https://www.eurekalert.org/pub_releases/2018-05/uosc-gdm050118.php.

[207] Ann Owens & Jennifer Candipan, *Racial/Ethnic Transition and Hierarchy Among Ascending Neighborhoods*, 55 Urb. Affs. Rev. 1550 (2018).

[208] Lanfear et al., *supra* note 149 at 15–18.

characteristics that negatively predict the degree to which Whites view neighbour relations as calm, trusting and helpful."[209]

This White attempt to redefine the color line through gentrification – or more derisively, "colonization"[210] – often actively relies on police participation. In many gentrifying neighborhoods, "residents may push local government to apply place-based policing initiatives that increase patrols and the probability of arrest for Black citizens" in newly claimed White spaces.[211] This approach has proven successful in criminalizing Black movement in White spaces, at least according to one study. After studying 246,000 arrest records associated with reactive policing to private citizen reports, three researchers from the University of Washington concluded that "black targets" of 911 calls were "more frequently subject to arrest overall" than non-Black targets, and that this was true "particularly in changing [gentrifying] neighborhoods when reporters are white."[212]

As gentrifying neighborhoods become whiter and wealthier, "the conspicuousness of black individuals in predominantly white neighborhoods" increased the probability of arrest in response to a White reporter – even for "nuisance" reports of criminal activity.[213] Indeed, Prendergast's conspicuous Blackness in the predominantly White Rialto suburb may more accurately explain her experience than the gentrification of the wider Rialto community. But her experience highlights how tenuous the existence of Black people can be in an area that has cemented itself as a White neighborhood in an otherwise diverse area.

Just ask James Juanillo. The Filipino CEO of Pack Heights, LLC, a dog-walking and pet-sitting service in San Francisco, has been tending to the furry friends of Pacific Heights millionaires for decades.[214] He also lives in Pacific Heights, by far the wealthiest neighborhood in the city and known as much for its residents (Nancy Pelosi, Danielle Steele, PayPal cofounder Peter Thiel, and Oracle CEO Larry Ellison) as for its panoramic views of the Golden Gate Bridge. While San Francisco remains one of the more diverse cities in the country, Mr. Juanillo's presence in such a wealthy (and White) neighborhood caught the attention of Lisa Alexander in June 2020. When Mr. Juanillo stenciled "Black Lives Matter" and "I Can't Breathe" on his home on June 15, 2020, Ms. Alexander demanded to know why he was defacing someone else's property and threatened to call the police.[215]

---

[209] Avery M. Guest et al., *Heterogeneity and Harmony: Neighbouring Relationships Among Whites in Ethnically Diverse Neighbourhoods in Seattle*, 45 URB. STUD. 501 (2008).

[210] *See* Jonathan L. Wharton, *Gentrification: The New Colonialism in the Modern Era.* Forum on Public Policy: A Journal of the Oxford Round Table 2008.

[211] Lanfear et al., *supra* note 149, at 1081.

[212] *Id.* at 1075.

[213] *Id.* at 1081, 1090.

[214] *CEO Apologizes for Pacific Heights Confrontation Over Black Lives Matter Sign*, KPIX5 (June 14, 2020, 2:17 p.m.), https://sanfrancisco.cbslocal.com/2020/06/14/ceo-apologizes-for-pacific-heights-confrontation-over-black-lives-matter-sign/.

[215] *Id.*

Mr. Juanillo's recording of the incident protected him when police arrived and later led to Ms. Alexander's firing from the cosmetics company she ran.[216]

Across town, Allison Ettel was working for her cannabis company in a recently gentrified area surrounding the San Francisco Giants ballpark when she followed through with threats to call 911 on an eight-year-old Black girl "illegally selling water without a permit" in front of her San Francisco apartment. When the girl's aunt began recording the incident, Ms. Ettel fearfully crouched behind a wall to evade detection for her 911 abuse. She was later dismissed from her company.[217] (And, to bring at least some positivity, the young girl's mother captured her delirious screams of joy when she found out musician Jonathon Brannon had bought her four tickets to Disneyland.)[218]

But young Mekhi Lee is not from San Francisco. He is from Brentwood, Missouri, an inner-ring suburb of St. Louis. St. Louis is richly and historically diverse, with an almost even split of White and Black residents as of 2017. Brentwood is not that. This quiet suburb is 85 percent White and 4 percent Black.[219] When Mekhi and two of his friends began shopping for prom outfits, they noticed store employees closely eyeing them and following them through the aisles. At one point, an elderly White woman referred to them as a "bunch of bums" and asked, "Would your parents and grandparents be proud of what you are doing?" When Mekhi and his friends reached the register to check out, they noticed the White store manager had escorted the elderly lady out of the store and overheard other White employees calling the police. When they exited the store, they were greeted by police, who said they had been alerted to three Black men shoplifting. The officers quickly determined that no crime had been committed and left.[220]

2.5 THE (WHITE) CORRIDORS OF POWER

Beyond the literal demographics of a changing neighborhood, American society's racial integration process is leading to increasing diversity in positions of power and prestige, settings "previously occupied only by whites."[221] Despite this more

---

[216] *Id.*

[217] Jessica Campisi, *After Internet Mockery, "Permit Patty" Resigns as CEO of Cannabis-Products Company,"* CNN (June 26, 2018, 10:47 p.m.), https://www.cnn.com/2018/06/25/us/permit-patty-san-francisco-trnd/index.html.

[218] Niraj Chokshi, *White Woman Nicknamed "Permit Patty" Regrets Confrontation over Black Girl Selling Water,* N.Y. Times (June 25, 2018), https://www.nytimes.com/2018/06/25/us/permit-patty-black-girl-water.html.

[219] United States Census Bureau, *Quick Facts: Brentwood city, Missouri,* https://www.census.gov/quick facts/fact/table/brentwoodcitymissouri/PST045219; *see also* Neighborhood Scout, *Brentwood Profile,* https://www.neighborhoodscout.com/mo/brentwood ("Brentwood is home to many people who could be described as 'urban sophisticates' ... who are both educated and wealthy ... [it] is not just about being educated and well-off financially: it is a point of view and state of mind.").

[220] *Nordstrom Rack Wrongly Accuses 3 Black Men of Theft, Apologizes,* CBS News (May 8, 2018), https://www.cbsnews.com/news/nordstrom-rack-wrongly-accuses-3-black-men-of-theft-apologizes/.

[221] Anderson, *supra* note 19, at 10.

pluralistic sharing of power, White reaction to Black presence in the corridors of power "reinforces a normative sensibility" that Black people are not expected, and thus to be treated with caution and even suspicion.[222] Black people fill a greater percentage of professional occupations in American society than ever before, but their presence as doctors, lawyers, or executives is incongruous with the "iconic ghetto" in which White society has categorized them.[223] As a result, the sense persists that they do not belong, that they are intruders, that they are imposters with nefarious, criminal motives.

What better example of this distrust of Black people in powerful, prestigious positions than the first Black man elected President of the United States? Having served as a United States senator and a state senator, and the president of the *Harvard Law Review* before that, he was nonetheless labeled an "outsider" and immediately confronted with spurious claims that he could not possibly be qualified for the job because he literally was not from this country. The fact that the man who succeeded Barack Obama to the presidency was the very man who breathed life into this conspiracy encapsulates weaponized racial fear almost too perfectly.

The White House is not the only prestigious space traditionally reserved for White people, however.

On April 21, 2018, Sandra Thompson, Myneca Ojo, and three other friends teed off to play eighteen holes of golf at the Grandview Country Club in Dover Township, Pennsylvania.[224] All five Black women were avid golfers and paying members at the mostly White club; they had played together for ten years. On the second hole, Steve Chronister, co-owner of the club, told the women their pace of play was "too slow" and threatened to revoke their memberships if they did not leave "our" premises. When the women ignored Chronister's demand and continued playing; he aggressively advised the women that police were on their way. Ms. Thompson, the president of the local chapter of the NAACP, began recording the encounter in part out of fear for her safety. The video shows Chronister sarcastically deriding the women as "real winners." Portions of the released 911 call capture Chronister telling the dispatcher that police needed to come and remove from the premises five women who were holding up other golfers:

DISPATCHER: *No weapons or anything like that, right?*

Chronister: *It's even worse than that, but anyway I can't . . .*

DISPATCHER: *Ok, sir, there's no weapons, right?*

Chronister: *No. Other than her mouth, there's not any weapons.*

DISPATCHER: *Ok. And they're just literally standing at the hole? They're not . . .*

---

[222] *Id.*

[223] *Id.* at 11.

[224] Marco & DelValle, *supra* note 190; Ryan Ballengee, *Black Women's Group Asked to Leave Pa. Golf Course Over Supposed Pace-of-Play Issue*, GOLF NEWS NETWORK (April 24, 2018, 11:38 a.m.), https://thegolfnewsnet.com/ryan_ballengee/2018/04/24/black-women-golf-group-asked-to-leave-pa-grandview-golf-course-racist-discrimination-109332/.

Chronister:	*I want her off the golf course. [Police are] gonna have to get out here quickly.*
DISPATCHER:	*How many people need to be removed?*
Chronister:	*There's two now. There were five.*
DISPATCHER:	*Are there any weapons?*
Chronister:	*No. Just her mouth.*[225]

Despite the obvious bias in the phone call and the lack of any clear emergency, the dispatcher coded the call and requested immediate law enforcement response. Several officers showed up a few minutes later and interviewed the women before realizing no crime had been committed – at least, not by the Black women enjoying their country club membership. Both the dispatcher call log and notes taken by officers at the scene confirmed that Mr. Chronister had clearly abused the 911 emergency call system for frivolous purposes, in violation of Pennsylvania law. Yet no citations were issued or charges filed against Mr. Chronister.

On May 8, 2018, African Studies graduate student Lolade Siyonbola fell asleep studying for finals in the common area of the Yale University Hall of Graduate Studies dormitory.[226] At 1:40 a.m., she was awoken by fellow graduate student Sarah Braasch, a White woman who did not live in the building. Ms. Braasch turned on the lights and exclaimed, "You're not supposed to be sleeping here. I'm going to call the police."[227] Ms. Siyonbola began filming the incident; she captured Ms. Braasch taking several photos and explaining, "I have the right to call the police on you." Three officers arrived approximately five minutes later, stating that they received a call of "somebody who appeared they weren't … where they were supposed to be."[228] The officers asked Ms. Siyonbola to prove her right to be in the building, though they did not make a similar demand of Ms. Braasch. Ms. Siyonbola provided her student identification card and then led the officers to her room, which she unlocked with her key so she could show them her belongings. The interrogation lasted for another forty-five minutes after Ms. Siyonbola showed the officers her ID and room.[229] Eventually, the officers relented and admitted that no criminal trespass had occurred. Siyonbola later told *Good Morning America* that she recorded and posted the video "just for my safety. I have always said to myself since Sandra Bland was killed I said to myself if I ever have an encounter with police, I'll film myself."[230]

Even being associated with the former President of the United States does not protect Black people from being suspected of fraudulently inhabiting the White

[225] Ed Mahon & Candy Woodall, *Grandview Golf Club: Listen to 911 Calls of Police Being Called on 5 black women in Pa.*, York Daily Record (May 30, 2018), https://www.ydr.com/story/news/2018/05/30/grandview-golf-club-listen-911-calls-cops-called-black-women/653205002/.
[226] O'Daly, *supra* note 197.
[227] Id.
[228] Id.
[229] Id.
[230] Id.

space. Two weeks before Lolade Siyonbola was questioned for being a Black woman in an Ivy League space, former Obama White House aide Darren Martin was questioned for being a Black man in the prestigious Upper West Side neighborhood of Manhattan.[231] Though not as glamorous as the Upper East Side, this "NYC nabe" ranks as among the wealthiest in the borough. It also does not mirror the diverse city around it; the Upper West Side has a 70 percent White population, and only 7 percent of its inhabitants are Black. When Mr. Martin began moving into his new apartment on the evening of April 28, 2018, a new neighbor called 911, claiming that he was breaking into the building with "a large weapon or a large tool." In fact, he had used his key.

Like Siyonbola, Martin recorded the subsequent encounter, which at one point included seven police officers, on the scene to investigate a breaking and entering. The video picks up a relay from the 911 dispatcher, who said the caller claimed to see "someone trying to break into the door … banging on doors … possibly a weapon, large tool."[232] Martin later admitted his fear that he could be profiled because of the way the "largely white, gentrified" neighborhood had looked at him earlier in the day when he wore a hoodie to move some boxes. "Maybe next time I'll wear a suit."

2.6 BROKEN WINDOWS RACISM

Among the most troubling types of racially motivated 911 abuse are those that summon armed police to investigate minor infractions, like using charcoal outside the proper zoning area or selling lemonade without a permit. The breakdown of informal social control mechanisms in these situations – the inability to resolve seemingly minor conflicts without police involvement – is unfortunate in its own right. But this breakdown in social cohesion and the aggressive response speaks also to a White fearful reaction that a minor rule violation or "nuisance crime" by a Black person may be a harbinger of things to come.

This type of "broken windows racism" evokes the racist and classist "broken windows" theory of policing popularized in the 1980s. The theory, first articulated in a 1982 article by George L. Kelling and James Q. Wilson, argued that "disorder and crime are usually inextricably linked," and claimed that any visible signs of antisocial behavior or civil disorder encourage further crime and disorder, including more serious crimes.[233] These criminologists claimed that "if a window in a building is broken and is left unrepaired, all the rest of the windows will soon be broken."[234] By extension, petty criminal behavior

[231] Rosenberg, *supra* note 192.
[232] Julia Jacobo & Erica Y. King, *'Profiling is Real': Former Obama Staffer Mistaken As Burglar While Moving into New York City Apartment*, ABC News (May 2, 2018), https://abcnews.go.com/Politics/profiling-real-obama-staffer-mistaken-burglar-moving-york/story?id=54877597.
[233] George L. Kelling & James Q. Wilson, *Broken Windows: The Police and Neighborhood Safety*, The *Atlantic* (March 1981), https://www.theatlantic.com/magazine/archive/1982/03/broken-windows/304465/.
[234] *Id.*

left unchecked will inevitably lead to more serious criminal activity. This theory, which drove widespread "quality of life" policing crackdowns in New York City and other major cities in the 1990s, has shown to not meaningfully reduce serious crime while criminalizing the behaviors of racial minorities and poor people viewed as "antisocial" by the dominant White, wealthy caste.[235]

While 911 abuse based on broken windows racism operates on a much shorter time frame than the gradual societal breakdown warned of by Kelling and Wilson, the analogy remains potent. For example, in June 2018, Felicia and Othniel Dobson were driving home to North Carolina when they stopped at Subway with their four children and aunt to eat dinner. After the family had been there for about an hour, eating, a Subway employee made a frantic 911 call:

> *Caller: I need someone to come through here please, ASAP. Now. There's about eight people in a van, and they've been in the store for about an hour. They keep going back and forth to the bathrooms by my back door. . . . maybe putting soda in water cups.*[236]

Putting soda (for which one must pay) in cups meant for water (given for free) is a violation of Subway's rules, but it is not uncommon. And it clearly is not the sort of emergency criminal behavior requiring a 911 call and "ASAP" armed police response. The Subway employee later claimed that she feared the family "might rob" her, in part because of their willingness to steal soda.

This fear is classic broken windows theory. Unless the minor infraction is aggressively snuffed out with armed police, more serious criminal activity will follow. It is also classic broken windows racism. Restaurant employees regularly witness patrons taking extra soda from fountains, but they only call the police in fear of an armed robbery when the patrons are "Black people in a van."

Take the experience of Tshyrad Oates, a Black man visiting an L.A. Fitness gym in Seacaucus, New Jersey, on a guest pass along with his Black friend, a longtime gym

---

[235] Bernard E. Harcourt & Jens Ludwig, *Broken Windows: New Evidence from New York City and a Five-City Social Experiment*, 73 U. CHI. L. REV. 271, 272 (2006) ("Taken together, the evidence . . . provides no support for a simple first-order disorder-crime relationship . . . nor for the proposition that broken windows policing is the optimal use of scarce law enforcement resources."); Greg St. Martin, *Do Broken Windows Mean More Crime?*, NORTHEASTERN NEWS (May 15, 2019), https://news .northeastern.edu/2019/05/15/northeastern-university-researchers-find-little-evidence-for-broken-windows-theory-say-neighborhood-disorder-doesnt-cause-crime/ (describing new study that "debunked the 'broken windows theory' . . . disorder in a neighborhood doesn't cause people to break the law, commit more crimes, or have a lower opinion of their neighborhoods"); Richard Delgado, *Policing and Race Law Enforcement in Subordinated Communities: Innovation and Response*, 106 MICH. L. REV. 1193, 1203 (2008) (observing that even if broken windows policing did "reduce crime slightly," it does so by "generated resistance in subordinated communities"); Dennis J. Baker, *The Moral Limits of Criminalizing Remote Harms*, 10 NEW CRIM. L.R. 370, 382 (2007) (quoting broken windows thesis co-creator James Wilson: "I still to this day do not know if improving order will or will not reduce crime . . . this was a speculation.").

[236] Breanna Edwards, *#EatingOutWhileBlack: Subway Employee Calls 911 on Black Family Because She Thought They Would Rob Her*, THE ROOT (July 5, 2018, 8:52 a.m.), https://www.theroot.com/ eatingoutwhileblack-subway-employee-calls-911-on-blac-1827358215.

member.[237] Both men were properly checked into the gym and had been exercising for about half an hour when an L.A. Fitness employee approached them and said their memberships had expired, they were trespassing, and they had to leave immediately. None of these assertions was true, and even if they had been true, this type of infraction appears unrelated to the kind of criminal activity that warrants a 911 call. Yet, three minutes later, five police officers arrived at the gym in response to the employee's "criminal trespass" call. In a discussion with police, the employee stated she feared they might cause damage because they were willing to work out without authorization. Mr. Oates recorded the half-hour conversation with police and took panoramic views of the gym, clearly showing that he and his friend were the only Black people in the gym. The population of Seacaucus, New Jersey, is less than 4 percent Black.[238]

2.7 NO HARM, NO FOUL?

In the 911 abuse incidents described so far, none of the targets of racial abuse were arrested or physically harmed. Some might wonder, then, what the fuss is all about. Some might even argue that a little politically incorrect inconvenience is worth it, just to be on the safe side. Better safe than sorry, right?

In fact, these arguments have been made in the middle of a racially biased 911 call. On October 9, 2018, Corey Lewis was babysitting his friend's two children in Marietta, Georgia, when he noticed a woman staring at him as he and the children exited a Walmart. The woman asked to speak with the children, and when Lewis refused, the woman followed him in her car out of the parking lot, to a gas station across the street, and eventually to his home. When Lewis arrived home, he was greeted by a Cobb County police officer asking why he had two children in the backseat.

The released 911 transcript illustrated the "better safe than sorry" reasoning in action:

CALLER: *I see this black gentleman with these two little white kids, so I just had a funny feeling. I rode around again and I said, "Let me see the little girl" and he goes, "No." . . . He just got gas now and he's pulling away. Should I follow him?*

DISPATCHER: *No, ma'am. I recommend not following him. . . .*

CALLER: *And if I'm wrong, that's great. I'm thrilled. But if I'm not, you know, then these kids are OK.*[239]

[237] Goldman, *supra* note 191.
[238] *QuickFacts: Secaucus Town, New Jersey*, U.S. CENSUS BUREAU, https://www.census.gov/quickfacts/fact/table/secaucustownnewjersey,NJ/PST045219.
[239] *"Things Look Weird": Woman Calls Police on Black Man Babysitting White Children*, ABC11 (October 12, 2018), https://abc11.com/black-babysitter-white-couple-atlanta-children-and/4467813/.

Some White communities have more or less expressly adopted better-safe-than-sorry racism as a security plan. For example, as Professor Addie Rolnick described in a recent law review article:

> [R]esidents of Mountain's Edge, a planned community on the southwestern outskirts of Las Vegas, created a community Facebook page to monitor suspicious activity and guard against a perceived crime wave. White residents posted photos of activity they deemed suspicious, including photos of Black children waiting for their parents to get home. These same residents sometimes followed their Black neighbors in order to take photos, and sometimes called security to report them. In response to complaints about racial profiling, the site organizer noted that the posts may "offend," but underscored the central goal of preventing crime. This pattern has been repeated across the country as residents use online neighborhood-based community groups to racially profile their neighbors.[240]

The danger of better-safe-than-sorry racism is twofold. First, as has become painfully clear, not every encounter between a police officer and an innocent Black person ends peacefully. Rashon Nelson, Donisha Prendergast, Corey Lewis, and Sandra Thompson are not household names. To the extent people know these individuals at all, they know them by the catchy hashtag that summarizes the absurdity of their encounters with police: "Sitting in Starbucks While Black," "Airbnbing While Black," "Babysitting While Black," "Golfing While Black." As personally humiliating and unjust as their experiences were, these people are lucky to have been largely forgotten, because their encounters did not end in tragedy. But in a different context, with a different first responder, any one of these individuals could have joined the long list of more well-known targets of racial fear: George Floyd, Michael Brown, Philando Castile, Eric Garner, Tamir Rice, Sandra Bland, Freddie Gray, Stefon Clark, Alton Sterling, and countless others.

Better safe than sorry – but safe for whom?

Each racially motivated 911 call creates an additional opportunity for unwarranted police violence against a Black individual. While every frivolous 911 call – and indeed, any police interaction – creates such an opportunity for the individuals involved, whatever their race, the risk is substantially greater for Black people and Black communities. In this sense, bias-motivated White callers truly are weaponizing their fear by sending an armed officer to confront an innocent Black person, who faces a greater chance that the confrontation will end in violence.

Although no adequate federal database of fatal police shootings exists,[241] a study from the University of California at Davis found "evidence of a significant bias in the killing

[240] Addie C. Rolnick, *Defending White Space*, 40 CARDOZO L. REV. 1639, 1715 (2019).
[241] Mark Tran, *FBI Chief: "Unacceptable" that Guardian Has Better Data on Police Violence*, THE GUARDIAN (October 8, 2015 9:49 a.m.), https://www.theguardian.com/us-news/2015/oct/08/fbi-chief-says-ridiculous-guardian-washington-post-better-information-police-shootings (quoting former FBI Director James Comey telling crime summit that it is "embarrassing and ridiculous" that the federal government has no federal database tracking police shootings in America).

of unarmed black Americans relative to unarmed white Americans in that the probability of being {black, unarmed, and shot by police} is about 3.49 times the probability of being {white, unarmed, and shot by police} on average."[242] This disparity cannot be explained by greater justification for shooting Black individuals. An independent analysis of *Washington Post* data on police killings found that, "when factoring in threat level, black Americans who are fatally shot by police are no more likely to be posing an imminent lethal threat to the officers at the moment they are killed than white Americans fatally shot by police."[243]

Disproportionate violence is not limited to fatal shootings. One Harvard study found that police officers are more likely to use their hands, push a suspect into a wall, use handcuffs, draw weapons, push a suspect onto the ground, point their weapon, and use pepper spray or a baton when interacting with Black individuals.[244] This study confirmed findings by the Center for Policing Equity, which found that "African-Americans are far more likely than whites and other groups to be the victims of use of force by the police, even when racial disparities in crime are taken into account."[245]

This disproportionality in the use of force is particularly apparent in the use of restraints. A Stanford study of police practices in Oakland, California, found that, in a thirteen-month period, "2,890 African Americans were handcuffed but not arrested ... while only 193 whites were cuffed [and not arrested]. When Oakland officers pulled over a vehicle but didn't arrest anyone, 72 white people were handcuffed, while 1,466 African Americans were restrained."[246]

[242] Cody T. Ross, *A Multi-Level Bayesian Analysis of Racial Bias in Police Shootings at the County-Level in the United States, 2011–2014*, PLOS ONE (November 5, 2015), https://journals.plos.org/plosone/article?id=10.1371/journal.pone.0141854 (observing that "the racial bias observed in police shootings in this data set [was] not explainable as a response to local-level crime rates").

[243] Wesley Lowery, *Aren't More White People than Black People Killed by Police? Yes, but No*, WASH. POST (July 11, 2016 6:41 AM), https://www.washingtonpost.com/amphtml/news/post-nation/wp/2016/07/11/arent-more-white-people-than-black-people-killed-by-police-yes-but-no/ (finding that the only significant factor in predicting whether someone shot and killed by police was unarmed was whether or not they were black, and that crime variables did not matter in terms of predicting whether the person killed was unarmed).

[244] Quoctrung Bui and Amanda Cox, *Surprising New Evidence Shows Bias in Police Use of Force but Not in Shootings*, N.Y. TIMES (July 11, 2016), https://www.nytimes.com/2016/07/12/upshot/surprising-new-evidence-shows-bias-in-police-use-of-force-but-not-in-shootings.html.

[245] Timothy Williams, *Study Supports Suspicion That Police Are More Likely to Use Force on Blacks*, N.Y. TIMES (July 7, 2016), https://www.nytimes.com/2016/07/08/us/study-supports-suspicion-that-police-use-of-force-is-more-likely-for-blacks.html. A similar study by researchers from UCLA, Harvard, Portland State University, and Boston University found that police used less force with highly stereotypical Whites, and this protective effect was stronger than the effect for non-Whites. *See* Kimberly Barsamian Kahn et al., *Protecting Whiteness: White Phenotypic Racial Stereotypicality Reduces Police Use of Force*, 7 SOC. PSYCHOL. & PERSONALITY SCI. 403, 405–06 (2016).

[246] Tom Jackman, *Oakland Police, Stopping and Handcuffing Disproportionate Numbers of Blacks, Work to Restore Trust*, WASH. POST (June 15, 2016), https://www.washingtonpost.com/news/true-crime/wp/2016/06/15/oakland-police-stopping-and-handcuffing-disproportionate-numbers-of-blacks-work-to-restore-trust/.

But perhaps no study illustrates the efficiency, efficacy, and danger of allowing racially fearful civilians to weaponize armed government agents more than a 2007 University of Chicago study assessing the ability of police officers to determine whether to shoot a target that flashed before them and comparing police reactions with those of a sample from the general population.[247] The targets featured a mix of armed and unarmed Black and White people.[248] While "[b]oth samples exhibited robust [anti-Black] racial bias in response speed," researchers concluded that "[o]fficers outperformed community members on a number of measures, including overall speed and accuracy."[249] In other words, not only did the police officers in the sample reveal deep anti-Black bias in choosing when to use deadly force, but they were also significantly more capable of using deadly force effectively than the average population. This study gives haunting insight into what it means to weaponize racial fear.

Increased attention to high-profile shootings of unarmed Black people preceded the increased attention to racially motivated 911 calls. But the link between the two is unmistakable. Over half of all police contacts with "suspicious" individuals occur as a result of a civilian complaint, and many of the now-infamous police shootings of unarmed civilians were initiated by nonemergency 911 calls.

Consider the case of Stephon Clark. On the night of March 18, 2018, Dave Reiling called 911 to report vandalism, stating that someone had "busted two of my windows in and he broke the car's window across the street from me."[250] The dispatcher instructed Reiling to go inside when two patrol cars and a police helicopter arrived on the scene. Shortly after, Reiling heard so many gunshots he assumed police and a suspect were involved in a shootout. Instead, police had spotted twenty-two-year-old Stephon Clark standing in his grandmother's backyard holding a cell phone.[251] Police approached Clark in the dark but did not announce that they were law enforcement.[252] Body camera footage showed officers shouting "Show me your hands!" immediately before firing dozens of bullets at Clark in rapid-fire succession; they had been on the scene less than twenty seconds.[253] Clark, an unarmed Black

[247] Joshua Correll et al., *Across the Thin Blue Line: Police Officers and Racial Bias in the Decision to Shoot*, 92 J. PERSONALITY & SOC. PSYCH. 1006 (2007).
[248] *Id.* at 1009.
[249] *Id.* at 1006.
[250] Nashelly Chavez, *Neighbor Regrets Call That Led to Stephon Clark Shooting*, VC STAR (April 11, 2018, 5:19 p.m.), https://www.vcstar.com/story/news/2018/04/11/neighbor-regrets-call-led-stephon-clark-shooting/509287002/.
[251] Frances Robles & Jose A. Del Real, *Stephon Clark Was Shot 8 Times Primarily in His Back, Family-Ordered Autopsy Finds*, N.Y. TIMES (March 30, 2018), https://www.nytimes.com/2018/03/30/us/stephon-clark-independent-autopsy.html.
[252] *Id.*
[253] *Id.* No officers approached Clark or offered him medical aid, instead continuing to shout at him to show his hands. Officers eventually handcuffed his lifeless body. Officers then uniformly muted the audio on their cameras. *See* Sam Levin, *"They Executed Him": Police Killing of Stephon Clark Leaves Family Shattered*, THE GUARDIAN (March 27, 2018), https://www.theguardian.com/us-news/2018/mar/27/stephon-clark-police-shooting-brother-interview-sacramento.

man who had two children and no criminal record, was shot eight times.[254] Reiling said the incident "makes me never want to call 911 again."[255]

The tragic case of Tamir Rice provides another poignant example. On November 22, 2014, officers responded to a 911 call reporting a person pointing a gun in a Cleveland park.[256] While the call itself clearly was not frivolous, neither was it an emergency. The caller expressly stated that the gun was "probably fake," that the Black individual was "probably a juvenile," and that he posed little danger to anyone.[257] However, the dispatcher did not relay these pieces of information to the responding officers.[258] Police officers pulled into the park in a cruiser and shot twelve-year-old Tamir Rice within two seconds of their arrival.[259] The car had not even come to a complete stop before the officers opened fire.[260] The officers neither approached Tamir nor provided him an opportunity to put his hands up.[261] Officers waited four minutes before approaching Tamir to provide medical aid, at which point they confirmed the gun was a toy.[262] Tamir died the next day.[263]

Some may argue that breaking car windows or flashing a gun in a public park are sufficiently serious to justify calling 911, even if the end results were "unfortunate." Even so, the trigger-happy response to these calls highlights the dangers of targeting Black individuals for armed police response. This reality exists even for minor infractions, like passing a counterfeit twenty-dollar bill, a clear nonemergency:

DISPATCHER: *How can I help you?*

CALLER: *Someone comes [in] our store and give us fake bills and we realize it before he left the store, and we ran back outside, they was sitting on their car. We tell them to give us their phone, . . . he was also drunk*

[254] Levin, *supra* note 253.

[255] Chavez, *supra* note 250.

[256] Brandon Blackwell, *Tamir Rice, 12-Year-Old Boy Shot Dead by Cleveland Police Officer, Had No Juvenile Court Record*, Cleveland.com (November 24, 2014), http://www.cleveland.com/metro/index .ssf/2014/11/tamir_rice_12-year-old_boy_sho.html.

[257] Elahe Izadi & Peter Holley, *Video Shows Cleveland Officer Shooting 12-Year-Old Tamir Rice Within Seconds*, WASH. POST (November 26, 2014), https://www.washingtonpost.com/news/post-nation/wp/ 2014/11/26/officials-release-video-names-in-fatal-police-shooting-of-12-year-old-cleveland-boy/.

[258] *Id.*

[259] *Id.*

[260] Bryan Adamson, *Reconsidering Pretrial Media Publicity: Racialized Crime News, Grand Juries and Tamir Rice*, 8 ALA. C.R. & C.L. L. REV. 1, 10 (2017) (quoting Judge Ronald B. Adrine, who remarked that "this court is still thunderstruck by how quickly this event turned deadly . . . On the video the zone car containing patrol officers Loehmann and Garmback is still in the process of stopping when Rice is shot.").

[261] Izadi & Holley, *supra* note 257.

[262] *Id.*

[263] *Id.* A grand jury declined to indict either officer, stating that the actions of the officers were "objectively reasonable" under the circumstances. This conclusion followed the recommendations of "an outside police expert . . . conclud[ing] that the officer acted reasonably given the information he had." Mark Berman, *Review Says Cleveland Police Officer Who Shot Tamir Rice Acted Reasonably*, WASH. POST (November 13, 2015), https://www.washingtonpost.com/news/post-nation/ wp/2015/11/13/review-says-cleveland-police-officer-who-shot-tamir-rice-acted-reasonably/.

> *and everything and return to give us our cigarettes back and so he can,*
> *so he can go home but he doesn't want to do that, and he's sitting on*
> *his car cause he is awfully drunk and he's not in control of himself . . .*

DISPATCHER: *. . . So, this guy gave a counterfeit bill, has your cigarettes, and he's*
              under the influence of something?

CALLER: *Something like that, yes. He is not acting right.*

DISPATCHER: *What's he look like, what race?*

CALLER: *Um, he's like tall and bald, about 6 . . . 6 ½, and she's not acting right*
              so and she started to go, drive the car.

DISPATCHER: *Okay so, female or male? . . .*

CALLER: *It is a man.*

DISPATCHER: *Okay. Is he white, black, Native, Hispanic, Asian?*

CALLER: *Something like that.*

DISPATCHER: *Which one? White, black, Native, Hispanic, Asian?*

CALLER: *No, he's a black guy.*[264]

Officers did not immediately shoot George Floyd dead when they arrived, as they did Stephon Clark and Tamir Rice. Instead, Officer Derek Chauvin sat with his knee in Floyd's neck, as he lay handcuffed face down on the sidewalk, for nine minutes and nineteen seconds, while three other officers stood and watched. All because someone called 911 to report a counterfeit twenty.

2.8 CEMENTING DISTRUST

Even those unnecessary police encounters that do not end in arrest or physical violence harden community distrust of police officers in the Black community, as officer responses to absurd, racially motivated complaints further delegitimize law enforcement. The ways officers respond to these frivolous calls further exacerbates this tension. Numerous surveys and studies confirm that Black targets of public reports are treated with greater distrust, disrespect, and suspicion by police officers than White targets.[265] In one study exploring the police response to civilian 911 complaints and comparing the community interactions between police and Black and White individuals, Black community members were consistently addressed with less respect than White individuals, after controlling for the race of the officer and

---

[264]   Faith Karimi, *Minneapolis Police Release 911 Call that Led to Encounter with George Floyd*, CNN (May 29, 2020, 5:15 p.m.), https://www.cnn.com/2020/05/28/us/minneapolis-george-floyd-911-calls/index.html.

[265]   Alex Shashkevich, *Police Officers Speak Less Respectfully to Black Residents than White Residents, Stanford Researchers Find*, STANFORD NEWS (June 5, 2017), https://news.stanford.edu/2017/06/05/cops-speak-less-respectfully-black-community-members/; Radley Balko, *There's Overwhelming Evidence that the Criminal Justice System Is Racist. Here's the Proof*, Wash. Post (June 10, 2020), https://www.washingtonpost.com/graphics/2020/opinions/systemic-racism-police-evidence-criminal-justice-system/ (collecting studies).

the location, severity, and outcome of the stop.[266] Beyond disrespectful treatment, "Black targets" of 911 calls were "more frequently subject to arrest overall," regardless of whether the reported conduct was criminal in nature or whether the Black suspect had actually committed a crime.[267]

This disproportionate treatment cannot be explained, at least not entirely, by structural racism within police forces. The same study found that "reactive police encounters [those arising from civilian complaints, including 911 calls] involving a Black suspect [were] substantially more likely to end in arrest, compared with proactive police stops" in which officers themselves initiated contact to investigate criminal activity.[268] In other words, police gave greater weight to the reporting of a 911 caller than their own professional experience when determining whether to arrest a Black suspect, a troubling finding given that police were significantly more likely to arrest Black targets "associated with nuisance crimes for White reporters" than the other way around.

This discriminatory treatment in response to frivolous 911 calls erodes community trust. Political science researchers have long demonstrated that people's views of and trust in government are most significantly correlated to their direct interaction with the government.[269] For many, that experience comes at the hands of a police officer. When police enforce racial biases of private citizens, they convert those biases into governmental discrimination, which undermines the legitimacy of law enforcement.[270] In fact, the single largest determinant in how an individual views the legitimacy and authority of police is the qualitative and quantitative personal interactions that person has with the police.[271] "People tend to focus on how police treat them – the process and interactions – rather than the final outcome of those interactions."[272]

Distrust arising from perceived mistreatment or disrespect at the hands of police can have deadly consequences. Individuals obey the law only partially to avoid

---

[266] Rob Voigt et al., *Language from Police Body Camera Footage Shows Racial Disparities in Officer Respect*, PNAS (June 20, 2017), https://www.pnas.org/content/114/25/6521.

[267] Lanfear et al., *supra* note 149; *see also* Balko, *supra* note 265.

[268] Lanfear et al., *supra* note 149.

[269] *See, e.g.*, Tom R. Tyler, *Trust and Law Abidingness: A Proactive Model of Social Regulation*, 81 B. U. L. Rev. 361, 365–80 (2001); TOM R. TYLER AND YUEN J. HUO, TRUST IN THE LAW: ENCOURAGING PUBLIC COOPERATION WITH THE POLICE AND COURTS 49–96 (2002).

[270] *See* Vesla Mae Weaver, *Why White People Keep Calling the Cops on Black Americans*, VOX (May 29, 2018 1:59 PM EDT), https://www.vox.com/first-person/2018/5/17/17362100/starbucks-racial-profiling-yale-airbnb-911 ("The gulf between how black America and white America experience the police is vast.").

[271] *Perceptions of Treatment by Police: Impacts of Personal Interactions and the Media*, NATIONAL INSTITUTE OF JUSTICE (March 17, 2014), https://nij.ojp.gov/topics/articles/perceptions-treatment-police-impacts-personal-interactions-and-media ("Personal interactions have the strongest impact on perceptions."; *see also* I. Bennett Capers, *Crime, Legitimacy, and Testilying+*, 83 Ind. L.J. 835, 852 (2008).

[272] NATIONAL INSTITUTE OF JUSTICE, *supra* note 271.

punishment.[273] In fact, the largest factor affecting obedience to police commands is legitimacy: "by increasing respect for the law as both fair and applied, lawmakers can in fact increase voluntary compliance with the law ... The more an individual regard[s] legal authorities as exercising legitimate authority, the more that individual [is] likely to obey the law. ... the relationship between legitimacy and compliance [is] linear: as legitimacy increases, so does compliance."[274] People who perceive that they receive "procedural justice" are also likely to perceive the police as legitimate and trustworthy, and thus are more likely to comply with police requests in the future.[275] Those who have not had positive experiences are more likely to respond to police requests with suspicion and even outright defiance. That suspicion and distrust can also heighten anxiety when police appear, leading to overreaction and further increasing the risk of an unnecessarily violent confrontation.[276] As a result of systemic, disproportionate abuse at the hands of police, Black communities are more likely than White communities to view law enforcement with suspicion and distrust.[277] This distrust is exacerbated when officers respond in force to racially motivated 911 calls.[278] These findings provide a partial, if incomplete, explanation for why Black individuals tend to have greater distrust of police – they are far more likely to have involuntary interactions with police, and those interactions are more likely to be adversarial, disrespectful, and violent.[279]

Distrust also contributes to both the overpolicing of Black neighborhoods and the underpolicing of those same neighborhoods. Underpolicing is driven both by police actions and by Black fear and distrust of police. That fear, driven by personal experience, significantly affects a person's decision to seek police protection, or not. One study of crime reporting in Portland, Oregon, "revealed that people's perception of the police – if they treat people well, take reported crimes seriously, and if they put effort into solving crimes – impact their likelihood of reporting less serious offenses. Individuals who view the police as more legitimate have an increased likelihood to ... report crime." In contrast, "individuals who have

---

[273] Tom R. Tyler & Jeffrey Fagan, *Legitimacy and Cooperation: Why Do People Help Police Fight Crime in Their Communities?*, 6 Ohio St. L.J. 231, 245 (2008).

[274] *Id.*

[275] *Id.*

[276] *Id.* ("For black individuals, racial anxiety is experienced as the fear of being victimized by police racism. These worries may result in black individuals approaching police interactions with heightened suspicion and anxiety. During their interaction, these mutual anxieties increase the risk that officers will conduct a frisk and that force will be used unnecessarily.").

[277] *See* L. Song Richardson & Phillip Atiba Goff, *Self-Defense and the Suspicion Heuristic*, 98 Iowa L. Rev. 293, 310 (2012).

[278] *See id.*; *see also Capers*, supra note 271 at 693; *Procedural Justice and Police Legitimacy*, POST, https://post.ca.gov/procedural-justice-and-police-legitimacy ("The public's perceptions about the lawfulness and legitimacy of law enforcement are ... important criteri[a] for judging policing in a democratic society. Lawfulness means that police comply with constitutional, statutory and professional norms. Legitimacy is linked to the public's belief about the police and its willingness to recognize police authority.").

[279] *See supra* Section 2.8 and notes 127–36.

experienced negative police interactions perceive the police as less legitimate" and are less likely to seek police protection in less than "life or death" situations.[280] Nationally, "Black victims report some [more serious] crimes at a higher rate than White victims," but are far less likely to report less serious crimes, out of a recognition of the "law's repressive and coercive capacities" for Black people, even Black victims of crime.[281] In other words, Black victims of crime turn to police for help only as a last resort and only when police help is urgently needed to address serious violent crime. Less serious social control issues go unchecked. The reason: victims' legitimate fear of reprisal from the very public servants charged with protecting them.

Public awareness of police abuse further chills participation in the public safety apparatus. One study examining resident response to a highly publicized case of police brutality in Milwaukee found that "all Milwaukee neighborhoods experienced a decrease in calls to the police after . . . [the] widely reported abuse." But this decrease "in White neighborhoods was small and quickly receded, whereas the effect was larger and more persistent in Black areas."[282]

These problems of over- and underenforcement can help explain why White individuals may use 911 more frequently than Black individuals to report non-emergencies. Police response to these calls exacerbates these disparities. White people tend to experience law enforcement as helpful, cooperative, and responsive as compared to African Americans.[283] A large study of White and Black drivers pulled over by police showed that "even when whites have involuntary contact with police, they overwhelmingly experience the police as helpful, benevolent, fair, and efficient problem solvers."[284] In contrast, "[n]onwhite people who try to enlist law enforcement for help are more likely than whites to themselves come under suspicion."[285] Moreover, officers are more likely to view Black individuals as defiant and uncooperative, and thus suspicious, for exercising constitutional rights, such as asking questions, refusing consent to enter or search premises, or asking officers to leave.[286] This "mismatch in experience equates to powerful incentives for people of one racial group to call the police," and a "powerful

---

[280] Lanfear et al., *supra* note 149, at 1077–78 (citing Schneider and Fagan/Tyler studies).

[281] *Id.* at 1078 (citing Skogan study).

[282] *Id.* at 1079 (citing Desmond study); *see also* Blacks in Law Enforcement of America, *Study: People Call 911 Less Often After High-Profile Instances of Police Brutality*, Bleausa.org (July 7, 2017), https://www.bleausa.org/study-people-call-911-less-often-after-high-profile-instances-of-police-brutality/ (citing Desmond study, which "found that 17 percent (22,200) fewer 911 calls were made in the following year compared with the number of calls that would have been made had the [high-profile beating of Frank] Jude [by Milwaukee police] never happened").

[283] CHARLES R. EPP, PULLED OVER: HOW POLICE STOPS DEFINE RACE AND CITIZENSHIP 98–104 (2014); *see also* Weaver, *supra* note 128.

[284] Weaver, *supra* note 270; *see also* Epp, *supra* note 283.

[285] Weaver, *supra* note 270.

[286] *Id.*

disincentive for black people to call the police in almost any situation except when their lives depend on it."[287]

2.9 FEEDING THE SYSTEM

Putting aside the disproportionately adverse outcomes of 911-generated reactive policing encounters, the encounter itself subjects Black targets to entry into the criminal-legal system, a system within which "Black individuals continue to be at a marked disadvantage." The result of this arbitrary entry into the criminal legal system – "mass surveillance and incarceration that disproportionately impact Black individuals and communities – provides a stark bookend to seemingly minor complaints to the police."[288]

Disproportionate incarceration rates for communities of color are an obvious and well-documented consequence of overpolicing in these communities.[289] Police responses to frivolous 911 calls contribute to disproportionate incarceration rates in two specific ways: disproportionate arrests rates for civilian "noncompliance" and mandatory "warrant checks." Intuitively, it might seem that a truly frivolous civilian complaint should not lead to an arrest because no crime actually occurred. But police officers are more likely to interpret a Black individual's lawful behavior – even constitutionally protected behavior – as hostile, adversarial, or violent.[290] Thus, not only are Black individuals less likely to comply when confronted by a police officer responding to a frivolous 911 call, but that officer is more likely to interpret even lawful refusal as illegal and make an unnecessary arrest.

Further, many police departments require that any officer responding to a 911 call conduct "warrant checks" on all individuals at the scene. These "warrant checks" are designed to find individuals with outstanding arrest warrants for, among other things, failure to pay traffic tickets or court fees and fines associated with prior

---

[287] *Id.* Moreover, recent studies have concluded that police take less seriously – and therefore, under-police – calls from predominantly black and Hispanic communities. For example, a review of Chicago Police Department practices found that police take longer to come to communities of color – and may not come at all; the average time to arrival after calls to police from nonwhite neighborhoods was twice as long as it was for predominantly white neighborhoods. *See Newly-Released Data Shows City Continues to Deny Equitable Police Services to South and West Side Neighborhoods*, ACLU ILLINOIS (March 31, 2014), https://www.aclu-il.org/en/press-releases/newly-released-data-shows-city-continues-deny-equitable-police-services-south-and.

[288] Lanfear et al., *supra* note 149, at 1075.

[289] *Id.*

[290] The study reviewing Chicago Police Department practices, for example, found that "[o]fficers expect and demand compliance even when they lack legal authority," and "are inclined to interpret the exercise of free-speech rights as unlawful disobedience, innocent movements as physical threats, [and] indications of mental or physical illness as belligerence." *See supra* note 258.

cases.[291] These checks more often result in arrests of Black people because the disproportionate arrest and conviction rates for Black individuals logically result in a disproportionate number of arrest warrants issued against people in these communities. Moreover, many of these communities have higher rates of poverty and thus are disproportionately affected by warrants issued for failure to pay fees and fines.[292] As one former police captain observed about mandatory warrant checks, "Warrants are what happen when one community is policed at a rate that is greater than others, making it unusual in some parts of a city to find young black males who don't have warrants."[293]

Donisha Prendergast recognized her luck in the weeks following her harrowing encounter with 911 abuse. She did not have a criminal history subjecting her to the merry-go-round of America's criminal justice system. She was not arrested or subjected to excessive force. She was not shot. But she was painfully aware that things could have turned out very differently:

> I'm still trying to fully digest the what, why and how of this. I am also deeply meditating on the why not. Why this should not have happened. Why they should not have reacted with such unnecessary force. . . . Why this is not a simple misunderstanding. Why this neighbor who was so fearful without any unjustified reason, should not have the power to potentially destroy another life because of the color of her skin.[294]

Collectively, these incidents illustrate the many ways Black people are subjected to arbitrary social expectations, and how they are punished for violating those expectations. Decades after the collapse of legal segregation, they also show that spaces like clothing stores, coffee shops, neighborhoods, and universities remain strongly controlled along racial lines.

At their core, these stories are about racial profiling, the concept that a person's race or ethnicity makes them an object of suspicion and subject to heightened scrutiny from law enforcement. From slave patrols to lynching to legal segregation, and in modern iterations like stop and frisk, racial profiling has long been used to maintain white authority by singling out the presence and behavior of people of

---

[291] *See* Torie Atkinson, *A Fine Scheme: How Municipal Fines Become Crushing Debt in the Shadow of the New Debtors' Prison*, 51 HARV. C.R.-C.L. L. REV. 189, 226–27 (2016) (describing disproportionate impact of "warrant checks" on communities of color).

[292] *Id.*

[293] David C. Couper, *Best Way to Respond to Foolish 911 Calls – Stop Sending Armed Cops*, USA TODAY (June 27, 2018), https://www.usatoday.com/story/opinion/policing/2018/06/27/911-calls-cops-policing-usaf32692002/; *see also* Atkinson, *supra* note 291, at 226–27 (noting that, in many jurisdictions where a majority of African Americans have outstanding warrants, "police ignore[] the reasonable suspicion requirement to run as many identifications as possible through the warrant system to identify 'offenders,' arrest them, and levy additional fines").

[294] *"Elderly White Woman" Calls 911 on Bob Marley's Granddaughter*, TELESUR (May 8, 2018), https://www.telesurenglish.net/news/Elderly-White-Woman-Calls-911-on-Bob-Marleys-Granddaughter-20180508-0001.html.

color – especially Black individuals – as requiring punishment. These systems rely on the participation of bystanders and observers to alert authorities to those deemed "suspicious." As we shall see in the next chapter, those frivolous, race-based judgments of suspiciousness are often legitimated by courts as reasonable citizen "tips" and are investigated by armed police, often with lethal consequences.

3

Just a Hunch

Elijah McClain committed the crime of being different. Elijah did not conform to the image of the stereotypical Black male. The twenty-three-year-old man was a soft-spoken, self-described introvert who loved animals. Friends and family described the professional massage therapist as a "spiritual seeker, pacifist, oddball, vegetarian, athlete, and peacemaker who was exceedingly gentle."[295] When Elijah was a young boy, his mother moved from Denver, Colorado, to the wealthy, predominantly White suburb of Aurora to avoid gang violence and decided to homeschool her son to alleviate his social anxiety.[296] In high school, Elijah taught himself how to play violin and guitar, and during lunch breaks he brought instruments to animal shelters to play for the animals there, believing the music put them at ease.[297]

Elijah also suffered from anemia, which made him susceptible to the cold. He sometimes wore a ski mask to protect his face from cold weather, and his family suspected he also wore it to hide his anxiety.[298] On the chilly evening of August 24, 2019, Elijah wore his ski mask as he walked to a convenience store in Aurora's Sable Altura neighborhood, a diverse but rapidly gentrifying area. He put his headphones on and began listening to music, dancing as he walked. That's when a passer-by called 911.

911 OPERATOR:	*Okay. Tell me exactly what happened?*
CALLER:	*So there's a guy, he's walking. . . . He has a mask on.*
911 OPERATOR:	*Okay.*
CALLER:	*And then when I passed by him, he puts his hands up and does all these kinds of signs. I don't know. He looks sketchy.*

[295] Grant Stringer, *Unlikely Suspect: Those Who Knew Elijah Balk at Aurora Police Account of His Death*, SENTINEL COLO. (October 27, 2019), https://sentinelcolorado.com/news/metro/unlikely-suspect-those-who-knew-elijah-balk-at-aurora-police-account-of-his-death/.

[296] *Id.*

[297] *Id.*

[298] *Elijah McClain Timeline: What Happened That Night and What Has Happened Since*, DENVER POST (August 23, 2020), https://www.denverpost.com/2020/06/26/elijah-mcclain-timeline-aurora-police/.

911 Operator:	*Okay.*
Caller:	*He might be a good person or a bad person.*
911 Operator:	*Yeah.*
Caller:	*But he has a full-on mask on.*
911 Operator:	*Okay. His arms.*
Caller:	*Yeah.*
911 Operator:	*Okay. I'm going to put a call in so officers can go see what's going on. . . . Were any weapons involved or mentioned?*
Caller:	*No.*
911 Operator:	*Okay. I already have a call in, okay. I need to get a full description. What race is he?*
Caller:	*I think he's a black male. . . .*
911 Operator:	*Okay. What color is the mask, or what does it look like?*
Caller:	*Black. . . .*
911 Operator:	*Okay. Is it like a ski mask, or what type of mask is it?*
Caller:	*Yeah, probably a ski mask. . . .*
911 Operator:	*I'm just adding notes. Are you or anyone else in danger right now?*
Caller:	*No.*[299]

Shortly after the caller hung up, three police officers stopped Elijah. One told him, "I have a right to stop you, because you're being suspicious."[300] The next fifteen minutes were captured on three separate police-worn body cameras. When police first physically approached Elijah, he explained, "I'm an introvert," and asked the officers to "please respect the boundaries that I am speaking." The police report asserted that Elijah resisted the officers, but body camera footage only shows Elijah being handcuffed and pinned to the ground. At one point in the video, an officer can be heard shouting, "He reached for your gun," though no video evidence confirms that warning. While Elijah was pinned to the ground, an officer applied a carotid control hold, also known as a chokehold, to cut off blood flow to the brain. Elijah began sobbing and vomiting; he repeatedly said, "I can't breathe."

Additional officers and a paramedic arrived on the scene approximately five minutes later, at which point one of the initial officers on the scene can be heard saying Elijah attacked them with "incredible strength." Another affirms, "Yeah, crazy strength." (Elijah was 5 feet 6 inches tall and weighed 140 pounds.)[301] A paramedic then injected Elijah with 500mg of ketamine, a sedative used to treat

[299] *Elijah McClain Killing 911 Call & Police Body Cam Footage Transcript*, Rev (August 25, 2019), https://www.rev.com/blog/transcripts/elijah-mcclain-killing-911-call-police-body-cam-footage-transcript.

[300] *Id.* Except where notes indicate otherwise, the description of Elijah McClain's encounter with police is drawn from this transcript.

[301] Erik Ortiz, *Elijah McClain Was Injected with Ketamine While Handcuffed. Some Medical Experts Worry About Its Use During Police Calls*, NBC News (July 3, 2020), https://www.nbcnews.com/news/us-news/elijah-mcclain-was-injected-with-ketamine-while-handcuffed-some-medical-experts-n1232697.

excited delirium.[302] Elijah suffered cardiac arrest on the way to the hospital that night, was pronounced brain dead three days later, and died on August 30, 2019.[303]

According to the body camera footage, Elijah's final words were:

> I can't breathe! I can't breathe, please stop! My name is Elijah McClain. That's all I was doing, I was just going home. I just needed money. I'm just different! That's all! That's all I was doing! I'm so sorry. I have no gun. I don't do that stuff. I don't do any fighting. Why would you taser me? I don't do drugs. I don't even kill flies! I don't eat meat. But I'm not a vegetarian. I don't judge people or anything. I try to live in secret. Forgive me! All I was trying to do was become better. But I will do it. I will do it. I don't do it. Even if I have to sacrifice my ID, I'll do it. You all are phenomenal. You are beautiful and I love you. You can try and forgive me. Officer, I'm a Pisces sun and a moon Gemini. Stop, stop! I'm sorry. That really hurts! That's the Gemini. Teamwork makes the dream work. It hurts so much! Yeah, I'm sorry. I wasn't trying to do that. I just can't breathe correctly.

Initially, Adams County District Attorney Dave Young investigated Elijah's death and determined that the officers had committed no criminal acts; no charges were filed against them.[304] In July 2020, nearly one year after Elijah's death, three Aurora police officers were fired and a fourth resigned when photos leaked showing them reenacting the chokehold that killed Elijah at the site of his death, near a makeshift memorial.[305] In September 2021, over two years after Elijah's death, a grand jury indicted several officers and paramedics on manslaughter and criminally negligent homicide charges.

Elijah's death was senseless, tragic, and preventable. As a young Black man in a gentrifying neighborhood, he blundered into the White space after sundown. He suffered the suspicions of an onlooker who admitted he was in no danger but who called 911 to report the emergency of an unarmed "sketchy" person who "puts his hands up." Based solely on the presence of a ski mask and the description of a "sketchy" person, the 911 operator dispatched three trained, armed agents of the government to restrain the man. Upon arrival, the officers found a skinny, admittedly "different," anxious Black man who did not conform to the prototype of the aggressive Black male. Their response was to conclude that he was "definitely on something" and choke him to death.[306]

Elijah's story connects two distinct aspects of the private policing of White space: the summoning of armed government agents to enforce the color line, and the violence used by those agents when they make contact with Black persons who cross that line. Private citizens uneasy with Black people they see as out of place – both physically and stereotypically – feel free to contact their "personal protection

[302] *Id.*
[303] *Elijah McClain Timeline, supra* note 298.
[304] *Id.*
[305] *Id.*
[306] *Id.*

agency." Police respond in force, having been trained in a "warrior cop" mentality that pits "us versus them," with the knowledge that their violent confrontations will go unchecked.

But a third actor enables this one-two punch of racial hierarchy: the United States Supreme Court. Elijah's death is tragic not only because it was utterly preventable, but also because it was likely justified under existing Supreme Court precedent. The Fourth Amendment to the United States Constitution protects Americans from "unreasonable searches and seizures." This phrase means that police cannot stop and interrogate citizens without sufficient justification, nor can they use excessive force in doing so. For nearly two centuries, any police stop not supported by probable cause was deemed automatically unreasonable. But the Supreme Court gutted that standard in 1968, when it held in *Terry v. Ohio* that police could stop and search anyone if they had "reasonable suspicion" the person was engaged in criminal activity.

In the half century since *Terry*, it has become painfully clear that the "reasonable suspicion" standard is no standard at all. Courts have repeatedly justified police harassment of individuals by finding reasonably suspicious the most threadbare facts: that the suspect was too nervous, not nervous enough, made eye contact, avoided eye contact, had an unusual travel plan, arrived at an airport early in the morning or late at night or in the middle of the day, deplaned first or last or in the middle, lived in a "high crime" neighborhood, or sought to avoid interaction with police.[307] While Supreme Court opinions give lip service to the notion that reasonable suspicion must be based on more than "just a hunch," in reality *Terry* and its progeny give carte blanche to police harassment of anyone who appears ever so slightly outside society's White-centric paradigm.

This change in the law has particular relevance to the policing of White spaces in two distinct ways.

First, it has legitimized the actions of the racially fearful "anonymous 911 caller." Applying *Terry*'s holding in subsequent cases, the Supreme Court has held that anonymous tips of criminal or suspicious activity, by themselves, provide adequate reasonable suspicion to justify an armed officer's forceful stop of the target of the tip.[308] Given this laughably low bar for reasonable suspicion, all but the most patently frivolous calls likely meet the standard, including calls from tipsters who allege no criminal activity or fear for personal safety but merely "sketchiness" in appearance or behavior. Regarding these tipsters, the Supreme Court has upheld

---

[307] For flight in a "high-crime" area as supporting reasonable suspicion, see *Illinois v. Wardlow*, 528 U.S. 119, 124 (2000) (reversing the Illinois Supreme Court). For the malleability of reasonable suspicion generally, see *United States v. Sokolow*, 490 U.S. 1, 13–14 (Marshall, J., dissenting).

[308] *Alabama v. White*, 496 U.S. 325, 331 (1990) (an anonymous tip provided reasonable suspicion for a stop even though officers had not managed to corroborate key elements of the tip); *Navarette v. California*, 572 U.S. 393 (2014) (finding reasonable suspicion of drunk driving in an anonymous phone tip, even though officers did not witness erratic driving when they followed the vehicle for five minutes).

police stops in response to anonymous 911 calls based on the fiction that anonymous callers to 911 are both inherently reliable and subject to sanction for lodging frivolous complaints.[309] The Court is wrong on both points. Shockingly so.

Second, the hunch-based nature of reasonable suspicion has given legitimacy to the private and public policing of Black movements and the criminalization of Black bodies in public. Essentially, to legally call 911, a citizen need only sense something out of place; far too often that "something out of place" is a Black person in the White space.[310] This "Spidey-sense" legal standard, combined with pervasive and pernicious implicit fears of the violent and subversive Black person, work to give legal cover to the formal social control of Black movements, including the violent actions to enforce that control. In this sense, the private "White caller criminal" finds his actions accepted, promoted, and enhanced by a willing police force and a court system that paves the way.

3.1 FROM PROBABLE TO REASONABLE

Police stops of civilians, whether at a traffic stop, on the street, or in response to a 911 call, are governed by the protections of the Fourth Amendment. An involuntary stop of a civilian by a police officer constitutes a "seizure" under the Fourth Amendment, which must be reasonable under the circumstances. Thus, whether an officer is justified in stopping the target of a 911 call depends on whether that seizure was reasonable.

The law governing what constitutes a reasonable seizure comes almost entirely from United States Supreme Court cases. For at least the last fifty years, the Supreme Court has steadily lowered the bar for what constitutes a "reasonable" search or seizure, making it far easier for officers to police the movement of Black people under the cover of "reasonable suspicion of criminal activity," including in response to frivolous and fearful 911 calls. The Court has done so by radically redefining the word "reasonable," from its original meaning of "probable cause" of criminal activity to "something more than a hunch" of criminal activity. In the process, the Court has eviscerated basic protections from police harassment, particularly for people of color, and provided its rubber stamp for all police responses to anonymous tips of criminal activity, whether the tip is about a Black man sitting in Starbucks, a Black woman sleeping in her dorm, or a Black man walking to the convenience store in a ski mask.

---

[309] *Navarette*, 572 U.S. at 400. See discussion later in this chapter, Section 3.5.

[310] Of course, the Fourth Amendment's reasonable suspicion standard governs state (police) conduct and not private conduct, and private 911 calls are not assessed on a threshold reasonable suspicion standard. But the legality of a 911 call does often depend on whether some basis existed to report an emergency, and given the Supreme Court's willingness to sanction trained police intervention in a range of nonemergency "reasonably suspicious" scenarios, it logically follows that the range of conduct lawfully recognized as "suspicious" to untrained private actors and giving rise to "legitimate" 911 intervention is extremely broad.

The fifty-four words of the Fourth Amendment are among the most examined, debated, and confusing in the United States Constitution. The entire text of the Amendment reads:

> The right of the people to be secure in their persons, houses, papers, and effects, against unreasonable search and seizures, shall not be violated, and no warrants shall issue, but upon probable cause, supported by oath or affirmation, and particularly describing the place to be searched, and the persons or things to be seized.

Among the many mysteries presented by the text of the Amendment is what connection, if any, is intended between the Reasonableness Clause, which forbids unreasonable searches and seizures, and the Warrant Clause, which requires probable cause to support the issuance of a warrant. Is one conditioned upon the other, such that a search or seizure is only "reasonable" if it is supported by probable cause and a warrant? Or is the reasonableness of an officer's search or seizure to be judged independently of warrants and by some standard other than probable cause?

For nearly 180 years, the Supreme Court adopted the first formulation and required searches or seizures to be justified by warrants supported by probable cause. Searches without a warrant were presumed unreasonable. The idea that "warrantless searches [and seizures] are per se unreasonable"[311] accords with common sense and the original purpose of the Fourth Amendment, although it may not necessarily be required by the text itself. The Fourth Amendment was adopted by the Framers in direct response to the broad abuses of colonial officers executing "writs of assistance" and "general warrants" that authorized broad, open-ended searches of the homes and belongings of colonists viewed as disloyal to the King of England.[312] Indeed, the American Revolution itself was as much a reaction to this oppressive police conduct as any general desire for freedom from the crown. Tightly restricting permissible searches and seizures to those premised upon probable cause and a particularized warrant ended this practice – the original intent of the Amendment. Moreover, in the absence of other textual guidance on what

---

[311]   *Katz v. United States*, 389 U.S. 347, 357 (1967).

[312]   Thomas Y. Davies is the foremost scholar of Fourth Amendment history and of the Supreme Court's undermining of the probable cause standard over the past century. In a series of articles, he excavates from the historical record a very different, more stringent meaning for the Fourth Amendment and shows that framing-era doctrine foresaw much stronger protections of the "right to be secure" in person and possessions than are supported by the generable reasonableness standard adopted by the modern Court. See *Recovering the Original Fourth Amendment*, 98 MICH. L. REV. 547 (1999); *The Fictional Character of Law-and-Order Originalism: A Case Study of the Distortions and Evasions of Framing-Era Arrest Doctrine in* Atwater v. Lago Vista, 37 WAKE FOREST L. REV. 239 (2002); *Correcting Search-and-Seizure History: Now-Forgotten Common-Law Warrantless Arrest Standards and the Original Understanding of "Due Process of Law,"* 77 MISS. L.J. 1 (2007); *The Supreme Court Giveth & the Supreme Court Taketh Away: The Century of Fourth Amendment Search & Seizure Doctrine*, 100 J. CRIM. L. & CRIMINOLOGY 933 (2010). *Can You Handle the Truth? The Framers Preserved Common-Law Criminal Arrest and Search Rules in "Due Process of Law" – "Fourth Amendment Reasonableness" Is Only a Modern, Destructive Judicial Myth*, 43 TEX. TECH. L. REV. 51 (2010).

constitutes "reasonable" police conduct, the Fourth Amendment's reference to probable cause supplies the most objective measure of reasonableness.

Tying reasonableness to probable cause had the additional advantage of clarity. The term "probable cause" has deep roots in English common law, predating the United States by more than a century, and most scholars agree that at the time the Fourth Amendment was adopted, it had a commonly accepted definition: more likely than not.[313] Requiring searches and seizures to be predicated on a showing that an individual more likely than not had committed a crime or that evidence of a crime more likely than not would be found created a clear, easily justiciable, and relatively high burden to justify governmental intrusion into the private lives of citizens.

That standard changed in 1968. For much of the 1960s, the Supreme Court, led by Chief Justice Earl Warren, granted significant sweeping victories to criminal suspects, recognizing the constitutional right to government-appointed counsel in criminal trials, requiring officers to inform suspects of their constitutional rights upon arrest (the *Miranda* warning), and mandating the exclusion from trial of evidence illegally obtained by police. These Warren Court decisions surprised many observers, who had expected that the Chief Justice's past as a former prosecutor and Attorney General of California whose father's murder went unsolved would shape the Court's response to these cases.[314] Many more Court watchers were furious, criticizing the Warren Court for "wrapping its flowing robes around all prisoners so as to virtually immunize them from police interrogations."[315] Indeed, Richard Nixon, a longtime political adversary of Warren's in California, harshly criticized the Warren Court's "pro-criminal" decisions in his successful 1968 "law and order" campaign for the presidency.[316]

But the last major Warren Court criminal procedure decision, also decided in 1968, swung the pendulum of power significantly back toward police, and in the process forever changed both Fourth Amendment jurisprudence and American policing. In *Terry v. Ohio*, the Court moved away from the default proposition that warrantless searches are per se unreasonable to the competing view that the appropriate test of police conduct "is not whether it is reasonable to procure a search warrant, but whether the search was reasonable."[317] This shift from "probable cause" to "reasonable suspicion" was momentous. Despite the Court's attempt to minimize the holding, noting its "quite narrow" scope, *Terry* expanded police power far more than a decade of Warren-era decisions had expanded the rights of criminal suspects

---

[313] Davies, *The Fictional Character of Law-and-Order Originalism, supra* note 312, at 285 ("In 1789, when the federal Frameers included 'probable cause' in the Fourth Amendment, 'probable' was still understood to mean at least more likely than not.").

[314] *See* Yale Kamisar, *How Earl Warren's Twenty-Two Years in Law Enforcement Affected His Work as Chief Justice*, 3 Ohio St. J. Crim. L. 11, 18 (2005).

[315] Shawn E. Fields, *Stop and Frisk in a Concealed Carry World*, 93 Wash. L. Rev. 1675, 1682 n.33 (2018) (citing Radley Balko, Rise of the Warrior Cop: The Militarization of America's Police Force (2014)).

[316] *See, e.g.*, Donald Braman, *Criminal Law and the Pursuit of Equality*, 84 Tex. L. Rev. 2097, 2109–10 (2006).

[317] *United States v. Rabinowitz*, 339 U.S. 56, 66 (1950).

and defendants. In the process, the Court stamped its approval on a police practice as oppressive to racial minorities as any government practice in the last fifty years: the stop-and-frisk.

Terry represented what would become a typical stop-and-frisk case.[318] A Cleveland beat cop observed two men standing on a street corner, then walking back and forth along an identical route multiple times in front of a department store, stopping each time to look inside the store window. Each completion of the route was followed by a conference between the two men on the corner. The two men eventually joined up with a third individual two blocks from the store. Suspecting the individuals of "casing a job, a stick-up," the officer stopped the three men and asked their names. When the men "mumbled something," the officer spun around suspect John W. Terry and patted down his outside clothing. He felt a pistol in Terry's overcoat pocket. After removing a revolver from Terry's coat pocket, he patted down the other two suspects and seized another revolver.

The Court found that the officer's actions amounted to a "search and seizure" under the Fourth Amendment – the officer "seized" Terry when he stopped him on the street and "searched" him when he patted down his outside clothing. But despite the absence of a warrant or even probable cause, the Court upheld the propriety of the officer's actions, observing that the Fourth Amendment protects only against *unreasonable* searches and seizures. The Court defined reasonableness as an objective test from the officer's perspective: "Would the facts available to the officer at the moment of the seizure or search 'warrant a man of reasonable caution in the belief' that the action taken was appropriate?'"[319] On the facts presented, the Court found that the officer, utilizing his years of experience apprehending thieves, had reasonable suspicion to suspect a crime was about to take place, and thus to stop the individuals.

Subsequent cases confirmed just how profoundly this decision unmoored the Fourth Amendment from its original probable cause analysis. In *United States v. Cortez*, the Court confirmed that "reasonable suspicion" to conduct a stop-and-frisk requires only a "particularized and objective basis for suspecting the particular person stopped of criminal activity."[320] In *Rodriguez v. United States*, the Court noted that, unlike probable cause, reasonable suspicion can be established by facts entirely consistent with innocent activity.[321] And in *United States v. Sokolow*, the Court stated emphatically that the required "level of suspicion" of criminality to justify a stop-and-frisk "is considerably less than proof of wrongdoing by a preponderance of the evidence."[322] Instead, only a "minimal level of objective

---

[318] *Terry v. Ohio*, 392 U.S. 1 (1968).
[319] *Id.* at 22.
[320] *United States v. Cortez*, 449 U.S. 411, 417 (1981).
[321] *Rodriguez v. United States*, 575 U.S. 348, 369 (2015).
[322] *Sokolow*, 490 U.S. at 7.

justification for making the stop" must be established by the officer.[323] The officer must point to at least some "specific and articulable facts" of suspicious activity; an "inchoate and unparticularized hunch" will not suffice.[324]

3.2 FROM EVIDENCE TO HUNCHES

At first blush, the standard remains objective. The *Terry* Court admonished that the "demand for specificity in the information upon which police action is predicated is the central teaching of [the] . . . Fourth Amendment."[325] But experience tells a different story, one of a "disturbingly formless and potentially permissive" standard based on hunches.[326] These "hunches" are often laundered into objective evidence of criminal activity through deference to the officer's "training and experience." In each stop-and-frisk case, courts not only look to the facts articulated by the police officer but also allow for rational inferences to be made from those facts, inferences guided by the officer's "training and experience" in ferreting out crime.

What results is the wholesale manufacture of reasonable suspicion based on an officer's use of a "criminal profile," ostensibly intended to help officers recognize behavior that may indicate criminal activity. These profiles, employed most frequently to identify drug couriers, use traits of past offenders to "create a probabilistic picture of those most likely to" engage in criminal activity.[327] But profiles are little more than "a scattershot hodgepodge of traits and characteristics so expansive that it potentially justifies stopping anybody and everybody."[328] Justice Thurgood Marshall warned of the overreliance on criminal profiles in his dissent in *Sokolow*, noting "the profile's chameleon-like way of adapting to any particular set of circumstances."[329]

The most infamous criminal profile is the drug courier profile used by the Drug Enforcement Agency in apprehending drug traffickers at airports. Described variously as a "rather loosely formulated" profile and an "informal, apparently unwritten checklist," the drug courier profile includes a list of characteristics purportedly associated with drug trafficking.[330] These characteristics, first examined by a judge considering challenges to this practice and later compiled into a list by Barry

---

[323] *Id.*

[324] *Id.*

[325] *Terry*, 390 U.S. at 21 n.18.

[326] Davies, *The Supreme Court Giveth, supra* note 312, at 988.

[327] Alberto B. Lopez, *Racial Profiling & Whren: Searching for Objective Evidence of the Fourth Amendment on the Nation's Roads*, 90 KY. L.J. 75, 87 (2002).

[328] DAVID COLE, NO EQUAL JUSTICE: RACE AND CLASS IN THE AMERICAN CRIMINAL JUSTICE SYSTEM 47 (1999), quoted in Alexander, *supra* note 113, at 86.

[329] *Sokolow*, 490 U.S. at 13–14 (Marshall, J., dissenting) (citation omitted).

[330] Charles Becton, *The Drug Courier Profile: "All Seems Infected that th' Infected Spy, Looks Yellow to the Jaundice'd Eye*, 65 N.C. L. REV. 417, 437 (1987); Angela Anita Allen-Bell, *The Birth of Crime: Driving While Black (DWB)*, 44 S.U. L. REV. 38 60 (2016).

Friedman in his book *Unwarranted: Policing Without Permission*, highlight the absurdity of these profiles:

> *Arrived at night*
> *Arrived early in the morning*
> *Walked rapidly through the airport*
> *Walked aimlessly through the airport*
> *Used a one-way ticket*
> *Used a round-trip ticket*
> *Carried brand-new luggage*
> *Carried a small gym bag*
> *Traveled alone*
> *Traveled with a companion*
> *Acted too nervous*
> *Acted too calm*
> *First to deplane*
> *Last to deplane*
> *Deplaned in the middle*
> *Wore expensive clothing and gold jewelry*
> *Dressed in dark slacks, work shirt, and hat*
> *Dressed in black corduroys, white pullover shirt, and loafers without socks*
> *Dressed in brown leather aviator jacket, gold chain, hair down to shoulders*
> *Flew to Washington National Airport on the LaGuardia Shuttle.*[331]

While drug courier profiles are most common, the use of expansive profiles goes well beyond airports and drug traffickers, ensnaring potentially everyone who steps outside. Courts have upheld involuntary police stops because suspects appeared nervous in their presence, despite the fact that nervousness around police is both natural and common.[332] But assuming someone can overcome their nerves and steel themselves around police, that calmness also arouses "reasonable" suspicion, as multiple courts have held.[333] On roadways, courts have upheld police stops of motorists solely because the motorist avoided eye contact with the officer, apparently a criminal attempt to evade notice.[334] But looking at the officer is no less suspicious. At least one court upheld a police stop because a motorist made eye contact with the officer as he drove by at the officer.[335]

---

[331]   Barry Friedman , Unwarranted: Policing Without Permission 152–53 (2017).

[332]   *E.g.*, *United States v. Mouscardy*, 722 F.3d 68, 76 (1st Cir. 2013); *United States v. Williams*, 271 F.3d 1262, 1268–69 (2001).

[333]   *E.g.*, *United States v. Himmelwright*, 406 F. Supp. 889, 892–93 (S.D. Fla. 1975); *see also United States v. McKnight*, 385 Fed. Appx. 547, 550 (6th Cir. 2010) (dismissing defendant's assertion that "calm demeanor" is exculpatory because "cooperating with an officer does not necessarily diminish other evidence of wrongdoing").

[334]   *United States v. Arvizu*, 534 U.S. 266, 270 (2002); *United States v. Garcia*, 118 Fed. Appx. 690, 693 (4th Cir. 2004).

[335]   *United States v. Lujan*, No. 4:17-cr-37, 2018 WL 3742452 (E.D. Tenn. Aug. 7, 2018).

If you're starting to think there is no way to avoid looking suspicious in public, you're right. Indeed, even behavior that is "too law-abiding" can arouse suspicion: the Florida Highway Patrol Drug Courier Profile cautions troopers to be suspicious of "scrupulous obedience of traffic laws."[336] In many ways, modern policing embodies the old adage that "all seems infected that th' infected spy, as all looks yellow to the jaundic'd eye."[337]

3.3 BLACK SKIN AND INCHOATE HUNCHES

The color arousing the suspicion of the infected eye today is not yellow, but black. And while there may be no way to avoid all suspicion in the eyes of such expansive criminal profiles, there is at least one way to arouse less suspicion: being White. No national data exists on police stop-and-frisk practices, but studies of particular cities confirm that police targets of suspicion-based stops are overwhelmingly Black and Brown. From 2004 through 2012, the New York Police Department conducted approximately 4.4 million *"Terry* stops."[338] Of those stops, 52 percent involved a Black target and 31 percent involved a Hispanic target; only 10 percent of those stopped were White. For reference, during this period, 23 percent of New York City's population was Black, 29 percent identified as Hispanic or Latino, and 33 percent of the population was White. That racial disparity has continued to the present day; one study found that Black and Latino New Yorkers were stopped and frisked nine times more frequently than their White counterparts through 2009, a number that only dropped slightly to six times between 2015 and 2020.[339]

Smart policing? Hardly. In 88 percent of the millions of stops and frisks conducted by the NYPD, no enforcement action was taken – no arrest, no ticket, nothing.[340] And when these stops did yield results, White suspects were more likely to be found carrying contraband drugs or firearms, suggesting that police made more targeted stops of reasonably suspicious White people while conducting suspicionless, drag-net-style sweeps of Black neighborhoods.[341]

---

[336] Fla. Dept. of Highway Safety & Motor Vehicles, Office of Gen'l Counsel, *Common Characteristics of Drug Couriers* § I.A.4 (1984), quoted in Alexander, *supra* note 113.

[337] Alexander Pope, *An Essay on Criticism: Part 2*, https://www.poetryfoundation.org/poems/44897/an-essay-on-criticism-part-2.; *see also* Becton, *supra* note 330.

[338] The statistics in this paragraph were developed during a class action suit alleging that the NYPD's stop-and-frisk policy and practice were unconstitutional. Floyd v. City of New York, 959 F. Supp. 2d 540, 573–75 (S.D.N.Y. 2013).

[339] Al Baker, *New York Minorities More Likely to Be Frisked*, NY Times (May 12, 2010), https://www.nytimes.com/2010/05/13/nyregion/13frisk.html; Alan Feuer, *Black New Yorkers are Twice as Likely to Be Stopped By the Police, Data Shows*, NY Times (September 23, 2020), https://www.nytimes.com/2020/09/23/nyregion/nypd-arrests-race.html (in 2018, Black people were six times more likely than Whites to be stopped).

[340] *Floyd*, 959 F. Supp. 2d at 575.

[341] Sharad Goel, Justin M. Rao, & Ravi Shroff, *Precinct or Prejudice? Understanding Racial Disparities in New York City's Stop-and-Frisk Policy*, 10 ANNALS OF APPLIED STATISTICS 365, 367 (2016).

Racial profiling in the name of reasonable suspicion is not limited to on-the-street pat-downs. Countless studies from across the country confirm that police engage in racial profiling when initiating traffic stops, highlighting the dangers of "Driving While Black." In 2019, the Stanford Open Policing Project released the results of a study analyzing more than 100 million traffic stops nationwide from 2011 to 2017. It found that "police stopped and searched Black and Latino drivers on the basis of less evidence than used in stopping white drivers, who are searched less often but are more likely to be found with illegal items."[342] A 2015 report by retired federal and state judges studying policing in San Francisco found significant "racial disparities regarding [San Francisco Police Department] stops, searches, and arrests [at traffic stops], especially for Black people."[343] In Chicago, a 2016 Police Accountability Task Force report found that "black and Hispanic drivers were searched approximately four times as often as white drivers."[344] Similarly, a 2015 analysis by the *New York Times* found that in Greensboro, North Carolina, police officers "used their discretion to search black drivers ... more than twice as often as for white motorists."[345] This study also found that "officers were more likely to stop black drivers for no discernable reason. And they were more likely to use force if the driver was black, even when they did not encounter physical resistance."[346]

Surely, such overwhelming statistical proof of racial bias could be used to challenge an individual act of racial profiling as just that, right? Wrong. While the Supreme Court has never held that a police officer can legally target an individual because of race, it also has turned a blind eye to clear racial profiling. In *Whren v. United States*, a unanimous Supreme Court held that the subjective motivations of a police officer in stopping someone are completely irrelevant, so long as there is some objectively reasonable basis to initiate the stop.[347] Thus, not only are pretextual stops constitutional, but the specific pretext is of no constitutional concern. The practical consequence is to constitutionalize racially profiled stops, particularly in the context of traffic stops. An officer may have overtly racist reasons for pulling over

---

[342] Erik Ortiz, *Inside 100 Million Police Traffic Stops: New Evidence of Racial Bias*, NBC NEWS (March 13, 2019). The study was published in *Nature Human Behavior*. Emma Pierson et al., *A Large-Scale Analysis of Racial Disparities in Police Stops Across the United States*, 4 NATURE HUMAN BEHAVIOR 736 (2020), https://5harad.com/papers/100M-stops.pdf.

[343] Kia Maiarechi, *What the Data Really Says about Police and Racial Bias*, VANITY FAIR (July 14, 2016), https://www.vanityfair.com/news/2016/07/data-police-racial-bias; *see also* KPIX, *Study Shows California Cops More Likely to Stop Black Drivers* (January 2, 2020), https://sanfrancisco .cbslocal.com/2020/01/02/study-shows-california-police-more-stop-black-drivers/.

[344] *Id.* The report is available for download. Police Accountability Task Force, Recommendations for Reform: Restoring Trust Between the Chicago Police and the Communities They Serve, Executive Summary (2016), https://chicagopatf.org/wp-content/uploads/2016/04/PATF_Final_Report_ Executive_Summary_4_13_16-1.pdf.

[345] Sharon LaFraniere & Andrew W. Lehren, *The Disproportionate Risks of Driving While Black*, N.Y. TIMES (October 24, 2015), https://www.nytimes.com/2015/10/25/us/racial-disparity-traffic-stops-driving- black.html.

[346] *Id.*

[347] *Whren v. United States*, 517 U.S. 806 (1996).

Black drivers. But so long as the officer observes some minor traffic infraction – driving one mile over the speed limit, utilizing the turn signal 150 feet before the intersection instead of 200 feet before the intersection, having an "obstructed" view because two leaves are stuck in a windshield wiper (all real life "Driving While Black" examples) – the officer may lawfully pull the car over and initiate his racially motivated encounter.[348]

This outcome was as foreseeable as it was preventable. In 1968, the year *Terry* was decided, the Kerner Commission foresaw an America with "two societies, one black, one white – separate and unequal."[349] What was true then is true now – cities and towns remain largely segregated due to a complex mixture of historical segregation and redlining, poverty, and cultural insulation and distrust. The Commission urged neighborhood integration and policing reforms to ease tensions and combat racial profiling. Instead, by unmooring police conduct from the "probable cause" standard and authorizing involuntary armed encounters based on minimal justification, the Supreme Court ushered in an era of legally sanctioned racial harassment.

Beginning in the early 1980s, police departments across the country began employing more "proactive policing" measures aimed at enforcing minor infractions and arresting suspects for littering or graffiti to deter people from committing more serious crimes. This "broken windows" theory of policing gave officers more opportunities to contact more individuals more aggressively for less serious violations of social order. This newfound power, predictably, was not deployed equitably; rather, these tactics became synonymous with racial profiling, racial discrimination, and overpolicing of minority neighborhoods. Stop-and-frisk was the tool of choice. The "irony, of course, is that the police power to 'frisk' suspicious persons is the product of a Supreme Court [the Warren Court] that did more to promote the legal rights of black Americans than any other court."[350]

But today, "the law not only allows police harassment of minorities, but also seems to encourage it. Courts have specifically approved race as a factor in the decision to stop and detain individuals."[351] For example, in *United States v. Brignoni-Ponce*, the Supreme Court found that having a "Mexican appearance" near the international

---

[348] *See, e.g.,* Isabella Gomez & Justin Lear, *Police in Kansas Handcuff Black Motorist over "Vegetation" in his Car Window,* CNN (May 23, 2018), https://www.cnn.com/2018/05/22/us/police-kansas-detain-man-vegetation-trnd/index.html.

[349] Clyde Haberman, *The 1968 Kerner Commission Report Still Echoes Across America,* N.Y. Times (October 7, 2020), https://www.nytimes.com/2020/06/23/us/kerner-commission-report.html. The Kerner Commission, so called because it was led by Illinois Governor Otto Kerner Jr., was officially named the National Advisory Commission on Civil Disorders. The commission's full report is available at https://belonging.berkeley.edu/system/tdf/kerner_commission_full_report.pdf?file=1&force=1.

[350] Tracey Maclin, Terry v. Ohio's *Fourth Amendment Legacy: Black Men and Police Discretion,* 72 St. John's L. Rev. 1271, 1275 (1998).

[351] Amy D. Ronner, *Fleeing While Black: The Fourth Amendment Apartheid,* 32 Colum. Hum. Rts. L. Rev. 383, 393 (2000).

border was sufficient to support reasonable suspicion that the individual was an undocumented immigrant.[352] Similarly, in *United States v. Weaver*, the Eighth Circuit held that the fact that an arriving airline passenger was a "roughly dressed young black male" was sufficient to create reasonable suspicion.[353] In her seminal article *Race and the Decision to Detain a Suspect*, Sheri Lynn Johnson explains, "Although no case condones race as the sole basis for an investigative stop, courts often allow it to tip the scales of probable cause or reasonable suspicion. ... Occasionally ... the coincidence of the suspect's and the perpetrator's race seems to be the *only* factor supporting the detention."[354]

The injection of flexible standards like reasonable suspicion, overbroad descriptions like the drug courier profile, and tactics like broken windows policing all give the green light for oppressive, often unconscious, overpolicing of minority communities. Angela Davis explained why malleable drug courier profiles in particular "permit the infusion of race in the detention discussion":

> Officers do not stop whites who exhibit the other innocent behaviors or characteristics as frequently as African-Americans. A white man dressed in a business suit who buys a roundtrip plane ticket with a quick turnaround time, travels with no luggage, and deplanes last may not be detained. But a young black man or woman casually dressed who acts and travels the same way may raise the suspicions of law enforcement agents. If a police officer who uses a profile treats similarly situated blacks and whites differently, then race becomes the defining factor which elevates a suspicion or hunch to reasonable suspicion or even probable cause.[355]

The use of race as a proxy for criminality, even unintentionally, is in some ways inevitable, given the long history of policing Black bodies as inherently criminal. But it is the Supreme Court's "reasonable suspicion" standard that gives bias-motivated policing its legal legitimacy. The concept of "reasonable suspicion" and its "totality of the circumstances" test allows "such a vast panoply of factors and inferences that it can easily mask police officers' racial prejudices."[356]

Those prejudices could be counterweighted by a stronger, more definite standard, like probable cause. "Clear and less malleable standards [would] ... alleviate the disproportionate impact of random, suspicionless searches in the minority community."[357] The Supreme Court's reluctance to impose any sort of bright-line

[352] *United States v. Brignoni-Ponce*, 422 U.S. 873 (1975).
[353] *United States v. Weaver*, 966 F.2d 391, 392 (8th Cir. 1992).
[354] Sheri Lynn Johnson, *Race and the Decision to Detain a Suspect*, 93 YALE L.J. 214, 225–26 (1983) (emphasis in original).
[355] Angela Davis, *Race, Cops, and Traffic Stops*, 51 U. MIAMI L. REV. 425, 430–31 (1997).
[356] Ronner, *supra* note 351, at 393.
[357] Ronner, *supra* note 351, at 393 n.46 (quoting William R. O'Shields, *The Exodus of Minorities' Fourth Amendment Rights into Oblivion: Florida v. Bostick and the Merits of Adopting a Per Se Rule Against Random Suspicionless Bus Searches in the Minority Community*, 77 IOWA L. REV. 1875, 1878 (1992)).

test for reasonableness legitimates a process permeated with bias, creating a system in which police can point to almost anything as evidence of suspicious activity:

> The indeterminate nature of the standard makes it easy for police officers who stop someone for discriminatory reasons, or for no reason at all, to later justify the stop by articulating other benign reasons. Because courts are routinely deferential to law enforcement officers, an officer can point to many aspects of the suspect's conduct and claim that in the totality of the circumstances, he or she was justifiably suspicious ... Moreover, the lack of specificity inherent in the reasonable articulate suspicion standard permits law enforcement agents to use race as a factor in justifying their suspicion.[358]

This masked racial prejudice largely goes unchallenged by courts charged with acting as neutral checks on police abuses of power. Courts routinely defer to officer discretion in decisions about stops and searches, even when those decisions are infected by subjective perceptions and biases that corrupt the law of search and seizure.

Some have defended these subjective racist biases as a claim of knowledge. This form of racism is sometimes called – oxymoronically – "reasonable racism." Reasonable racism refers to the view that the stereotypes about Black men are true, that reacting defensively to Black people is reasonable. "It inheres in 'the notion that black males really do share a dangerous tendency to violence, or mayhem, or crime,' in the notion that this stereotyping is really 'common sense.'"[359] This notion can also function as excuse: "The 'Reasonable Racist' asserts that, even if his belief that Blacks are 'prone to violence' stems primarily from racism ... he should be excused for considering the victim's race ... because most similarly situated Americans would have done so as well."[360] Thus, even when a court does not expressly endorse race as a controlling factor in the reasonable suspicion analysis, it may nevertheless defer to the "reasonable police officer" who – like the rest of us – views Black persons with inherent distrust.

What allows this elision is the fact that "reasonable" is often defined by courts as what is typical or common, not what ought to be deemed just and fair. Or as Jody David Armour puts it, "[t]he role of the courts, from this perspective, is to *observe* rather than *define* the attributes of the reasonable man."[361] This narrative relies on a peculiar concept of harm. In criminal law, harm is understood as an element of an *actus reus*, or criminal act. An individual must do something or at least attempt to do something to be guilty of a crime. You become a criminal if – and only if – you make

---

[358] *Id.* (quoting Randall S. Susskind, *Race, Reasonable Articulable Suspicion and Seizure*, 31 AM. CRIM. L. REV. 327, 332–33 (1994)).

[359] D. Marvin Jones, *"He's a Black Male ... Something Is Wrong with Him!" The Role of Race in the Stand Your Ground Debate*, 68 U. MIAMI L. REV. 1025, 1029 (quoting D. MARVIN JONES, RACE SEX, AND SUSPICION: THE MYTH OF THE BLACK MALE 3 (2005)).

[360] JODY DAVID ARMOUR, NEGROPHOBIA AND REASONABLE RACISM: THE HIDDEN COSTS OF BEING BLACK IN AMERICA 19 (1997).

[361] *Id.* at 32 (emphasis in original).

a particular choice and act on it. But the reasonable racism framework does not require a criminal act as that concept has been traditionally understood. For Black persons, their guilt is not a result of what they have done, but of who they are. The core notion is that "this kind" is dangerous per se – an idea harking back to seventeenth-century characterizations of Black slaves as a "heathenish brutish" and "dangerous kinde of people" who had to be controlled.[362]

But racist acts cannot be excused as legally reasonable simply because they are common. The job of the Court in assessing reasonableness should not be reduced to empirical observations of widely held racist beliefs. Were it otherwise, Fourth Amendment reasonableness would be reduced to a codification of centuries-long irrational racial fear of Black people in America.

3.4 CRIMINALIZING BLACK MOVEMENTS

In 1996, in *Whren v. United States*, the Rehnquist Court specifically permitted racist cops to stop Black people for pretextual reasons.[363] Four years later, the Court lent objective legitimacy to such racial profiling in *Illinois v. Wardlow*, when it held that reasonable suspicion of criminal activity can be founded on nothing more than presence in a "high crime area" and an unwillingness to engage with police officers.[364]

In *Wardlow*, two uniformed police officers in the special operations section of the Chicago Police Department were driving the last car in a four-car caravan that converged on an area known for heavy narcotics trafficking to investigate the drug transactions in progress. One of the officers noticed Sam Wardlow, a young Black man, standing next to a building holding an opaque bag. When Wardlow saw the police officers, he fled. Officers gave chase on foot, stopped and frisked Wardlow, and found an unregistered .38-caliber handgun in the bag. Wardlow challenged the stop, saying the officers did not have "specific and articulable facts of criminal activity" sufficient to create the reasonable suspicion required to justify the seizure.

The Supreme Court disagreed. The Court first reiterated that reasonable suspicion to justify an involuntary stop-and-frisk requires only some "minimal level of objective justification."[365] The Court then found that presence in a "high crime area" can be one such objective factor; "nervous, evasive behavior," such as flight from a police officer, is another.[366] Those two factors could justify a warrantless stop-and-frisk, the Court held. Thus, by a vote of 5–4, the Supreme Court held that

---

[362] From the Barbados Slave Code of 1661. Quoted in Maalik Stansbury, *Barbados Slave Codes*, *supra* note 28.

[363] *Whren v. United States*, 507 U.S. 806 (1996).

[364] *Illinois v. Wardlow*, 528 U.S. 119 (2000).

[365] *Id.* at 124.

[366] *Id.*

presence in a high crime area coupled with nervous behavior in the presence of a police officer constituted sufficient indicia of criminality to justify an armed government agent's stop-and-frisk of an otherwise law-abiding citizen.

Arguably no case has done more to promote the enforcement of White spaces in American public life than *Wardlow*. Despite its disingenuous refusal to acknowledge the role of race either in the police's stop of Wardlow or in its decision, the Court's rule had immediate, adverse impacts on communities of color in two dimensions.

First, the Court did not require any sort of empirical or other evidentiary showing that a particular neighborhood was in fact a "high crime area," leaving that decision to the discretion of the police officer. In reality, "high crime area" was then and is now a proxy phrase for "poor, Black neighborhood" – the ghetto. By constitutionalizing the idea that mere presence in such an area provides an important hallmark of suspicious activity, the Supreme Court traveled far down the road toward criminalizing people's presence in their own neighborhoods, particularly when those neighborhoods disproportionately are occupied by the very marginalized groups with more legitimate reason to fear – and flee – the cops. At a minimum, the Court's ruling contributed significantly to the criminalization of Blackness and poverty in "high crime" areas, fostering a culture of "segregation policing" and further entrenching the idea of suspicious Black spaces and safe White spaces.[367] And it gave carte blanche to police departments around the country to continue over-policing these neighborhoods and engaging in aggressive, racially motivated stop-and-frisk sweeps.

Second, the Court's finding that nervousness, including flight, in the presence of a police officer is suggestive of criminality ignores Black Americans' centuries-long experience of indignity, harassment, physical violence, and death at the hands of police officers. "Some people, especially members of minority groups ... have perfectly legitimate reasons to avoid police, as they may have been subjected to unjustified detentions and searches, harassment, or even physical abuse in the past."[368] As David Harris explained seventeen years before *Wardlow*:

Many African-American males can recount an instance in which police stopped and questioned them or someone they knew for no reason, even physically abusing or degrading them in the process. While the causes of this phenomenon are no doubt complex – among other factors, racism and simple ignorance surely play a role – the effect is undeniable: African Americans, as more frequent targets of undesirable treatment by police than whites, are naturally more likely to avoid

---

[367] *See* Monica C. Bell, *Anti-Segregation Policing*, N.Y.U. L. REV. 650, 675 (2020); Molly Griffard, *Bias-Free Predictive Policing Tool? An Evaluzation of the NYPD's Patternizr*, 47 FORDHAM URB. L.J. 43, 53–55 (2019) (describing the role the Court, relying on faulty social science, promotes the criminalization of poverty).

[368] Ronner, *supra* note 351, at 396 n.56 (quoting David A. Harris, *Particularized Suspicion, Categorical Judgments: Supreme Court Rhetoric Versus Lower Court Reality Under* Terry v. Ohio, 72 ST. JOHN'S L. REV. 975, 996 (1998)).

contact with the police. They wish to avoid harassment, baseless stops and frisks, and even more extreme actions, such as beatings, at the hands of police.[369]

That experience of abuses large and small has had a profound effect not only on individual Black Americans, but on Black culture. White parents talk to their children about peer pressure, alcohol, and drugs; Black parents talk with their children about what to do when they are stopped by police. "Black males learn at an early age that confrontations with the police should be avoided: Black teenagers are advised never to challenge a police officer, even when the officer is wrong . . . Such an encounter often engenders distinct feelings for the Black man. Those feelings are fear of possible violence or humiliation."[370]

Ubiquitous media images and news stories detailing police abuse of Black civilians reinforces this fear and the consequent desire to avoid police at all costs. A 1993 NAACP study found that Black men who encountered police could not help but think of the savage, videotaped beating of Rodney King three years earlier.[371] More recently, Rayshard Brooks was shot and killed as he fled from police less than three weeks after George Floyd's murder. Surveillance footage showed Brooks struggling with and evading police before being gunned down as he ran away. Brooks's wife, Tomika Miller, later said they had watched the video of Floyd's lynching "over and over" and that may have led Brooks to resist: "So especially [after] watching this video of George Floyd over and over again, his reaction may have been, 'I'm not getting put in handcuffs.' We can't just toss it out because he resisted – George Floyd didn't and it ended the same way."[372]

In the immediate aftermath of *Wardlow*, one scholar rightly opined that the decision created a form of "Fourth Amendment apartheid."[373] White Americans are free to move throughout their "low crime neighborhoods" and walk confidently by police without fear of harassment, while Black Americans remain subject to constant, pervasive police contact, which in turn conditions them to avoid police, which under *Wardlow* suggests criminality and justifies involuntary detention:

> Police use Terry stops aggressively in high crime neighborhoods; as a result, African Americans and Hispanic Americans are subjected to a high number of stops and

---

[369] *Id.* (quoting David A. Harris, *Factors for Reasonable Suspicion: When Black and Poor Means Stopped and Frisked*, 69 IND. L.J. 659, 680 (1994)).

[370] Tracey Maclin, *"Black and Blue Encounters" – Some Preliminary Thoughts About Fourth Amendment Seizures: Should Race Matter?*, 26 VAL. U. L. REV. 243, 255 (1991).

[371] *NAACP Study Cites Wall Between Police and Black Communities*, UPI ARCHIVES (March 31, 1993), https://www.upi.com/Archives/1993/03/31/NAACP-study-cites-wall-between-police-and-black-communities/2482733554000/ (describing study reported in CHARLES J. OGLETREE, M. PROSSER ET AL., BEYOND THE RODNEY KING STORY: AN INVESTIGATION OF POLICE MISCONDUCT IN MINORITY COMMUNITIES (1994)).

[372] Dannielle Maguire, *Rayshard Brooks's Family Have Spoken About His Death. Here Are the Most Powerful Moments from Their Press Conference*, ABC NEWS (June 16, 2020), https://www.abc.net.au/news/2020-06-16/rayshard-brooks-family-press-conference-police-shooting-atlanta/12360760.

[373] Ronner, *supra* note 351.

frisks. Feeling understandably harassed, they wish to avoid the police and act accordingly. This evasive behavior (in their own) high crime neighborhoods gives the police that much more power to stop and frisk.[374]

One enduring irony of *Wardlow* is that it established a clear, bright-line rule for reasonable suspicion – something the Court has otherwise steadfastly refused to provide, preferring to rely instead on the "totality of the circumstances" analysis. Police departments across the country immediately read *Wardlow* to mean "High Crime Area + Flight = Green Light," and courts almost universally have agreed. Thus, while the Supreme Court refuses to place any bright-line guardrails around police use of *Terry* stop-and-frisks, it willingly adopted a bright-line permission slip for police officers to engage in suspicionless racial profiling. The enforcement of the color line in American cities became that much easier.

Four years after *Wardlow*, the nation's largest police department – the NYPD – implemented its quasi-dragnet style stop-and-frisk policy in New York City's poorest minority neighborhoods, dramatically increasing its use of on-the-street stops and frisks to crack down on petty crimes. From 2004 to 2012, NYPD officers stopped-and-frisked 4.4 million New Yorkers, over 80 percent of whom were Black or Brown.[375] This was no accident, as at least one commanding officer admitted during a taped roll call, during which he instructed his officers to frisk "the right people at the right time, the right location . . . and I have no problem telling you this, male blacks 14, to 20, 21."[376]

In a US Department of Justice Special Report, *Contacts Between Police and the Public, 2015*, the Bureau of Justice Statistics painted a grim picture of the ways in which Black civilians are overpoliced on the street, on the roadways, and in the use of force by officers.[377] The report noted that "a greater percentage of blacks than whites experienced police-initiated contact" despite there being more than six times as many White people as Black people in America.[378] Black people were more likely than Whites to be stopped on the street, pulled over in their cars,[379] stopped as a result of police-initiated contact, and stopped as a result of a citizen-initiated contact (911 or other call to police).[380] And Black people stopped by police were more than twice as likely to experience the threat or use of force than White people

[374] *Id.* at 422 (quoting Harris, *supra* note 75, at 681).

[375] *Floyd*, 959 F. Supp. 2d at 573–75.

[376] John Del Signore, *NYPD Commanding Officer Caught on Tape Ordering Cops to Stop and Frisk Young "Make Blacks,"* GOTHAMIST (March 22, 2013), https://gothamist.com/news/nypd-commanding-officer-caught-on-tape-ordering-cops-to-stop-and-frisk-young-male-blacks.

[377] ELIZABETH DAVIS ET AL., BUREAU OF JUSTICE STATISTICS, CONTACTS BETWEEN POLICE AND THE PUBLIC, 2015 (October 2018), https://www.bjs.gov/content/pub/pdf/cpp15.pdf.

[378] *Id.* at 9.

[379] *Id.* at 2.

[380] *Id.* at 10, tbl.9.

stopped by police.[381] But regardless of the type of stop, less than 3 percent of all persons stopped were arrested.[382]

Even when these police contacts do not result in an arrest, the unnecessary, racially motivated contact further hardens distrusts and traumatizes an already marginalized community. Nor should the "mere inconvenience" of a stop-and-frisk be minimized. As Justice Scalia noted in a concurring opinion in *Minnesota v. Dickerson*:

> I frankly doubt ... whether the fiercely proud men who adopted our Fourth Amendment would have allowed themselves to be subjected, on mere *suspicion* of being armed and dangerous, to such indignity, which is described as follows in a police manual:
>
> "Check the subject's neck and collar. A check should be made under the subject's arm. Next a check should be made of the upper back. The lower back should also be checked.
>
> A check should be made of the upper part of the man's chest and the lower region around the stomach. The belt, a favorite concealment spot, should be checked. The inside thigh and crotch area also should be searched. The legs should be checked for possible weapons. The last items to be checked are the shoes and cuffs of the subject."[383]

3.5 THE ANONYMOUS TIPSTER'S HUNCH

Much of the foregoing discussion involves police officers developing reasonable suspicion of criminal activity based on personal observations interpreted through the racially tinged lens of the criminal profile. But what about the racially fearful private citizen who senses something "sketchy" or observes someone out of place? Can this hunch-driven method of lawful policing also protect private enforcers of the color line?

In a strictly legal sense, the answer must be no. The Fourth Amendment only applies to government conduct. Thus, the Fourth Amendment's reasonable suspicion standard governs only police and other official activity, not private conduct. To the extent a private citizen attempts to "search or seize" another private citizen, that conduct is governed and redressed through civil and criminal sanction, not constitutional litigation.

But in a much larger sense, the answer must be yes. If trained law enforcement professionals are entitled to react on the basis of race-based hunches, then certainly similar reactions of untrained private citizens are at least equally excusable. The Supreme Court has repeatedly authorized police stops of Black people on

---

[381] *Id.* at 16–17.

[382] *Id.* at 10.

[383] *Minnesota v. Dickerson*, 508 U.S. 366, 381–82 (1993) (Scalia, J., concurring) (quoting J. MOYNIHAN, POLICE SEARCHING PROCEDURES 7 (1963) (emphasis in original)).

threadbare, often racially charged facts. Courts routinely uphold these stops even though the overwhelming majority of the stops uncover no wrongdoing whatsoever, and even in the face of compelling empirical evidence that many of the "articulable facts" trotted out by police bear no relation at all to criminal activity. The Supreme Court allows such stops even when the express, stated motivation of the police officer has nothing to do with the suspicious activity purportedly justifying the stop, but with conducting a suspicionless fishing expedition to uncover other crimes. These pretextual stops are often motivated by one fact: race. Yet the Supreme Court says that fact is irrelevant and allows the stop anyway.

If these are the standards governing the investigations of experts trained in criminal behavior, how can private citizens be held to a higher standard of conduct? If an officer can perceive the nervous presence of someone in a high-crime area as sufficiently indicative of criminal activity to necessitate a forceful, compelled detention, then shouldn't a private citizen observing someone out of place, asleep in a college dormitory or dancing in the dark with a mask on, have the right to request a police response to this "suspicious" behavior? If an officer sworn to uphold the law can effectuate a traffic stop for something as frivolous as vegetation in a windshield wiper when the true purpose of the stop was to profile a Black man, then why should we expect different behavior when a private citizen sees a minor barbecuing violation and frantically calls 911 to stop the Black man from committing more serious crimes?

To be clear, I am not arguing that private actors should have the right to engage in this type of fact-free, hunch-based racial profiling. But I am suggesting it should come as no surprise that *they do have such a right*, when the highest court in the land protects identical racist behavior by the government agents both charged with protecting society from harm and purportedly restrained by the Constitution from inflicting it.

This hunch-based standard of policing has another, more direct safe haven for racially fearful 911 abuse, one expressly endorsed by the Supreme Court. In a stunning failure to recognize the realities of 911 abuse, the Supreme Court held in *Navarette v. California* that anonymous 911 callers are presumed to be credible and reliable and thus that a 911 caller's report of *any* criminal or suspicious behavior provides reasonable suspicion to justify a police response and forceful stop of the target of the call.[384] By broadly protecting officers who respond to all but the most frivolous 911 calls, the Court both implicitly insulated White caller criminals from liability and ensured the success of the White caller criminal's intentions – to summon an armed government agent to police the color line.

A short discussion of the development of this anonymous tipster case law shows how the Supreme Court eroded Fourth Amendment protections for 911 abuse targets, building on its erosion of those protections in *Terry*, *Whren*, and *Wardlow*.

---

[384]   *Navarette v. California*, 572 U.S. 393 (2014).

The Court first addressed the question of whether information from an informant – as opposed to direct observation or investigation – could provide reasonable suspicion in *Adams v. Williams.*[385] In *Adams*, the police received a tip at 2:15 a.m. that a man seated in a nearby vehicle was carrying narcotics and had a gun in his waist. The tipster did not explain how he knew this information, but the officer responded to the tip anyway because "[t]he informant was known to him personally and had provided him with information in the past."[386] In fact, the informant had previously called in a single tip about homosexual activity that did not result in an arrest, because the "sodomy" could not be corroborated.[387] When the officer arrived on the scene, he approached the vehicle, found the man described by the informant, and immediately searched the informant's person pursuant to *Terry*. The Court acknowledged that the officer lacked probable cause to search or arrest the target, but held that he did have reasonable suspicion, because information from an informant known to be reliable carried sufficient "indicia of reliability" to justify a stop.[388]

Notably, the Court contrasted the case of a known informant providing readily verifiable information with an anonymous phone tip, finding the informant to be more reliable precisely because of the risk of a false report: "The informant here came forward personally to give information that was immediately verifiable at the scene... under Connecticut law, the informant might have been subject to immediate arrest for making a false complaint had the officer's investigation proved the tip incorrect."[389]

The Court had the opportunity to consider the reliability of an anonymous tip two decades later, in *Alabama v. White.*[390] In *White*, the tipster called police and described not only the alleged crime – transport of cocaine – and the perpetrator, but the car she would drive, the route she would take, and her destination. The Court held that the tip, standing alone, was insufficient to supply reasonable suspicion. However, the specificity of the tip allowed for its partial corroboration by police, who identified the vehicle and followed it as it took the journey described by the tip.[391]

The Court held that "the independent corroboration by the police of significant aspects of the informer's predictions imparted some degree of reliability to the other allegations made by the caller," providing the required "indicia of reliability" to

---

[385] *Adams v. Williams*, 407 U.S. 143 (1972).

[386] *Id.* at 147.

[387] *Id.* at 156 (Marshall, J., dissenting).

[388] *Id.* at 147.

[389] *Id.* at 146–47.

[390] *Alabama v. White*, 496 U.S. 325 (1990). Significantly, *Illinois v. Gates* came between *Adams* and *White*; *Gates* considered an anonymous tip in the context of probable cause. The Court held that, while the tip itself was not sufficient absent "something more," probable cause was created by the totality of the circumstances, including police corroboration of the details of the tip. *Gates*, 462 U.S. 213, 227 (1983).

[391] *White*, 496 U.S. at 332.

support reasonable suspicion.[392] In other words, the tipster not only provided detailed information about the suspect but was able to accurately predict what the suspect would do in the future, suggesting that the caller had inside information about the suspect's activities and plans. Once the police corroborated those predictions, the Court concluded that the tip was sufficiently reliable to provide reasonable suspicion, although "it [was] a close case."[393]

Ten years later, the Court squarely confronted the type of anonymous 911 call more closely associated with the Living While Black phenomenon. In *Florida v. J.L.*, the Court considered an anonymous tipster who described a Black teenager standing at a bus station, told police where to find him, and alleged he was carrying a gun.[394] The verifiable information the tipster provided – including the person's description, attire, and current location – was openly available to any passerby. Thus, that information alone did not provide any demonstration "that the tipster [had] knowledge of concealed criminal activity" like the illegal possession of a handgun.[395] The tipster did not and could not explain how he knew the suspect had a gun on him. The Court rejected this type of tip as a basis for reasonable suspicion, because reasonable suspicion "requires that a tip be reliable in its assertion of illegality, not just its tendency to identify a determinate person."[396] Thus, an anonymous tip cannot merely identify a (Black) person existing in public and lob unobserved, unsubstantiated allegations of criminal conduct about them. The tip must allege some personally observable criminal or otherwise suspicious behavior.

Florida v. J.L. appeared at first to be a victory for restraining White caller criminals and other anonymous 911 abusers. Unfortunately, in *Navarette v. California*, the Court retreated from this standard.[397] In *Navarette*, the Court upheld the legality of a traffic stop based on an anonymous tip that a truck had run the caller off the road, even though police officers followed the truck for five minutes and observed no dangerous driving. The Court held that "the call bore adequate indicia of reliability" to support reasonable suspicion, pointing to the apparent eyewitness nature of the report, the contemporaneity of the report with the incident (judged by the truck's location when the police found it), and the use of the 911 system to make the report.[398]

While permitting a traffic stop based on an anonymous tip of drunk driving might seem prudent, the reasoning in *Navarette* created a dangerous bright-line rule that anonymous tips delivered via the 911 system are per se reliable for the purposes of

[392] *Id.*
[393] *Id.*
[394] 529 U.S. 266 (2000).
[395] *Id.* at 272.
[396] *Id.*
[397] *Navarette v. California*, 527 U.S. 393 (2014).
[398] *Id.* at 398–99.

creating reasonable suspicion.[399] Writing for the majority, Justice Thomas claimed that the entirely anonymous tip was inherently reliable precisely because the caller used 911:

> A 911 call has some [technological] features that allow for identifying and tracing callers, and thus provide some safeguards against making false reports with immunity. . . . The caller's use of the 911 system is therefore one of the relevant circumstances that, taken together, justified the officer's reliance on the information reported in the 911 call.[400]

This naïve view of 911 uses and abuses is dangerously out of touch with reality, where over half of all calls are frivolous and virtually no one is punished.[401] But in accepting the tip in *Navarette* as an acceptable basis for reasonable suspicion, in the absence of corroborating evidence of the alleged illegal activity, the Supreme Court effectively abandoned its bar against "reliance on bare assertions of criminal activity from anonymous tipsters" and "undermine[d] the rigor of [its] reasonable suspicion analysis."[402]

For their part, the four *Navarette* dissenters took a more clear-eyed and accurate approach to 911 abuse. Writing for the dissent, Justice Scalia observed that "unnamed tipsters can lie with impunity," and the use of the 911 system does nothing to diminish that fact.[403] The dissent closed with a prescient warning:

> All the malevolent 911 caller need do is assert a traffic [or other] violation, and the targeted car will be stopped, forcibly if necessary, by the police. If the driver turns out not to be drunk (which will almost always be the case), the caller need fear no consequences, even if 911 knows his identity. After all . . . his word is as good as his victim's.[404]

---

[399] Joshua Aberman, *Culpability Through Anonymity: Why* Navarette v. California *Vastly Lowers the Standard for Reasonable Suspicion Based Solely on Anonymous Tips*, 48 Loy. L.A. L. Rev. 539, 551 (2014). This assumption perhaps seems even more of a reach after the events of the past few years.

[400] *Navarette*, 527 U.S. at 400–01.

[401] *See generally supra* Chapter 2.

[402] George M. Dery III & Kevin Meehan, *The Devil is in the Details: The Supreme Court Erodes the Fourth Amendment in Applying Reasonable Suspicion in* Navarette v. California, 21 Wash. & Lee J. Civil Rts & Soc. Just. 275, 286, 293 (2015).

[403] *Navarette*, 527 U.S. at 406 (Scalia, J., dissenting) (quoting Florida v. J.L. 529 U.S. 266, 275 (Kennedy, J., concurring)).

[404] *Id.* at 413–14.

4

Defending White Space

Weaponizing phone lines to enforce White spaces has proven an effective tool for the passively fearful. In most cases, it lends anonymity, allowing a racially fragile citizen to lodge a complaint and recede into the shadows as armed agents assume responsibility. Akin to keyboard warriors and internet trolls, 911 abusers can lob unsubstantiated attacks and escape involvement or scrutiny themselves.[405]

But this type of color line enforcement is a step removed from the action. It relies on a 911 dispatcher and a police officer to act on the frivolous, race-baiting tip. Some White space defenders want to be more involved, to take the law into their own hands under the guise of self-defense. Thanks to gun rights lobbies and state legislatures across the country, now they can. No trend better encapsulates the State's increasing acquiescence to civilian weaponization of racial fear than Stand Your Ground laws. These laws fly in the face of traditional self-defense doctrine, posing a serious threat to public safety "by encouraging armed vigilantism."[406]

Under traditional self-defense law, citizens can use force to defend themselves anywhere, but when they are outside their home, they cannot use force that is likely to kill or seriously injure someone if it can be safely avoided.[407] This traditional law respects both the individual right to self-defense and the sanctity of human life by requiring a person to avoid taking a life when a clear and safe alternative exists.[408]

---

[405] Many thanks go to Professor Addie Rolnick of the University of Nevada Law Vegas School of Law, from whose 2019 Cardozo Law Review article this chapter owes its name. *See generally* Rolnick, *supra* note 240. Professor Rolnick's work has been instrumental in my understanding and development of the issues described in the next two chapters.

[406] Everytown for Gun Safety, *The Inherent Danger of Stand Your Ground Laws*, EVERYTOWN RSCH. & POL'Y (January 8, 2021), https://everytownresearch.org/report/the-inherent-danger-of-stand-your-ground-laws/.

[407] *See* Tamara Rice Lave, *Shoot to Kill: A Critical Look at Stand Your Ground Laws*, 67 U. MIAMI L. REV. 827, 832–34 (2013) (analyzing the difference between Florida's Stand Your Ground law and more traditional self-defense laws); Cynthia V. Ward, *"Stand Your Ground" and Self-Defense*, 42 AM. J. CRIM. L. 89, 93–104 (2015) (discussing the historical and legal development of the traditional self-defense rule in criminal law).

[408] *See Guns in Public: Stand Your Ground*, GIFFORDS L. CTR. TO PREVENT GUN VIOLENCE, http://lawcenter.giffords.org/gun-laws/policy-areas/guns-in-public/stand-your-ground-laws/.

The centuries-old exception to this rule – the castle doctrine – allows a person inside his home to defend himself with force even if he could have safely walked away.[409] Under traditional law, an affirmative self-defense claim absolves a person of criminal culpability for killing another human being because, in the eyes of the law, the killing was reasonable and necessary. Self-defense claims have always been fraught with racial discrimination. The pervasive, implicitly fearful "anti-Blackness" mindset created by centuries of violent stereotyping has made juries far quicker to justify the killing of a Black person as a "reasonable" act of self-defense than that of a White person.

Stand Your Ground laws expand the opportunity for policing of White spaces to masquerade as self-defense by erasing the duty to retreat. These laws expand the scope of the "castle" to any public space, allowing people to use deadly force in public even when a clear and safe alternative is available. At least thirty-nine jurisdictions have adopted some version of Stand Your Ground in the last two decades, through legislative enactment or judicial order.[410]

These laws are indisputably linked to elevated homicide rates.[411] Moreover, they have proven an effective and deadly tool for enforcing the color line. By eliminating any requirement to de-escalate tense situations and expanding castle doctrine protections to any public place, Stand Your Ground laws provide cover for White vigilantes intent on defending their castle of White space and attacking as suspicious any Black person who dares step outside the iconic ghetto. And juries abide. When White shooters who kill Black victims assert a Stand Your Ground defense, the resulting homicides are deemed justifiable at least five times more frequently than when the shooter is Black and the victim is White.[412]

Of course, Stand Your Ground laws did not create the misconception that racial minorities are inherently more violent or more aggressive and thus more deserving of

---

[409] Catherine L. Carpenter, *Of the Enemy Within, the Castle Doctrine, and Self-Defense*, 86 MARQ. L. REV. 653, 667 (2003) ("In the case of defense of habitation, the Castle Doctrine allows the resident to stand ground and use deadly force against the intruder to protect the sanctity of the home from the attempted atrocious felony because the duty to retreat would be incompatible with the goal of preventing the commission of the felony.").

[410] *Guns in Public, supra* note 408.

[411] A.B.A., NATIONAL TASK FORCE ON STAND YOUR GROUND LAWS: REPORT AND RECOMMENDATIONS 10–14 (September 2015). Many of the Stand Your Ground laws are based on form legislation drafted by the American Exchange Council (ALEC) and the National Rifle Association. Elizabeth Megale, *A Call for Change: A Contextual-Configurative Analysis of Florida's Stand Your Ground Laws*, 68 U. MIAMI L. REV. 1051, 1079–84 (2014).

[412] Everytown for Gun Safety, *Stand Your Ground Laws Are A License to Kill*, Everytown Research & Policy (January 25, 2021), https://everytownresearch.org/report/stand-your-ground-laws-are-a-license-to-kill/ (citing Roman, *supra* note 32). A previous Everytown fact sheet claimed that these deaths were deemed justifiable eleven times more frequently. *See* Fields, *supra* note 30 at 985 n.340 (citing to previous Everytown for Gun Safety Fact sheet from 2019, which is no longer available). A study by the Marshall Project of all homicides in the FBI dataset between 1980 and 2014 found similar patterns. In the Marshall Project analysis, Black-on-Black homicides were found justified about 2 percent of the time, similar to the overall rate, but White-on-Black homicides were found justified eight times as often as other homicides. Lathrop & Flagg, *supra* note 33.

suspicion, especially when they step into the White spaces. But as the Reverend Leonard Leach observed, these laws fan the flames of racial fear, "perpetuat[ing] a foolish bravado of those who feel a bold security when they have a gun in their hand, and exonerating an arrogance and/or ignorance."[413] The willingness of states to promote and protect such armed confrontation in the face of clear racial bias further reflects, at best, official actors' ambivalence toward private racial enforcement.

More cynically, this legislative rush to protect racially motivated private violence can be seen as an effort to, in effect, subcontract segregation. As Addie Rolnick noted in the 2019 article from which this chapter derives its name, "[b]y expanding the categories of permissible violence, state legislatures can authorize private parties to carry out violence while appearing to reign [sic] in state-sponsored [police] violence."[414] After all, "state-sponsored race discrimination of any kind is prohibited by federal law, while private race discrimination, particularly violence, is illegal . . . only in its most extreme and blatant forms."[415]

This chapter considers the common-law origins of self-defense claims and the historic use of self-defense doctrine as a tool of White supremacy and racial segregation. It then explores how the unprincipled expansion of no-retreat self-defense rules – Stand Your Ground laws – from the home to all public spaces not only brings the racially problematic assessment of "reasonable self-defense" into the public square but actively works to promote the violent protection of White space from Black "invaders."

4.1 "TRADITIONAL" SELF-DEFENSE LAW

The recognition of self-defense as a justification for homicide has deep roots in Anglo-American law. The killing of another human being is illegal in virtually all circumstances, and intentionally killing another person carries with it the most severe punitive consequences. Further, American law generally discourages self-help measures involving the use of physical force, against persons or property. The legal principles permitting the use of deadly force in self-defense thus "present a very limited exception to the rule that killing is illegal."[416] At common law, a person who is not an aggressor is justified in using force upon another only if he reasonably believes that such force is necessary to protect himself or others from imminent risk of death or serious bodily injury. That force must also be proportional: deadly force can only be used to prevent the use of deadly force. And in most jurisdictions, at common law, a person was prohibited from using deadly force against an aggressor if any safe avenue of retreat existed – in other words, if the use of force was not

[413] A.B.A., *supra* note 411, at 24.
[414] Rolnick, *supra* note 240, at 1647.
[415] *Id.*
[416] *Id.* At 1658.

necessary. The DC Circuit Court of Appeals outlined these essential elements in *United States v. Peterson*:

> There must have been a threat, actual or apparent, of the use of deadly force against the defender. The threat must have been unlawful and immediate. The defender must have believed that he was in imminent peril of death or serious bodily harm, and that his response was necessary to save himself therefrom. These beliefs must not only have been honestly entertained, but also objectively reasonable in light of the surrounding circumstances. It is clear that no less than a concurrence of these elements will suffice.[417]

These four elements – imminence of threat, necessity, proportionality, and reasonableness – form the legal bounds of traditional self-defense doctrine. Both the non-aggressor requirement and the duty to retreat implicate the necessity element. At common law, the use of deadly force was deemed not necessary if an aggressor provoked the confrontation or if a safe and nonviolent avenue of retreat existed. Society simply was not prepared to recognize as legitimate the killing of another human being when it was not absolutely necessary to preserve another life.

One exception to the duty to retreat, the "castle exception," has roots as ancient as the doctrine of self-defense itself. The castle exception, or "castle doctrine," states that a non-aggressor need not retreat before using deadly force to repel an aggressor in her own home, even if she has a completely safe avenue of retreat. This exception is based on the common-law view that a person's home is her castle, a natural sanctuary from external aggression. But historically, that exception had been limited strictly to the home and surrounding enclosed yard or field (curtilage).

As in many areas of law, the thorniest and most racially problematic aspect of self-defense is the reasonableness requirement. A non-aggressor must *reasonably* believe her life is imminently in danger. Adjudicating reasonableness in self-defense cases presents challenging problems implicated by the inherent subjectivity of the shooter's mental state and the intersection of the incident with larger societal issues related to race, gender, age, and other demographic markers. Furthermore, in American law and culture, "reasonableness" has long been defined from the perspective of the reasonable White man.[418] And what is viewed as "reasonable" in any given circumstance may very well have implicit or explicit racist contours – for instance, "reasonable racists" argue that fear of Black people is itself reasonable.[419]

---

[417]   *United States v. Peterson*, 483 F.2d 1222, 1229–30 (D.C. Cir. 1973).

[418]   *See* Camille A. Nelson, *Consistently Revealing the Inconsistencies: The Construction of Fear in the Criminal Law*, 48 St. Louis L.J. 1261, 1272 (2004) ("[T]he content and character of the 'reasonable person' test has not changed and is still, essentially, the reasonable White man in disguise."); Leon Trakman, *Plluralism in Contract Law*, 58 Buff. L. Rev. 1031, 1086–87 (2010) (pointing out that the judiciary "use[s] paternalistic principles of contract law to mask substantive inequalities between parties and treats the reasonable person as a reasonable white man"); Rolnick, *supra* note 410 ("The hypothetical reasonable person is likely to be a reasonable White man.").

[419]   *See supra* Chapter 3.

4.2 IT'S ALL ABOUT RACE

To succeed with a traditional self-defense claim, the defendant must show that he honestly believed that deadly force was necessary to prevent an imminent use of deadly force against him. That belief must also have been objectively reasonable – that is, any other "reasonable" person, in his position at that time, would have had the same belief. Although reasonableness in this context does not equate to what the "average" person would do, some level of statistical similarity in reaction across society is inherent in the reasonableness inquiry. Moreover, a reasonable belief that deadly force is necessary is almost certainly accompanied by a reasonable fear of death or injury.

But who is the "reasonable person," and what factors may we consider in answering this question? Some cases provide insight. Take, for example, *People v. Goetz*, perhaps the most infamous and controversial self-defense case in recent American legal history.[420] In the early afternoon of December 22, 1984, Bernhard Goetz, a three-time mugging victim, boarded a New York City subway in which four African American teenagers were riding. Shortly after Goetz boarded, two of the teenagers approached Goetz and either requested or demanded five dollars. Goetz responded by backing away, pulling an unlicensed .38 caliber handgun from his waistband, and firing five shots at the group, hitting all four of them. In a later videotaped statement, Goetz explained that he planned a "pattern of fire" from left to right; he later admitted that "his intention at that point was to 'murder [the four youths], to hurt them, to make them suffer as much as possible."[421] At trial, Goetz claimed self-defense.

The case drew notoriety in part because it raised critical questions about what constituted the "reasonable person."[422] Is it a reasonable person with the defendant's prior experiences and background, which in *Goetz* would include being a three-time crime victim? Is it a reasonable person experienced with petty thefts on New York City subways, as Goetz claimed to be? Is it a reasonable person with beliefs about people like the alleged aggressors, in this case young Black men, similar to those of the defendant? What if those beliefs are based on inaccurate stereotypes? What if those beliefs are widely, indeed universally, shared? And what if those beliefs are implicit and unchangeable, at least in the moment of confrontation?

These questions, generated by *Goetz* and the countless self-defense cases before and after it, highlight the reality that any focus on reasonable fear in deadly force cases is inherently vulnerable to racial bias. This has been and would be true even without dangerous Stand Your Ground expansions of the self-defense doctrine. The requirement of objective reasonableness, which is supposed to operate as a check on

---

[420]   *People v. Goetz*, 68 N.Y.2d 96 (N.Y. 1986).

[421]   *Id.* at 101.

[422]   *See, e.g.,* Editorial, A *"Reasonable Man" Named Goetz*, N.Y. Times (April 29, 1986), at A26, https://www.nytimes.com/1986/04/29/opinion/a-reasonable-man-named-goetz.html.

individual biases, may instead operate to rubber-stamp individual bias if the deci-sion-maker shares the psychological and cultural fears that led the defendant to kill. A "prosecutor's or jury's after-the-fact assessment of whether fear was reasonable is, at its core, a question of whether the members of the jury would have assessed the threat similarly."[423] At its root, then, the question is not whether a fear is reasonable but whether the fear is shared. Because biases that characterize Black people as aggressive, violent, and prone to crime are widespread, connecting perpetrators, judges, and potential jurors, the reasonableness requirement that should provide a check against race-based vigilantism may offer only illusory protection against self-defense law providing cover for racial violence.

Furthermore, the reasonableness test may only accommodate some versions of shared fear. The hypothetical reasonable person is often viewed from the perspective of the person with society's dominant, "normalized" characteristics – that is, White people, often men.[424] When measured against this standard, the fears of women and non-White people may not register. As a result, their potential self-defense claims may not appear reasonable by this standard.

Indeed, the potential for racial bias is built into the core doctrine of self-defense. The question of whether private violence is justifiable as self-defense, and therefore legal, centers on whether the killer feared the victim and whether that fear was reasonable. While many Americans expressly disavow racial bias, humans' psycho-logical processes combined with entrenched cultural myths reveal an inescapable association between Blackness and threat.[425] Mapped onto bodies, this tendency means that individuals are more likely to fear Black strangers, and police, prosecu-tors, judges, and juries are more likely to understand that fear as reasonable. In this sense, all self-defense cases involving stranger assailants are at least in part "about race."

Self-defense law "legalizes violence in response to a perceived threat, as long as the perception is reasonable (that is, it would be shared by others)."[426] Those perceptions are generated by imperfect information about the potential aggressor, and in short encounters between strangers people often have little else on which to rely than easily ascertainable characteristics like size, gender, dress, and skin color.[427]

None of these characteristics are particularly reliable, but race nonetheless plays an outsized role in what is considered "reasonable" in the self-defense calculus because of ingrained stereotypes about race and violence. "Blacks serve as our mental prototype (i.e., stereotype) for the violent street criminal"[428] and "[w]hen

[423] Rolnick, *supra* note 240 at 1673.
[424] *See supra* note 419.
[425] *See infra* Chapter 6.
[426] Rolnick, *supra* note 240 at 1675.
[427] *Id.*
[428] Richardson & Goff, *supra* note 277 at 310.

the person being judged fits a criminal stereotype, ... [an] actor more easily [can] believe honestly – but mistakenly – that the person poses a threat and that deadly force is necessary."[429] That widely shared stereotype impacts every step of the self-defense calculus, including what violence juries deem acceptable, according to Professor Cynthia Lee:

> If most individuals would be more likely to "see" a weapon in the hands of an unarmed Black person than in the hands of an unarmed White person and are thus more likely to shoot an unarmed Black person when they would not shoot a similarly situated White person, then jurors in self-defense cases may also be more likely to find that an individual who says he shot an unarmed Black person in self-defense because he believed the victim was about to kill or seriously injure him acted reasonably, even if he was mistaken.[430]

Thus, "it would be reasonable, if unjust, to expect that self-defense doctrine is more likely to exonerate people who kill Black victims." Here again the reasonable racist rears his unjust head – if more people are more likely to feel their lives are threatened when faced with a Black person than a White person, is it not "reasonable" to more aggressively use deadly force in "self-defense"? And by extension, would it not be more reasonable to find such race-based violence justifiable? Certainly, such a world is not just, but it is the world we have. Federal homicide data shows that gun killings of Black people by White people were ruled justified 35 percent of the time, compared with killings of While people by Black people being ruled justified in only 3 percent of cases.[431] Moreover, "killings of Black men by White people (including private and police killings) were eight times more likely to be found justifiable than any other [racial] combination."[432]

4.3 SELF-OFFENSE

Given the potential for racial bias to infect split-second decisions about the use of deadly force and the high cost of mistaken self-defense claims, it would be reasonable to expect self-defense claims to be tightly circumscribed, available only in the most extreme scenarios and subjected to close legal scrutiny.

Yet, the opposite is true. Over the past two decades, most states have adopted a constellation of additional rules that relax the traditional requirements. These rules make self-defense easier to claim, excuse many cases from legal review, and make the defense available in more situations. Some of these rules have deep roots in common law and are intended to address gaps left by strict application of the core principles. Others, however, are relatively new; these are the collection of recent

[429] *Id.* at 314.
[430] Cynthia Lee, *Making Race Salient: Trayvon Martin and Implicit Bias in a Not Yet Post-Racial Society*, 91 N.C. L. REV. 1555, 1584–85 (2013).
[431] Rolnick, *supra* note 240 at 1669; Roman, *supra* note 32 at 8.
[432] Rolnick, *supra* note 240 at 1676.

laws and judicial decisions often collected under the heading of "Stand Your Ground." Most strikingly, many of the newer laws do not appear to address a clear gap in existing law: their primary effects are symbolic (they reinforce the desirability of self-defense) and procedural (they insulate a person who kills in self-defense from review by a jury).

These laws expand self-defense by loosening the once-narrow requirements for self-defense: imminence, proportionality, necessity, and reasonableness. They also expand the "castle doctrine" exception, once limited to the home, to allow private citizens to "stand their ground" and use deadly force against alleged aggressors in a growing range of public spaces – even if a completely safe retreat is clearly available.[433] These laws dangerously broaden what was once a very narrow justification for homicide and encourage armed vigilantism, to the detriment of Black people in White spaces.

Even before the proliferation of Stand Your Ground legislation, individual states extended the castle doctrine's "no retreat" exception beyond the home to include vehicles, boats, workplaces, and neighborhood streets.[434] Some of these states do not even require the intruder to be actively intruding, but only near the structure, stretching the meaning of the word "imminent" to a degree that strains credulity.[435] Moreover, many states have eliminated the requirement that the person acting in self-defense even be in the building, car, or other protected space to which the intruder seeks entry; he need only witness the potential criminal entry to justifiably use deadly force to stop the entry.[436] Thus, in at least some states, the law of self-defense no longer requires a showing that deadly force was necessary to prevent the imminent use of deadly force, but rather a showing that a property crime might occur in the future. In these jurisdictions, the words imminence, necessity, and proportionality no longer play any apparent role in limiting private violence.

These expansions of self-defense law protect private violence under a "castle doctrine" theory but redefine the "castle" to include public areas, like office buildings and suburban communities. The natural consequence, if not the intent, of these laws is to sanction the forcible segregation of public spaces into "us" and "them" spaces and authorize the violent enforcement of invisible property lines, by those who belong against the suspiciously out-of-place. They also communicate to those who attract greater suspicion in society, particularly Black and other darker-

---

[433] *Hearing on "Stand Your Ground" Laws: Civil Rights and Public Safety Implications of the Expanded Use of Deadly Force Before the S. Judiciary Comm. Subcomm. On the Const., Civil Rts., and Hum. Rts.*, 113th Cong. (testimony of John R. Lott Jr., president, Crime Prevention Research Center) ("The difference between 'Stand Your Ground' and 'Castle Doctrine' laws is over where they apply, not what they rule is. Both laws remove the duty to retreat. Castle Doctrine laws apply to attacks within one's home ... Once you step off your property ... Stand Your Ground laws apply.").

[434] *See* Rolnick, *supra* note 240, at 1681; Daniel Sweency, *Comment, Standing Up to "Stand Your Ground" Laws*, 64 CLEV. ST. L. REV. 715, 730–33 (2016).

[435] Rolnick, *supra* note 240, at 1681.

[436] *Id.*

skinned people, that they move through public spaces at their own peril. The "reasonable person" in the United States harbors implicit racial biases and an ingrained sense of "Black violent threat."[437] When threatened, that reasonable person makes split-second decisions, categorizing information crudely by what appears to belong and what appears out of place – categories shaped by those innate biases. Thus, the reasonable person may feel a vague fear of violent threat when a Black person stands at the door of a house in a predominantly White gated community or next to an expensive luxury car. For centuries, that inchoate fear would not justify the use of deadly force. Not anymore.

This unprincipled relaxation of the imminence and necessity requirements can have devastating consequences for a Black person moving into a predominantly White neighborhood, who might not be recognized by his White neighbors. This is not a far-fetched scenario.

For example, on April 28, 2018, officers in New York City responded to a 911 call claiming "somebody was trying to break into the door" of an apartment building, with "possibly a large weapon or tool."[438] When police arrived, they met twenty-nine -year-old Darren Martin, a former White House staffer who was in the process of moving into his apartment in the wealthy Upper West Side neighborhood of Manhattan. Deputies quickly determined that Martin had a right to be there and did not have a weapon, but they continued questioning him, in public, for another fifteen minutes. Martin, who recorded the incident on Instagram Live, later told reporters, "We have the power to document these scenarios now and prove we're not just making this stuff up. I think people need to know it's a reality. I'm just happy to be here telling the story. A lot of men and women of color don't have that opportunity."[439] Arguably, the neighbor who called 911 could have skipped that step, shot Martin, and claimed self-defense under the relaxed imminence standard.

Or take the case of Henry Louis Gates Jr., the Alphonse Fletcher University Professor and Director of the Hutchins Center for African and African American Research at Harvard University. On July 20, 2009, Professor Gates returned home from a trip to find his front door damaged.[440] He called for his Black taxi driver to assist him in opening the door. A neighbor, seeing two Black men in a White Cambridge neighborhood trying to force a door open, called 911. Police responded; Gates was arrested for disorderly conduct when he accused the officers of racial profiling. In some states with relaxed imminence requirements (not Massachusetts), Professor Gates could have been gunned down by the neighbor, who could have

[437] *See infra* Chapter 6.
[438] Shayna Freisleben, *Black Former White House Staffer Was Moving into New Apartment When Someone Called Police*, CBS News (May 3, 2018), https://www.cbsnews.com/news/black-former-obama-staffer-moving-into-new-apartment-someone-reported-burglary-called-police/.
[439] *Id.*
[440] Abby Goodnough, *Harvard Professor Jailed; Officer Is Accused of Bias*, N.Y. Times (July 20, 2009), https://www.nytimes.com/2009/07/21/us/21gates.html.

pled self-defense, arguing that the homicide was justified because the men appeared to be breaking into a dwelling – even if that neighbor felt no particular threat.

Of course, not all such incidents end merely in arrest. In April 2018, fourteen-year-old Brennan Walker missed the bus and got lost trying to walk to his high school outside Detroit. When he walked up to Jeffrey Ziegler's house and knocked on the door for help, Ziegler grabbed his shotgun and fired at Brennan, narrowly missing. Ziegler's wife, Dana, later testified in court about what led to such a violent response from her White husband: "I saw a black person standing at my door and I screamed at him and I asked him what he was doing there. He tells me he is going to school and at that point he approaches the door, forward momentum, comes forward, opens the screen door, and puts his hand on the door handle again, as though he's coming into my house." Ziegler was later convicted of assault with intent to do great bodily harm.[441]

A far more controversial expansion of self-defense involves statutes that allow a private citizen to shoot to stop a fleeing felon. Texas law, for example, permits a private citizen to use lethal force against "the other who is fleeing immediately after committing burglary, robbery, aggravated robbery, or theft during the nighttime."[442] This statute dispenses with all traditional understanding of the word "proportional." It allows the use of deadly force in response to nonphysical property crime and allows deadly force even when the threat itself has vanished. In fact, this permission for private citizens to gun down fleeing felons exceeds even the authorization to use deadly force enjoyed by law enforcement. In holding that the Fourth Amendment prohibited police officers from shooting an unarmed fleeing felon absent probable cause that such force was necessary to prevent death or great bodily injury, the United States Supreme Court declared in *Tennessee v. Garner* that "it is not better that all felony suspects die than that they escape."[443] In Texas at least, it appears the state has subcontracted this type of vigilante justice to private actors who are beyond the reach of the Fourth Amendment.

Georgia codified its vigilante justice scheme in its now-infamous "citizen's arrest" law, which permits "a private person [to] arrest an offender if the offense is committed in his presence or within his immediate knowledge."[444] If "the offense is a felony and the offender is escaping or attempting to escape, a private person may arrest him upon reasonable and probable grounds of suspicion"[445] and use all necessary force to do so, including deadly force.

As in other vigilante justice regimes, one community in particular bears the brunt. On February 23, 2020, an anonymous tipster in Satilla Shores, Georgia, called 911 to

[441] Caitlin O'Kane, *Michigan Man Who Shot at Black Teen on Front Porch Found Guilty*, CBS News (October 13, 2018), https://www.cbsnews.com/news/michigan-man-who-shot-at-black-teen-who-knocked-on-his-door-found-guilty/.

[442] Tex. Penal Code Ann. § 9.42(2)(B) (West 2019).

[443] *Tennessee v. Garner*, 471 U.S. 1, 11 (1985).

[444] Ga. Code Ann. § 17-4-60 (2020).

[445] *Id.*

report a Black man inside a house that was under construction.[446] The caller neither reported a crime nor gave any further description of the "suspect." At about the same time, Ahmaud Arbery was jogging on a deserted road nearby. During his run, a white pickup truck attempted to run him off the road. In footage captured on a cell phone video, a White man jumped out of the truck bed with a shotgun in his hand and chased down Arbery.[447] During a struggle for the shotgun, a second White man in the truck bed pulled out a handgun and shot Arbery dead.

It is unclear whether Arbery was the man identified by the 911 caller. But when approached by police investigating the homicide, the two White men – father and son Gregory and Travis McMichael – claimed they approached Arbery to make a citizen's arrest because they thought he was "a burglary suspect."[448] The McMichaels admitted they never saw Arbery commit a crime and never felt endangered by Arbery, but they nevertheless lay in wait for him and attacked him as he jogged. For nearly three months, neither police nor prosecutors took up the case despite having seen the video footage, claiming the McMichaels acted within the bounds of Georgia's citizen's arrest and Stand Your Ground laws.[449] Only after the damning video became public and went viral did a fourth prosecutor finally arrest the two men for murder. The men were later convicted.

4.4 THE WORLD IS MY CASTLE

Prior to 2005, these expansions of self-defense law were mostly ad hoc and addressed discrete aspects of a particular state's approach. But beginning in the early 2000s, the American Legislative Executive Council (ALEC), in concert with the National Rifle Association (NRA), began crafting a detailed set of model statutory reforms designed to loosen restrictions on private gun ownership and use and expand the right to use deadly force in self-defense.[450] The first set of proposals helped usher in a wave of deregulation authorizing the concealed and public carrying of a range of firearms with little or no restriction. In advocating for the second set of self-defense reforms,

[446] Alexandra Kelley, *"I Just Need to Know What He's Doing Wrong": Two 911 Calls Made Before Ahmaud Arbery Killing,* THE HILL (May 7, 2020), https://thehill.com/changing-america/respect/equality/496722-i-just-need-to-know-what-hes-doing-wrong-two-911-calls-made.

[447] *Video Appears to Show Fatal Shooting of Ahmaud Arbery,* WASH. POST (May 11, 2020), https://www.washingtonpost.com/video/national/video-appears-to-show-fatal-shooting-of-ahmaud-arbery/2020/05/11/346cb94e-c0e5-418e-b30b-34b52cdbb62d_video.html.

[448] Brakkton Booker, *Lawyer for Arbery Shooting Suspect: "This Is Not Some Sort of Hate Crime,"* NPR (May 14, 2020), https://www.npr.org/2020/05/15/857146729/lawyer-for-arbery-shooting-suspect-this-is-not-some-sort-of-hate-crime.

[449] Cleve R. Wootson Jr. & Michael Brice-Saddler, *It Took 74 Days for Suspects to Be Charged in the Death of a Black Jogger. Many People Are Asking Why It Took So Long.,* WASH. POST (May 8, 2020), https://www.washingtonpost.com/national/outraged-by-the-delayed-arrests-in-killing-of-black-jogger-protesters-in-georgia-demand-justice/2020/05/08/8e7d212a-90a9-11ea-9e23-6914ee410a5f_story.html.

[450] Bill Berkowitz, *ALEC, the NRA, and the Killing of Trayvon Martin,* HUFFPOST (March 23, 2012), https://www.huffpost.com/entry/alec-the-nra-and-the-murd_b_1375836.

which have come to be known as Stand Your Ground laws, the NRA expressly tied public gun possession to self-defense, claiming that "this type of legislation empowers innocent victims . . . the process for approving an application for a gun permit may take too long for some victims."[451] Indeed, when the first Stand Your Ground law was proposed in Florida in 2004, "the NRA argued that laws expanding self-defense were designed to protect women."[452] Since then, the NRA has continued to "advocat[e] for gun ownership as a solution to intimate partner violence and other forms of gendered violence."[453]

Florida passed the nation's first Stand Your Ground law in 2005. While the legislation, and subsequent laws modeled after it, actually incorporate a constellation of reforms to self-defense law, the name "Stand Your Ground" reflects the most radical change to common-law self-defense doctrine: the complete elimination of the duty to retreat. Whereas the castle doctrine represented a narrow exception to the duty to avoid using deadly force if possible and prior state reforms expanded the doctrine to certain other locations, Stand Your Ground laws allow private citizens to use deadly force against aggressors *anywhere* – even if a safe avenue of retreat exists.

This incredible expansion of self-defense law has had three immediate impacts. The first, and most obvious, impact was to authorize private citizens to stand and fight and fire upon anyone, at any time, in any place, whether during a bar fight, a heated office argument, or a dispute over a parking space. Before 2005, the public location of these confrontations would have required retreat in many states. Not surprisingly, these laws "are associated with clear increases in homicides."[454] A 2012 study by researchers at Texas A&M University found that all twenty-one of the jurisdictions the researchers identified as Stand Your Ground jurisdictions examined saw a significant increase in homicide rates, with an average of more than 600 additional homicides per year.[455]

Defenders of the "no retreat" rule point to the fact that in all of these situations the traditional requirements of imminence, necessity, proportionality, and reasonableness still temper automatic rubber stamps of vigilante shootings. But the second impact of Stand Your Ground casts doubt on that argument. Most of the thirty-nine states with Stand Your Ground rules have also incorporated presumption of threat rules and other procedural changes that give the benefit of the doubt to defendants claiming self-defense. While self-defense has traditionally been viewed as an affirmative defense to be raised and proven by a criminal defendant at trial, Florida and

---

[451]   Samone Ijoma, *False Promises of Protection: Black Women, Trans People & the Struggle for Visibility as Victims of Intimate Partner and Gendered Violence*, 18 U. Md. L.J. Race Relig. Gender & Class 255, 259 (2018).

[452]   *Id.* at 263.

[453]   *Id.* at 256.

[454]   A.B.A. *supra* note 411, at 11–12.

[455]   Cheng Cheng & Mark Hoekstra, *Does Strengthening Self-Defense Law Deter Crime or Escalate Violence? Evidence from the Castle Doctrine* 4, 18 (Nat'l Bureau of Econ. Rsch., Working Paper No. 18134, 2012), https://www.nber.org/system/files/working_papers/w18134/w18134.pdf.

other states have adopted the opposite approach. In these jurisdictions, criminal defendants claiming self-defense under Stand Your Ground are presumed to have acted reasonably; the burden is on prosecutors to demonstrate in pretrial hearings that the killing was *not* justified.[456] Florida's legislature went further in 2017, allowing a judge to dismiss the case before trial unless the prosecution proved by clear and convincing evidence that the Stand Your Ground immunity did not apply.[457] Unsurprisingly, given the extent of these immunizing protections, homicides in Florida deemed to be "justified" tripled in the years following passage of the state's Stand Your Ground legislation.[458]

The immunity these laws provide to aggressors is perhaps the most troubling effect of Stand Your Ground laws. At common law, an aggressor who initiated the violent confrontation could not claim self-defense. That moral admonition no longer applies in Stand Your Ground jurisdictions. Now, "a resident who sees a suspicious person in their neighborhood can follow and confront that person. If violence results, stand your ground laws and [related] immunity laws make it more likely the suspicion-based violence will be legal."[459]

That is precisely what happened to seventeen-year-old Trayvon Martin. On February 26, 2012, George Zimmerman called the police from his gated townhome community in Sanford, Florida, to report "a real suspicious guy ... This guy looks like he is up to no good or he is on drugs or something. It's raining and he's just walking around and looking about."[460] Two minutes into the call, Zimmerman – who had made nearly fifty calls to police in the past eight years to report Black males he believed to be suspicious[461] – stated that "these assholes, they always get away," before pursuing Trayvon on foot.[462] Six minutes after Zimmerman placed his call, he shot Trayvon Martin dead, approximately seventy yards from Trayvon's house. At the time of his death, Trayvon was carrying a bag of skittles and a can of tea.[463]

---

[456] Brendan Farrington, *Florida Law Shifts "Stand Your Ground" Burden of Proof*, NEWS-PRESS (June 11, 2017), https://www.news-press.com/story/news/local/2017/06/10/stand-ground-law-shifts-burden-proof-prosecutors/102721106/. This approach has been criticized as creating a "presumption of fear," meaning that police are more likely to see a justified killing if the victim looks dangerous; for many, "Black" equals "dangerous." Michael Yaki, *Statement of Commissioner Michael Yaki, in* U.S. COMM'N ON CIVIL RTS., EXAMINING THE RACE EFFECTS OF STAND YOUR GROUND LAWS AND RELATED ISSUES: BRIEFING REPORT 21 (February 2020) (quoting Kathryn Russell-Brown, *Go Ahead and Shoot, The Law Might Have Your Back: History, Race, Implicit Bias, and Justice in Florida's Stand Your Ground Law, in* DEADLY INJUSTICE: TRAYVON MARTIN, RACE, AND THE CRIMINAL JUSTICE SYSTEM (D. Johnson et al. eds., 2015)).

[457] Farrington, *supra* note 456.

[458] *Id.*

[459] Rolnick, *supra* note 240, at 1688.

[460] *Transcript of George Zimmerman's Call to the Police*, GENIUS, https://genius.com/George-zimmerman-transcript-of-george-zimmermans-call-to-the-police-annotated.

[461] Associated Press, *New Recordings Show Zimmerman's Many Police Calls*, FOX NEWS (November 28, 2015), https://www.foxnews.com/us/new-recordings-show-zimmermans-many-police-calls.

[462] *Transcript, supra* note 460.

[463] Greg Botelho, *What Happened the Night Trayvon Martin Died*, CNN (May 23, 2012), https://www.cnn.com/2012/05/18/justice/florida-teen-shooting-details/index.html.

Zimmerman's defense team chose not to seek a pretrial dismissal of murder charges under Florida's Stand Your Ground laws, seeking instead an acquittal based on traditional self-defense.[464] However, as required by Florida's Stand Your Ground provision on jury instructions, the judge instructed jurors that Zimmerman had no duty to retreat and in fact had a right to stand his ground and use deadly force if he reasonably believed doing so was necessary to defend himself.[465] The jury acquitted him.

In the aftermath of George Zimmerman's acquittal, radio talk show host Tavis Smiley commented, "It appears to me, and I think many other persons in this country, that you can in fact stand your ground unless you are a black man."[466] Numerous studies since that time have confirmed this suspicion. An Everytown for Gun Safety Research & Policy report cited three influential studies that found:

> Across all states, homicides in which white shooters kill Black victims are deemed justifiable far more frequently than when the situation is reversed. In Stand Your Ground states, these homicides are deemed justifiable five times more frequently than when the shooter is Black and the victim is white. Controlling for other factors – such as who initiated the confrontation and whether or not the victim was armed – Florida Stand Your Ground cases involving minority victims are half as likely to lead to conviction, compared to cases involving white victims.[467]

Moreover, a 2018 study by Professor Justin Murphy, examining hundreds of Stand Your Ground cases over nearly a decade, provided even more compelling evidence of the discriminatory impact of Stand Your Ground laws.[468] Murphy controlled for fifteen variables, including the race and gender of the victim and defendant, whether the victim initiated the confrontation, whether the victim was "clearly committing a crime," whether the defendant pursued the victim, whether the defendant could have retreated, whether the defendant had a gun, the presence of witnesses or physical evidence, and whether the victim died. The results were alarming, if not surprising: a Stand Your Ground defense "has *nearly zero* probability of succeeding

---

[464] CNN Staff, *Zimmerman to Argue Self-Defense, Will Not Seek "Stand Your Ground" Hearing*, CNN (May 1, 2013), https://www.cnn.com/2013/04/30/justice/florida-zimmerman-defense/index.html.

[465] Ta-Nehisi Coates, *How Stand Your Ground Relates to George Zimmerman*, THE ATLANTIC (July 16, 2013), https://www.theatlantic.com/national/archive/2013/07/how-stand-your-ground-relates-to-george-zimmerman/277829/.

[466] The comment was made on a broadcast of *This Week with George Stephanopoulis*; it was reported by ABC News and others. Alyssa Giannirakis, *Tavis Smiley: You Can "Stand Your Ground Unless You Are a Black Man,"* ABC NEWS (July 14, 2013), https://abcnews.go.com/blogs/politics/2013/07/tavis-smiley-you-can-stand-your-ground-unless-you-are-a-black-man.

[467] Everytown for Gun Safety, *supra* note 412 (citing Roman, *supra* note 32; Everytown analysis of FBI Supplementary Homicide Report, 2014 to 2018; Nicole Ackermann et al., *Race, Law, and Health: Examination of "Stand Your Ground" and Defendant Convictions in Florida*, Soc. Science & Medical 142, 194–201 (2015), https://www.sciencedirect.com/science/article/abs/pii/S0277953615300642?via%3Dihub).

[468] Justin Murphy, *Are "Stand Your Ground" Laws Racist and Sexist? A Statistical Analysis of Cases in Florida, 2005–2013*, 99 Soc. Sci. Q. 439 (2018).

when the victim is white and the defendant is a person of color. This finding remains true after accounting for more than 10 objective factors related to the crime."[469] While the probability of conviction remained high for all defendants across the board – between 80 and 90 percent – Murphy found that "the probability of conviction for a black defendant in an otherwise objectively equivalent case approach[ed] 100 percent."[470]

Other data from the study confirms just how much Stand Your Ground legislation has broadened and perverted the concept of "self-defense." In 78 percent of cases, the victim was not committing a crime, and in nearly 55 percent of cases the victim did not even initiate the conflict. In contrast, in 59 percent of cases the defendant could have safely retreated but did not, and in 28 percent of cases the defendant actually pursued a retreating victim.[471] Shockingly, none of these variables correlated significantly with a greater or lesser likelihood of conviction.[472]

Interestingly, one variable that correlated significantly with a greater likelihood of acquittal was whether the defendant was armed. Defendants armed with a gun were "less likely to be convicted . . . to a statistically significant degree."[473] This finding casts significant doubt on claims by John R. Lott and other gun rights advocates that racial disparities in outcomes in self-defense cases can be explained by the "fact" that Black people are more likely to use guns in violent crimes, "the assumption being that guns rather than colored skin tend toward convictions."[474] In other words, this argument suggests, because Black people are more likely to be armed with a gun when committing a crime or otherwise engaging in violent confrontation (itself an unsubstantiated claim), it stands to reason that more defendants will be acquitted on self-defense grounds when repelling an attack from these armed Black criminal assailants. If that were true, then why are virtually no Black defendants ever acquitted?

In reality, claims like these traffic in the same racially fearful stereotyping that pervades society – that suspecting all Black individuals of criminal aggression is reasonable because, statistically speaking, Black people are both more prone to crime and more prone to be armed. Neither claim is true. But both are believed and repeated to such a degree that they form a collective reasonable racism that metastasizes, lurking in the mind of the trigger-happy neighborhood watchman who sees a Black man with *something* in his hand, the prosecutor who declines to bring first-degree murder charges, and the jury that acquits because the cell phone or the bag of Skittles in the victim's hand *could have* been a gun.

---

[469] *Id.* at 439 (emphasis added).
[470] *Id.* at 451.
[471] *Id.* at 443, tbl.2.
[472] *Id.*
[473] *Id.* at 444.
[474] *Id.* at 444–46.

Here again, we find the ugly spectre of the "reasonable racist," the person who asserts that:

> even if his belief that Blacks are "prone to violence" stems primarily from his racism – that is, from a belief in the genetic predisposition of Blacks toward greater violence, from uncritical acceptance of the Black cultural stereotype, or from personal racial animus – he should be excused for considering the victim's race before using force because most similarly situated Americans would have done so as well. . . . "Therefore," he concludes, "an individual racist in a racist society cannot be condemned for an expression of human frailty as ubiquitous as racism."[475]

Jody David Armour's eloquent description of the "slippery oxymoron"[476] of the Reasonable Racist fairly captures the experience of affirmative self-defense claims in this country and helps explain why a Black man claiming self-defense is eleven times less likely to succeed than a similarly situated White man.

Notably, Armour wrote this in 1997, eight years before Florida passed the nation's first Stand Your Ground law. In other words, the "reasonableness" calculus assessed in self-defense claims was already racially tinged. Stand Your Ground laws did not change that racial undertone, but they did radically expand the places in which the racially tinged reasonableness calculus would be relevant. As a result, the fear of many minority communities has been confirmed: "Stand Your Ground law sits side-by-side with racial profiling; the ticket to vigilante justice."[477]

4.5 THE SUBURBAN HOUSEWIFE . . . IN 2020

On June 23, 2020, during the height of nationwide protests demanding racial justice following the murder of George Floyd, President Trump tweeted directly to "The Suburban Housewives of America," claiming that Joe Biden would "destroy your neighborhood and your American Dream. I will preserve it, and make it even better!"[478] The tweet linked to a New York Post article describing how Biden would reinstate an Obama-era fair housing regulation aimed at combating segregation in suburbs and providing federal funding for low-income housing in desirable suburban areas. Trump doubled down on the claim on August 12, tweeting that "The 'suburban housewife' will be voting for me. They want safety & are thrilled that I ended the long running program where low-income housing would invade their neighborhood."[479]

---

[475]   Armour, *supra* note 360, at 19.

[476]   *Id.*

[477]   A.B.A., *supra* note 411, at 24 (quoting testimony of Miami criminal defense attorney Ed Shohat before task force).

[478]   Morgan Phillips, *Trump Tells Voters Who Live in Suburbs They "Will No Longer Be Bothered" by Low-Income Housing*, Fox News (July 29, 2020), https://www.foxnews.com/politics/trump-suburban-voters-housing-rule.

[479]   Adam Shaw, *Trump Says "Suburban Housewife" Will Vote for Him over Biden, Cites Low-Income Housing Policies*, Fox News (August 12, 2020), https://www.foxnews.com/politics/trump-suburban-housewife-biden-low-income-housing

Media attention to these barely disguised racist dog whistles focused mainly on Trump's hopelessly outdated sexist appeal to "suburban housewives." But the appeal to White wealthy homeowners, in the thinly veiled promise to protect them from an "invasion" of racial minorities, marked a shocking attempt by the President of the United States to assert the integrity of the White space. Indeed, in the month between Trump's tweets, he quietly scrapped the Affirmatively Furthering Fair Housing provision of the 1968 Fair Housing Act, an act ostensibly directed at protecting the property values of "true Americans."[480]

These race-baiting appeals for votes reflect reality in urban and suburban areas across the country. The White space exists in all cities. De jure segregation in the nineteenth and early twentieth centuries set the formal parameters of White and Black spaces, which among other things concentrated Black and other minority communities in less desirable neighborhoods beset by noise and air pollution from nearby industrial plants. In urban centers, these neighborhoods overwhelmingly were located on the eastern side of cities, as cities placed industrial plants on the eastern part of town so West-to-East continental winds would blow air pollutants away from town instead of over it.[481] This practice, combined with the "industrial slavery" of convict leasing and the overwhelming disruption of racial terror lynching and other forms of private violence, cemented neighborhood-by-neighborhood wealth disparities among White and Black spaces in cities large and small across the country.

Redlining further exacerbated this wealth disparity. Post-World War II federal programs that created post-World War II suburbs through funding for mortgages, highways, and utilities were administered in a way that ensured the new suburbs would be White spaces.[482] Federal agencies assessed the lending risk of various city neighborhoods through a color-coded system in which green (good investment) was assigned to White neighborhoods and red (bad investment) was assigned to Black and other minority neighborhoods.[483] These lending practices, which continued well past the formal end of private segregation in 1968, further concentrated wealth

[480] *See* Nick Vadala, *What is the Fair Housing Rule and How Will Its Repeal Affect Philly?*, Phila. Inquirer (August 2, 2020), https://www.inquirer.com/news/affh-fair-housing-rule-philadelphia-trump-obama-20200801.html.

[481] Leo Benedictus, *Blowing in the Wind: Why Do So Many Cities Have Poor East Ends?*, Guardian (May 12, 2017), https://www.theguardian.com/cities/2017/may/12/blowing-wind-cities-poor-east-ends. A study of British cities found that "past pollution explains up to 20% of the observed neighbourhood segregation" and noted that "the deprivation of an area faded when the pollution did." *Id.* In other words, the closing of factories that created economic hardship for residents of these neighborhoods also opened the way to the gentrification that later displaced them.

[482] *See, e.g.*, Katie Nodjimbadem, *The Racial Segregation of American Cities Was Anything but Accidental*, Smithsonian Mag. (May 30, 2017), https://www.smithsonianmag.com/history/how-federal-government-intentionally-racially-segregated-american-cities-180963494/.

[483] Tracy Jan, *Redlining Was Banned 50 Years Ago. It's Still Hurting Minorities Today*, Wash. Post (March 28, 2018), https://www.washingtonpost.com/news/wonk/wp/2018/03/28/redlining-was-banned-50-years-ago-its-still-hurting-minorities-today/.

toward White spaces and away from Black spaces. This economic segregation remains in place today. Recent explosive growth of suburbs and exurbs in fast-growing cities like Phoenix, Las Vegas, Raleigh, and Austin continue to follow the familiar, highly segregated patterns of the previous century.

This century-plus history of legal, social, and economic segregation reinforces the suspicion felt by White people when a Black person moves into a White space, especially a White residential space. Professor Rolnick explains how the architectural layout of these White suburban neighborhoods promotes that suspicion:

> In Western and Sun Belt suburbs, clusters of carefully planned neighborhoods are built around cul-de-sacs, marked by a single entrance, and often enclosed by a wall or gate. These features minimize the likelihood that a stranger might pass through the neighborhood for an innocent reason, giving residents a further basis for believing that an unfamiliar person is out of place or up to no good. Access may be restricted by guards and identification requirements. Many of these communities were built long after legal segregation ended, giving them a sort of post-racial status, but many are still "white spaces" where Black residents and visitors risk being seen as "out of place."[484]

These "gated communities churn a vicious cycle by attracting like-minded residents who seek shelter from outsiders and whose physical seclusion then worsens paranoid groupthink against outsiders."[485]

This suspicion of someone who appears to be out of place served as the pretext for many of the surveillance-based 911 calls discussed in Chapter 2. But current expansions of self-defense laws justifying confrontational, even hot-pursuit, public violence based on nothing more than "reasonably racist" assumptions about a dark-skinned person's intentions in a gated community dramatically increase the stakes in private enforcement of the color line. Indeed, as Boston University School of Law Dean Angela Onwuachi-Willig and Professor Jeannine Bell have passionately argued, this type of violent protection of a neighborhood's homogenous identity has always been a part of maintaining the White residential space. In making sense of Trayvon Martin's death as the consequence of a "Black intruder" invading a predominantly "White space," Onwuachi-Willig explored the urgent need for White communities to "preserv[e] the material benefits and the psychological wages of whiteness."[486] For White residents of White spaces, expanded self-defense laws are a reminder that the law permits them to use violence, even lethal violence, to defend themselves, their families, and their homes from Black "intruders."[487]

---

[484] Rolnick, *supra* note 240, at 1704–05.

[485] Rich Benjamin, *The Gated Community Mentality*, N.Y. Times (March 29, 2012), https://www.nytimes.com/2012/03/30/opinion/the-gated-community-mentality.html.

[486] Angela Onwuachi-Willig, *Policing the Boundaries of Whiteness: The Tragedy of Being Out of Place from Emmett Till to Trayvon Martin*, 102 Iowa L. Rev. 1113, 1119 (2017).

[487] Rolnick, *supra* note 240, at 1690.

Indeed,

> as the typical legal tools of segregation ... have been repealed or rejected, modern segregation has come to be viewed as a social or economic problem rather than a legal one. Segregation is still reinforced by law, but one may need to look more deeply to see the relationship. Self-defense law, which is unavoidably linked to racial fear and which states have consistently expanded despite its potential for bias, is one legal tool that reinforces modern segregation by offering government approval and encouragement to private neighborhood violence in service of racial fears.[488]

4.6 STATE-SPONSORED WEAPONIZATION

The result of these changes to Stand Your Ground laws, when combined with the requirements and immunities described in Chapters 2 and 3, is a perverse system of state-sponsored incentives that encourage the weaponization of racial fear by biased civilians. In particular:

(1) Civilians are allowed to call 911 for frivolous, racially motivated reasons with virtual *impunity*.

(2) Police officers are *required* to respond to all 911 calls, even frivolous calls clearly motivated by racism.

(3) When responding to these calls, police officers are authorized to use any amount of "reasonable" force, including deadly force, and almost always are *immunized* from discipline or prosecution if they use excessive force.

(4) Civilians are permitted to stand their ground, even if a clear and safe path of retreat exists and may *kill other unarmed civilians* if they feel threatened.

(5) When responding to these homicides, some states *prevent* police officers from making arrests if the homicides plausibly fit within this expanded definition of self-defense, regardless of whether facts indicate a clear racial motive.

(6) If an arrest is made, some states require prosecutors to affirmatively *prove* in pretrial hearings that the killing was not justified by a Stand Your Ground law, rather than putting the onus on the defendant to raise the affirmative defense at trial.

When placed side by side, this complex web of requirements, immunizing doctrines, and burdens of proof facilitates the civilian weaponization of racial fear, ensuring the support of state legislatures and armed police officers in the process. While each of the incentives, individually, may serve a different underlying policy purpose, they collectively protect racially motivated civilians, allowing them to summon the official criminal justice apparatus to reinforce and accommodate their racial fear.

---

[488] *Id.* at 1691.

5

Unqualified Immunity

On March 13, 2013, Wayne Jones was walking in the street near downtown Martinsburg, West Virginia, when officer Paul Lehman stopped the Black man and told him it was a crime to walk in the street.[489] When Lehman asked Jones if he had a weapon, Jones, who was schizophrenic and confused, asked, "What's a weapon?" When the officer explained, Jones replied that he did have "something." Lehman demanded that Jones place his hands on the squad car and, when Jones did not respond to any of his questions, tased him. A second officer arrived, in response to Lehman's call for backup, and tased Jones as well, at which point Jones broke away from the officers and ran. Three more officers arrived, one of whom caught Jones and placed him in a chokehold until he lay motionless. One officer saw a "fixed blade knife in [Jones's] hand," at which point the five officers formed a semicircle around Jones and fired twenty-two bullets into the homeless man while he lay face down. When Jones's family sued the officers for violating his Fourth Amendment right to be free from excessive force, the United States District Court for the Northern District of West Virginia granted all five officers qualified immunity, finding it was not "clearly established" that shooting a man twenty-two times as he lay motionless was unlawful; the suit was dismissed.[490]

Three years later, Shase Howse was standing outside his home in Cleveland, Ohio, when several men pulled up next to him in an unmarked vehicle.[491] One of the men asked Howse if he lived at the house. When Howse replied that he did, the man asked if he was *sure* he lived there. Agitated and confused, Howse replied, "Yes, what the fuck?" The man then leapt from the car, said Howse had a bad attitude, and after asking a third time if he lived there, put Howse's hands behind his back and said he was going to jail. At no point did any of the men identify themselves as police

---

[489] This narrative is largely adapted from the Fourth Circuit's description of events. *Estate of Jones v. City of Martinsburg, W. Va.*, 961 F.3d 661, 664–66 (2020).

[490] *Estate of Jones v. City of Martinsburg, W. Va.*, N. 3:13-CV-68, 2018 WL 4289325, at *6 (N.D.W. Va. September 7, 2018).

[491] This narrative is adapted from the Sixth Circuit's description of events. *Howse v. Hodous*, 953 F.3d 402, 405–06 (6th Cir. 2020).

officers. When Howse resisted, another plainclothes police officer exited the unmarked police cruiser and began beating Howse, punching him repeatedly in the head as Howse's head hit the pavement. Howse's suit was also dismissed after the court granted the police qualified immunity, because, in the dissent's formulation of the issue, the court could find no "clearly established constitutional right" that forbids "an officer to throw a person to the ground in order to arrest that person without probable cause."[492]

The previous chapter explored the legislative march to protect armed civilian vigilantes using deadly force in "self-defense" to protect the White space and the tortured redefinition of words like "imminent" and "necessary" in service of that goal. During roughly the same period that Stand Your Ground legislation swept through the nation's statehouses, the United States Supreme Court charted a parallel course to promote a similar culture of impunity within law enforcement. This jurisprudential turn also relied heavily on a creative reimagining of once-established legal concepts like "reasonableness" under the Fourth Amendment and "qualified" immunity for public officials. And like the legislative experience with Stand Your Ground, the Supreme Court's protection of trigger-happy policing neither finds support in constitutional or common law nor reckons honestly with the havoc it has wreaked on Black communities.

This chapter challenges legislative and judicial efforts to immunize police officers from all but the most outrageous misconduct by finding "objectively reasonable" virtually all uses of force by officers and providing "qualified immunity" in the rare instance when force is deemed excessive. This failure to provide any sort of check or deterrent against the use of force by armed, implicitly biased officers improperly strengthens the weapon of the racially fearful and further empowers bias-motivated individuals to act on their biases.

Police officers have long enjoyed "an immunity from scrutiny" for using unnecessary force in encounters with civilians.[493] The law, as developed in state legislatures and federal courts, has affirmatively "encouraged such favoritism."[494] The doctrines of "objective reasonableness" and "qualified immunity" account for much of this protection from prosecution. The law regarding use of force and qualified immunity has evolved over the last two decades to provide a near-blanket protection for even the most egregious, unwarranted, and racially charged police misconduct.[495]

---

[492] *Id.* at 414 (Cole, C.J., dissenting).
[493] Cynthia Lee, *Reforming the Law on Police Use of Deadly Force: De-Escalation, Preseizure Conduct, and Imperfect Self-Defense*, 2018 U. Ill. L. Rev. 629, 633 (2018).
[494] *Id.*
[495] *See* Diana Hassel, *Living a Lie: The Cost of Qualified Immunity*, 64 Mo. L. Rev. 123, 130–31 (1999) (highlighting the diminishing importance of questions of fact in excessive force cases given the power of the qualified immunity defense); *see also Saucier v. Katz*, 533 U.S. 194, 206 (2001) (finding that qualified immunity protects defendants when their actions fall on the "sometimes 'hazy border between excessive and acceptable force'" (quoting *Priester v. City of Riviera Beach*, 208 F.3d 919, 926–927 (11th Cir. 2000)).

5.1 USE OF FORCE AND "OBJECTIVE REASONABLENESS"

The law regarding police use of force has been developed primarily by United States Supreme Court case law, with state statutes and court decisions mirroring the Court's essential rulings. The Supreme Court first attempted to define a precise legal standard for excessive force in *Tennessee v. Garner.*[496] In *Garner,* a police officer responding to a report of a prowler observed a Black teenager named Edward Garner running across the backyard of a home that had just been burglarized.[497] When Garner began climbing over the fence, the officer shot him in the back of the head, fearing that if Garner made it over the fence, he would elude capture. Garner was taken to a hospital, where he died on the operating table.

In *Garner,* the Supreme Court criticized the common-law rule permitting an officer to use whatever force was necessary, including deadly force, to effectuate the arrest of a fleeing felon.[498] Rejecting that rule, the Court held that "the use of deadly force to prevent the escape of all felony suspects, whatever the circumstances, is constitutionally unreasonable."[499] The Court explained that it is constitutionally reasonable to prevent escape by using deadly force only where an officer has probable cause to believe the suspect poses a threat of serious physical harm, either to the officer or to others.[500]

This straightforward, bright-line rule had a direct and immediate impact on officer-involved shootings: "The number of persons shot and killed by police decreased dramatically after the *Garner* decision, in large part because many police departments, which had previously embraced the common law rule, changed their policies to conform to the decision."[501]

But only four years after it decided *Garner,* the Supreme Court retreated from its embrace of clearly defined guidelines for police use of deadly force. In *Graham v. Connor,* the Court instead held that whether an officer has unconstitutionally used excessive force would be judged by an "objective reasonableness" standard.[502] This vague and imprecise standard is easily malleable and bends inexorably in favor of police officers rather than injured or killed civilians.

In *Graham,* a diabetic man named Dethorne Graham asked a friend, William Berry, to drive him to a nearby store so he could buy some orange juice to stave off a developing insulin reaction.[503] Graham went into the store and noticed a long line

---

[496]   471 U.S. 1 (1985).

[497]   This narrative is adapted from the Supreme Court's description of events. *Id.* at 3–4.

[498]   *Id.* at 15 ("In short, though the common-law pedigree of Tennessee's rule [allowing deadly force to stop a fleeing felon] is pure on its face, changes in the legal and technological context mean the rule is distorted almost beyond recognition when literally applied.").

[499]   *Id.* at 11.

[500]   *Id.* at 11–12.

[501]   Lee, *supra* note 493, at 642 (citing Abraham N. Tennenbaum, *The Influence of the Garner Decision on Police Use of Deadly Force,* 85 J. CRIM. L. & CRIMINOLOGY 241, 255–56 (1994)).

[502]   90 U.S. 386, 397 (1989).

[503]   This narrative is summarized from the Supreme Court's description of events. *Id.* at 388–90.

of people waiting to check out; knowing that he needed the juice quickly, Graham immediately exited the store. Officer Connor, who saw Graham quickly enter and exit the store, suspected him of robbery. As Graham and Berry pulled away from the store, Connor followed them. After approximately half a mile, he pulled them over and instructed both men to wait in the car while he called for backup. By this point, Graham was entering a state of diabetic shock, symptoms of which may include confusion, anxiety, and slurred speech. He exited the car in a frantic state, ran around it twice, and then fell down unconscious.

While Graham was unconscious, several officers arrived at the scene; one of them handcuffed Graham's hands tightly behind his back. Several officers then lifted Graham's unconscious body up and placed him face down on the hood of Berry's car. When Graham regained consciousness, he asked the officers to check his wallet for a diabetes decal that he carried. One of the officers responded by telling him to "shut up" and shoved his face against the hood of the car. Four officers then grabbed Graham and threw him headfirst into the police car. Sometime later, Officer Connor received a report that Graham had done nothing illegal at the convenience store, at which point the officers drove him home and released him.

Graham suffered a broken foot, cuts on his wrists, a bruised forehead, and an injured shoulder. He later sued the officers for using excessive force, but the district court granted a directed verdict for the officers before the case could go to the jury, finding that the amount of force used by the officers was reasonable under the circumstances and therefore did not amount to a constitutional violation under the Due Process Clause.[504] The Fourth Circuit affirmed.[505]

On review, the US Supreme Court reversed and remanded the case for further proceedings because, it held, the courts had analyzed the case under the wrong provision of the Constitution. Excessive force cases, the Court held, implicate the Fourth Amendment's search and seizure reasonableness requirement, not the Due Process Clause of the Fourteenth Amendment.[506] The Court then expressly retreated from the bright-line rule provided by *Garner*, holding that "[d]etermining whether the force used to effect a particular seizure is 'reasonable' under the Fourth Amendment requires a careful balancing of . . . the individual's Fourth Amendment interests against the countervailing governmental interests at stake."[507] Acknowledging that this balancing test "is not capable of precise definition or mechanical application," the Court observed that some relevant factors include "the severity of the crime at issue, whether the suspect poses an immediate threat to the safety of officers or others, and whether he is actively resisting arrest or attempting to evade arrest by flight."[508]

---

[504] *Graham v. City of Charlotte*, 644 F. Supp. 246, 249 (W.D.N.C. 1986).
[505] *Graham v. City of Charlotte*, 827 F.2d 945 (4th Cir. 1987).
[506] *Graham*, 490 U.S. at 388.
[507] *Id.* at 396 (internal quotation marks and citations omitted).
[508] *Id.* (internal quotation marks and citations omitted).

The Court explained that in conducting the balancing analysis, courts should apply an objective standard of reasonableness.[509] The officer's actual intent or motive is irrelevant in this objective inquiry.[510] This portion of the holding – that an objective standard would now govern police use-of-force cases – "was a breakthrough."[511] Civil rights advocates believed that imposing an objective standard and absolving the injured victim from having to prove malicious intent on the part of the officer would give civilians more protection against police abuses.[512]

But elsewhere in the opinion, the Court defined "reasonableness" in terms that were unmistakably deferential to law enforcement:

> The "reasonableness" of a particular use of force must be judged from the perspective of a reasonable officer *on the scene*, rather than with the 20/20 vision of hindsight. . . . The calculus of reasonableness must embody allowance for the fact that police officers are often forced to make *split-second judgments* – in circumstances that are tense, uncertain, and rapidly evolving – about the amount of force that is necessary in a particular situation.[513]

This seminal paragraph has been at the center of an intense and growing debate over the proper standard by which to judge officer use of deadly force. On the one hand is the law enforcement community defending "objective reasonableness" as a practical, necessarily flexible acknowledgement of the tense, split-second decisions officers make every day. On the other hand are reform advocates and a large chorus of scholars who view this vague standard as inuring solely to the benefit of officers and justifying police brutality in case after case of unarmed (mostly Black) people gunned down by police.

5.2 "SPLIT-SECOND SYNDROME"

Several aspects of the "objective reasonableness" test, as articulated in *Graham* and expanded by lower courts, pose problems for plaintiffs pursuing excessive force claims. First, "[t]his idea of reasonableness is circumscribed very tightly by time."[514] Rather than allowing juries to consider what a reasonable officer would do in general, taking into account all of the information the officer on the scene had

---

[509] *Id.* at 397.

[510] *Id.*

[511] *More Perfect: Mr. Graham and the Reasonable Man*, RADIOLAB (November 30, 2017), https://www .wnyc.com/story/mr-graham-and-reasonable-man (statement of Graham's attorney, articulating belief that the objective standard would provide better protections for civilians against police violence).

[512] *Id.*

[513] *Graham*, 490 U.S. at 396–97 (emphasis added). The Court also noted that an officer does not have to be correct in his assessment of the need to use force. "The Fourth Amendment is not violated merely because an officer was mistaken, as long as his mistake was reasonable." Lee, *supra* note 493, at 645 (citing *Graham*, 490 U.S. at 396).

[514] *More Perfect, supra* note 511.

prior to the use of force and the calculations a reasonable officer would have made with that information, courts and juries may only consider what a reasonable officer would have done in that "split-second."[515] As baked into constitutional jurisprudence and, now, police use-of-force training, this "split-second syndrome can overwhelm other decision processes and lead to instantaneous assessments of risk and threat" that ignore both the broader context of the encounter and alternatives to lethal force.[516] And this very narrow temporal scope alone defeats the overwhelming majority of use-of-force claims.[517]

Indeed, under *Graham*, "situations in which an officer perceives an immediate threat do not require a risk calculation wherein the officer first considers a menu of actions before deciding how to respond."[518] James J. Fyfe, a former NYPD lieutenant and leading criminologist whose work influenced the Supreme Court's decision in *Garner*, strongly criticized the valorization of police use of deadly force that split-second syndrome promoted and advised that courts ask whether alternatives existed that would have reduced serious injuries or fatalities.[519] Instead, the Court has gone in the opposite direction, holding in *Scott v. Harris* in 2007 that *no* uses of deadly force are clearly impermissible in any situation, so long as the use is objectively reasonable under the circumstances.[520] The Court steadfastly refused to consider whether less lethal alternatives existed, stating that no "magical on/off switch ... triggers rigid preconditions whenever an officer's actions constitute 'deadly force.'"[521]

Split-second syndrome is exacerbated by the toxic mentality of the "warrior cop." A growing number of police recruits are trained in proper use-of-force tactics in warlike settings better suited for military combat than civilian peacekeeping.[522] Private training contractors like RealWorld Tactical, often owned and operated by military special forces veterans, "preach[] that police work is inherently violent, and

---

[515] *Graham*, 490 U.S. at 396–97. Any event taking place immediately prior to the use of force – the superseding event – breaks the chain of causation up to that point, rendering anything that happened prior to that moment irrelevant. See *County of Los Angeles v. Mendez*, 137 S. Ct. 1539, 1546 (2017) (considering whether the incident giving rise to a reasonable use of force is an intervening, superseding event breaking the chain of causation from a prior, unlawful entry).

[516] Jeffrey Fagan & Alexis D. Campbell, *Race and Reasonableness in Police Killings*, 100 B.U. L. Rev. 951, 965 (2020).

[517] See Michael L. Wells, *Scott v. Harris and the Role of the Jury in Constitutional Litigation*, 29 Rev. Litig. 65, 95 (2009); *see also* More Perfect, *supra* note 511 (summarizing interviews with police officers and finding that, rather than providing a victory for civil rights advocates, "officers look at *Graham* as their First Amendment").

[518] Fagan & Campbell, *supra* note 516, at 962.

[519] *Id.* at 964.

[520] *Scott v. Harris*, 550 U.S. 372, 383 (2007).

[521] *Id.* at 382.

[522] Alain Stephens, *The "Warrior Cop" Is a Toxic Mentality. And a Lucrative Industry*, Slate (June 19, 2020), https://slate.com/news-and-politics/2020/06/warrior-cop-trainings-industry.html. *See also* Seth Stoughton, *Commentary: Law Enforcement's "Warrior" Problem*, 128 Harv. L. Rev. F. 225, 234 (2015) https://harvardlawreview.org/2015/04/law-enforcements-warrior-problem/.

that officers represent the last opportunity for law and order in an increasingly dangerous society."[523] As law professor and former police officer Seth Stoughton explained, "They are taught that they live in an intensely hostile world. A world that is, quite literally, gunning for them."[524] From this perspective, the only thing stopping an officer from "becoming a statistic" is his willingness to "take the fight to the bad guys," which more often than not means using excessive force in even the most peaceful encounters.[525]

While the warrior cop narrative has existed for decades, a "flood of funding and surplus military equipment made available to police departments" has literally weaponized the police force, driving "a cottage industry of police consultants, which charge departments thousands of dollars to teach tactics more suited for war than civil society."[526] These consultants teach courses on topics ranging from tactical knife fighting and using military sniper rifles in "unique applications" such as disabling vehicles, to recognizing "radical Islam" and preventing departments from falling victim to "false evidence of racial disparities."[527] Already implicitly primed by the general culture to view Black people with suspicion, officers are now expressly primed to view any encounter with a civilian as a potentially fatal threat and to respond accordingly. Former Minneapolis police officer Jeronimo Yanez attended a department-funded "Bulletproof Warrior" seminar in 2016, which primed its attendees with a single question: "Are you ready to kill?" A few weeks later, Yanez shot and killed Philando Castile at a traffic stop in front of his four-year-old daughter. Yanez stated he "feared for his life" after Castile informed him that he was a licensed gun owner and had a firearm in his car, as he was required to do by Minnesota law. At no point in the encounter did Castile reach for his gun.[528]

5.3 REASONABLE RACISM, REASONABLE FORCE

Predictably, a use-of-force doctrine that both asks what a vaguely "reasonable" or "average" officer would do in the moment and limits consideration of reasonableness to the very instant at which force is used has led to a generation of court cases that almost uniformly justify the use of deadly force by police officers. It also encourages overreliance on "heat of the moment" heuristics that disproportionately lead to use of force against Black individuals. When pervasive, implicit racial stereotypes infect the automatic processing of officers and civilians alike, the average decisions of average police officers under conditions of perceived threat result in

---

[523] Stephens, *supra* note 522.
[524] Stoughton, *supra* note 522.
[525] *See id.*, and Stephens, *supra* note 522.
[526] Stephens, *supra* note 522.
[527] *Id.*
[528] *Id.*

disproportionate killings of the sources of those perceived threats: Black men and women, girls and boys.

Implicit racial stereotypes can and do affect perceptions of whether an officer's use of force was reasonable. Black Americans are often associated – both implicitly and explicitly – with aggression, violence, and criminality.[529] Far from retraining the mind away from these stereotype cues, police training remains primed with "crime stereotypes of risky places and groups of (nonwhite) people," which "perceptually cue the sense of risk from these social contexts."[530] The "prototypical criminal" or "symbolic assailant" in police training remains to this day "a Black male in an inner-city neighborhood," reinforcing "tropes about crime and race that shape the sense of danger for police."[531]

This biased priming creates thousands of dangerous scenarios across the country every day. As police patrol Black neighborhoods more intensively, based in part on the false stereotype of Black criminality, they initiate contact with Black civilians far more frequently than they do with other groups.[532] Modern policing prioritizes police-initiated contact in places considered "high risk" or "high crime," which frequently serves as a proxy for "Black neighborhood."[533] This crude delineation of safe and dangerous spaces into White and Black spaces further cements the risk of racially disparate responses in the "split-second" before force is used.

The pervasiveness of these biases offers two opportunities for racist stereotypes to infect the "objective reasonableness" inquiry. First, if an "average" officer confronting a Black individual is more likely to view that individual as a threat, whether or not that feeling is accurate or reasonable, should that subjective, racist feeling justify the officer's actions as objectively reasonable? Second, if the average civilian juror considering the reasonableness of the officer's use of force also harbors the same implicit racial biases, is it not "reasonable" to expect her to consider race a legitimate factor in the analysis?

Of course, the answer to both questions should be no. Race cannot and should not be considered a legitimate factor in the reasonableness analysis. Yet Professor Armour's reflection on the oxymoronic concept of the "reasonable racist," the average person who acts on his racist impulses just like everyone else, appears to find a home in the Supreme Court's objective reasonableness jurisprudence. Indeed, central to the *Graham* use of force standard "is that the *accuracy* of … why officers thought they were in imminent danger matters less than what the officer *felt* in *that* moment at *that* scene" and whether another officer "would have *felt* the same urgency."[534]

[529] *See generally* discussion *infra* Chapter 6.
[530] Fagan & Campbell, *supra* note 516, at 972.
[531] *Id.*
[532] *Id.*, at 973.
[533] *Id.*
[534] *Id.* at 965 (emphasis in original).

After all, in the moment, Tamir Rice was not a twelve-year-old boy holding a BB gun, but a Black-twelve year-old boy holding a gun. Saheed Vassell was not a bipolar man holding a welding pipe in an exaggerated manner, but a Black man pointing a device. In the moment, Michael Brown, Eric Garner, George Floyd, and Jacob Blake were not unarmed men, but unarmed Black men.

5.4 THE "WEAPON" OF RACIAL FEAR

The racial implications of objective reasonableness are not theoretical or anecdotal. Police officers in the United States have killed more than 1,000 civilians each year since 2013.[535] For decades, empiricists have argued about why people of color generally and Black individuals specifically are killed at far higher rates – both in absolute numbers and relative to their representation in the general population – than White individuals. In May 2020, Jeffrey Fagan and Alexis D. Campbell published a groundbreaking study that analyzed data from 3,933 recent police killings and assessed the connection between race and split-second factors relevant to whether the killing was reasonable under the circumstances. The results were shocking if not surprising: "Black suspects are more than twice as likely to be killed by police than are persons of other racial or ethnic groups, including shootings where there are no obvious reasonable circumstances."[536]

Notably, the use of deadly force against Black and White civilians remained consistently disproportionate when controlling for the presence of a firearm and for a physical attack on an officer. In other words, when the civilian either was perceived to be carrying a gun or had engaged in an attack on an officer, Black civilians were approximately twice as likely to be killed as White civilians (not in absolute numbers, but relative to the number of police encounters studied).[537] Black civilians were more likely to be killed by police officers than White civilians when fleeing from officers.[538] Indeed, confirming the retreat from *Garner*'s short-lived bright-line rule against killing fleeing felons, a full 30 percent of all fatalities studied by Fagan and Campbell involved civilians shot and killed by police while fleeing from the officer.[539]

These racially disproportionate results cannot be explained solely by the higher rate of contact with Black civilians, though the unjustified overpolicing of communities of color certainly increases the threat of racially motivated use of force. A massive 2019 study by the Stanford Computational Policy Lab found a significant correlation between officer patrol density in minority neighborhoods and racial disparity in police

---

[535] *Id.* at 955 (citing *Fatal Force*, WASH. POST (April 14, 2020), https://www.washingtonpost.com/graphics/investigations/police-shootings-database/).

[536] *Id.* at 961.

[537] *Id.* at 994.

[538] *Id.*

[539] *Id.* at 991.

stops.[540] Of course, it has long been known that "police patrol Black and other nonwhite neighborhoods more intensively and are thus more likely to initiate contact with local residents once in those neighborhoods."[541] It also has been well known that this policing of Black movement in "Black space" involves harsher interactions, including more frequent uses of force. But even controlling for increased contact with Black civilians, one study found that "between 2007 and 2014, there were 61,000 more police uses of force against Black civilians than there would have been if force was used at the same rate against white civilians."[542] That same study found that deadly force was used in an additional 1,800 cases against Black civilians.[543]

The consequences for the victims of racially fearful 911 abusers are obvious, but also empirically demonstrable. A 2018 study by Charles Lanfear, Lindsey Beach, and Timothy Thomas found that racial disparities are similarly pronounced in police arrests and use of force when the contact with Black people is initiated by a 911 call rather than by an officer on patrol.[544] These researchers found that reactive police stops (in which police react to a citizen complaint) involving a Black suspect were significantly more likely to end in arrest compared to proactive police stops, even though indicators of probable cause were less prevalent with Black suspects. In reactive policing cases involving nuisance crimes and other highly discretionary types of crimes, both the arrest rate and the police use of force rate was significantly higher for Black suspects than for White suspects.[545] Thus, in a very real sense, the primed, aggressive, and immunized police officer becomes an effective and deadly weapon for the racially fearful White caller criminal.

5.5 "TESTILYING"

Graham's objective reasonableness standard not only fails to provide guidance to officers; it also "fails to provide meaningful guidance to lower courts, attorneys, and litigants regarding whether and when a police officer's use of deadly force is justified."[546] The result has been near-uniform deference to officers and a lowering of

---

[540] Emma Pierson et al., *A Large-Scale Analysis of Racial Disparities in Police Stops Across the United States* (2019), https://5harad.com/papers/traffic-stops.pdf [https://perma.cc/WMH9-X32P] (correlating patrol density in minority neighborhoods to racial disparity in police stops).

[541] Fagan & Campbell, *supra* note 516, at 973.

[542] *Id.* at 973 (citing Rory Kramer & Brianna Remster, *Stop, Frisk, and Assault? Racial Disparities in Police Use of Force During Investigatory Stops*, 52 LAW & SOC'Y REV. 960, 987 (2018)).

[543] *Id.*

[544] Lanfear et al., *supra* note 149 at 1087–88.

[545] *Id.* at 1089.

[546] Lee, *supra* note 493, at 647–48 ("*Graham* permits courts to consider any circumstance in determining whether force is reasonable without providing a standard for measuring relevance, it gives little instruction on how to weigh relevant factors, and it apparently requires courts to consider the severity of the underlying crime in all cases, a circumstance that is sometimes irrelevant and misleading in determining whether force is reasonable." (quoting Rachel Harmon, *When Is Police Violence Justified?*, 102 Nw. U. L. REV. 1119, 1130 (2008))).

"objective reasonableness" to a near nullity. For example, in *Jennings v. Pare*, the district court considered "conflicting testimony" about the reasonableness of an officer's use of an "ankle turn control technique" that resulted in a broken ankle, well after the suspect had stopped resisting.[547] Despite the conflicting evidence on what appeared to be a critical issue, the court granted summary judgment, finding that the plaintiff "failed to present any evidence that, under the circumstances confronting [the officer], 'no objectively reasonable officer' would have applied the ankle turn control technique in the manner the [officer] did."[548]

Deference to the officer's threat assessment in the field is coupled with deference to the officer's testimony in the courtroom, further insulating officers from excessive force claims. Numerous scholars, criminologists, and officers themselves report that an officer's testimony is routinely given greater inherent credibility by courts and juries than conflicting testimony from the victim of police use of force.[549] Whether this deference is normatively justified, one problematic consequence has been the self-reported practice of police officers committing perjury by manufacturing circumstances to justify their or their partner's use of excessive force. A commission studying the NYPD found that perjury was "so common in certain precincts that it has spawned its own word: 'testilying.'"[550] But "[d]espite the common knowledge that law enforcement perjury occurs, prosecutions are extremely rare."[551] Indeed, except in cases of lethal force or egregious displays of abuse, "law enforcement officers can engage in otherwise sanctionable and criminal behavior usually without fear of consequences."[552]

5.6 QUALIFIED IMMUNITY

Even if a judge finds sufficient evidence that an officer used excessive force, a second layer of protection – qualified immunity – almost always shields officers from prosecution. What first developed as a doctrine designed to balance the rights of individuals to be free from government abuse with the need to protect government actors from frivolous lawsuits "has metastasized into an almost absolute defense to all but the most outrageous conduct. The values of deterrence of unlawful behavior and compensation for civil rights victims have been overshadowed by the desire to protect government agents, particularly police officers, from almost all claims against them."[553]

[547] 479 F.3d 110, 115 (1st Cir. 2007).
[548] *Id.*
[549] *See* Hassel, *supra* note 495, at 125; *see also* Capers, *supra* note 271 at 867–68.
[550] Capers, *supra* note 271, at 836 (quoting MILTON MOLLEN, ET AL., COMM'N TO INVESTIGATE ALLEGATIONS OF POLICE CORRUPTION AND THE ANTI-CORRUPTION PROCEDURES OF THE POLICE DEP'T, CITY OF N.Y., COMMISSION REPORT 36 (1994)).
[551] *Id.* at 837.
[552] *Id.* at 837.
[553] Diana Hassel, *Excessive Reasonableness*, 43 IND. L. REV. 117, 118 (2009).

If a court or jury finds that an officer used force beyond what was "objectively reasonable," then this force amounts to an "unreasonable seizure" that violates the Fourth Amendment. Importantly, this violation of the Fourth Amendment neither negates the arrest of the arrested victim of police brutality nor affects the admissibility of evidence that may have been discovered as a result of the force. In short, to the extent a victim of police brutality is arrested and faces trial on criminal charges, the brutality to which he was subjected has no bearing on the criminal proceedings at all. Instead, the victim of state-sponsored violence must turn to the civil system to seek vindication through a civil rights lawsuit.

Among the three "Reconstruction Amendments" to the United States Constitution passed after the Civil War, the Fourteenth Amendment most directly addressed the brutal civil rights abuses against Black people by state and local government officials like police officers and private actors working in concert with such officials. It did so by guaranteeing that citizens were protected from unconstitutional actions by *state* authorities and not just *federal* authorities. Shortly after the Civil War, Congress passed the Civil Rights Act of 1871 "to enforce the Provisions of the Fourteenth Amendment to the Constitution of the United States."[554] This act, which became known as the Second Ku Klux Klan Act, was designed in large part to protect Black people from state-sponsored Klan violence by giving those deprived of a constitutional right by someone acting "under color of law" the right to seek relief in a federal court.[555] The Supreme Court later interpreted "under color of law" to mean anyone acting in an official government capacity, including law enforcement officers.[556] This Act was later codified in the federal code at 42 U.S.C. § 1983; civil rights lawsuits alleging constitutional violations by government actors are now widely known as "Section 1983 actions."

Courts rarely took Section 1983 actions seriously during the height of Jim Crow and the age of racial terror lynchings through the end of the nineteenth and first half of the twentieth centuries – arguably when such enforcement actions could have been most useful. But the Supreme Court reinvigorated and reinforced the scope of Section 1983 actions in 1961, in *Monroe v. Pape*, which allowed a Chicago family's suit against police officers to move forward after officers burst into their home, forced the entire family to stand naked in their living room while police searched the house, then detained the head of the household for more than ten hours, interrogating him about a recent murder without allowing him to contact family members or his attorney, before releasing him without charge.[557] Ten years later, in *Bivens v. Six Unnamed Agents of Federal Bureau of Narcotics*, the Supreme Court held that civil

---

[554] Civil Rights Act of 1871, 42 U.S.C. § 1983.

[555] *Id.* (The defendant must have acted "under color of any statute, ordinance, regulation, custom, or usage, of any State or Territory or the District of Columbia.").

[556] *Monroe v. Pape*, 365 U.S. 167 (1961).

[557] *Id.*

rights claims similar to Section 1983 actions could be brought against federal officials acting "under color of law."[558] Thus, whether a citizen claiming civil rights violations by law enforcement brings a Section 1983 action or a *Bivens* action depends on whether the officer involved is a state or local police officer or a federal agent.

The text of Section 1983 provides no immunities or defenses for violations of a citizen's constitutional rights. However, between *Monroe* and *Bivens*, the Supreme Court created such an immunity out of whole cloth, in the 1967 decision *Pierson v. Ray*.[559] In that case, the Supreme Court expressed doubt that Congress intended, by the plain language of Section 1983, to abolish longstanding "common-law immunities" and read into the statute immunity for two categories of state actors: judges, who were given absolute immunity, and police officers, who could defend their actions on the basis of "good faith and probable cause."[560] This defense echoed the good-faith defense long available for public officials at common law, which immunized public officials from lawsuits for actions taken in good faith. This defense to Section 1983 claims created by the Court in *Pierson* – a defense found nowhere in the text or legislative history of the Congressional statute and limited, with little explanation, only to police officers – formed the basis for the modern qualified immunity doctrine.

In the absence of Supreme Court guidance in applying this newly created defense, lower courts looked to the common-law good-faith defense, which included a subjective component. Thus, over the next two decades, lower courts settled on an alternative two-part test to determine whether qualified immunity applied. Plaintiffs could overcome immunity by showing either that a police officer acted in subjective bad faith in violating an individual's constitutional rights or that the officer objectively knew or should have known that his actions violated the Constitution.[561] The subjective component was similar to the good-faith defense available under common law.[562] In 1982, however, in *Harlow v. Fitzgerald*, the Supreme Court significantly shrank a plaintiff's ability to defeat qualified immunity by abolishing the subjective test.[563] In other words, a victim of police brutality who had compelling evidence that an officer personally chose to use force for bad faith, even illegal, reasons – including reasons motivated by race – still could not prevail unless the plaintiff showed that a "reasonable officer" objectively knew or should have known that the use of force was not permitted under the Fourth Amendment.[564]

---

[558]   *Bivens v. Six Unknown Named Agents of the Federal Bureau of Narcotics*, 403 U.S. 388 (1971).
[559]   *Pierson v. Ray*, 386 U.S. 547 (1967).
[560]   *Id.* at 557.
[561]   *See* Gasperini DeMarco, *The Qualified Immunity Quagmire in Public Employees' Section 1983 Free Speech Cases*, 25 Rev. Litig. 349, 360 (2006); Andrew W. Weis, *Qualified Immunity For "Private" 1983 Defendants After Filarsky v. Delia*, 30 Ga. St. U.L. Rev. 1037, 1060 (2014).
[562]   *See Pierson*, 386 U.S. at 555–56 (validating officers' claims "that they should not be liable if they acted in good faith and with probable cause in making an arrest" because the doctrine of qualified immunity includes "the defense of good faith").
[563]   457 U.S. 800 (1982).
[564]   *Id.* at 817–18.

Just as troubling as the Court's elimination of the subjective test, the Court created an extraordinarily high bar for what constituted an "objective" violation of a constitutional right sufficient to overcome qualified immunity. The Court held that "government officials . . . generally are shielded from liability for civil damages insofar as their conduct does not violate *clearly established* statutory or constitutional rights of which a *reasonable person* would have known."[565] The Court later clarified in *Ashcroft v. al-Kidd* that qualified immunity shields federal and state officials from money damages unless the plaintiff can prove both "(1) that the official violated a statutory or constitutional right, and (2) that the right was 'clearly established' at the time of the challenged conduct."[566] In other words, it no longer was enough to establish that a constitutional right was violated to overcome qualified immunity. Now, a plaintiff had to show that this right was "clearly established" and that a "reasonable officer" would have known he was violating such a clearly established right.

The Court's redefinition of the phrases "reasonable officer" and "clearly established" in the four decades since *Harlow* illustrates a clear, unilateral desire to expand the defense into a near-absolute immunity for all police misconduct. For example, the Court redefined "a reasonable person" to "a reasonable officer" and clarified that the standard encompassed "any reasonable officer," meaning that "the right violated must be so clear that its violation . . . would have been obvious . . . to the least informed, least reasonable 'reasonable officer.'"[567] In other words, an officer's misconduct will not be judged "objectively unreasonable," and thus not shielded by qualified immunity, unless the officer's actions were more egregious and more plainly illegal than what even the worst officer in the United States would have done. This absurdly low standard contradicts all common understandings and applications of "reasonableness" in every other area of law, a perception the Court appeared to confirm in 2015 in *Mullenix v. Luna*, when it stated that qualified immunity protects "all but the plainly incompetent."[568]

Moreover, the Court's treatment of what constitutes a "clearly established" constitutional or statutory right all but guarantees absolute immunity for even the most "plainly incompetent" police conduct. Traditionally, to find that a right is "clearly established," courts require controlling precedent from the US Supreme Court, a relevant federal circuit court, or the highest court in the state acknowledging that right. Here, the terminology can get confusing. The Fourth Amendment clearly establishes a right to be free from "unreasonable seizures," and no controlling court

[565] *Id.* at 818 (emphasis added).
[566] *Ashcroft v. al-Kidd*, 563 U.S. 731, 735 (2011); *see also* Hassel, *supra* note 553, at 123–24 ("The objective qualified immunity standard was seen to represent the proper balance between conflicting interests: the interest in providing compensation for, and deterring unconstitutional conduct against the need to protect against frivolous lawsuits and to encourage vigorous enforcement of the law.").
[567] Scott Michelman, *The Branch Best Qualified to Abolish Qualified Immunity*, 93 Notre Dame L. Rev. 1999, 2004 (1999).
[568] *Mullenix v. Luna*, 577 U.S. 7, 12 (2015) (quoting *Malley v. Briggs*, 475 U.S. 335, 341 (1986)).

case is required to establish that right. But whether a particular action clearly violates that right (or, in other words, whether one has a clearly established right to be free from a particular action) requires a controlling case to so hold. For example, a plaintiff could point to the Supreme Court's decision in *Tennessee v. Garner* to claim that an officer's decision to shoot an unarmed fleeing person in the back of the head violates a clearly established Fourth Amendment right to be free from such an "unreasonable seizure." At least in theory.

In reality, however, the Supreme Court has so narrowly defined "clearly established" in the context of qualified immunity that virtually no police action is a clear violation of a constitutional right. In *Mullenix*, the Court explained, "The dispositive question is whether the violative nature of *particular* conduct is clearly established,"[569] and plaintiffs must show "not just that the relevant right existed, but also that the specific action the officer took violated that right."[570] Doing so requires plaintiffs to prove that it is beyond debate that the particular action the officer took, in that exact context and under those exact circumstances, violated the Fourth Amendment. By equating "clearly established" with "beyond debate," the Court implicitly expanded qualified immunity to protect all police misconduct unless a plaintiff can point to a published, controlling court decision in which an officer engaged in identical behavior under identical circumstances – a virtual impossibility.

No better example confirms this reality than *Mullenix* itself. In that case, Israel Leija, Jr., a twenty-four-year-old Latino male, led police on a high-speed chase after an officer approached his car and informed him that he was under arrest.[571] Officer Mullenix joined the effort to catch Leija and suggested shooting at Leija's car to disable it, even though spike strips had already been placed on the road to disable the vehicle. Approximately three minutes after Officer Mullenix exited his vehicle, he spotted Leija's vehicle and fired six shots at it. Four of the six shots hit Leija, killing him.

Leija's estate sued Officer Mullenix and successfully defeated a motion for summary judgment, with the district court finding genuine issues of fact regarding whether the officer acted recklessly.[572] The United States Court of Appeals for the Fifth Circuit went further, concluding that Mullenix acted objectively unreasonably because "there were no innocent bystanders . . . and Mullenix's decision was not a split-second judgment."[573] The Fifth Circuit noted that officers had already placed spike strips down directly in Leija's path, that the spike strips represented a de-escalation technique that was not only required by police protocol but also

---

[569] *Id.*

[570] Michelman, *supra* note 567, at 2004.

[571] This narrative is summarized from the Supreme Court's description of events. *Mullenix*, 577 U.S. at 8–10.

[572] *Luna v. Mullenix*, No. 2:12-CV-152-J, 2013 WL 4017124, at *6 (N.D. Tex. August 7, 2013).

[573] *Mullenix*, 577 U.S. at 11.

likely to end the chase with minimal injury, that Officer Mullenix knew the spike strips had been placed down, and that Officer Mullenix chose to fire anyway, even though he clearly was not in any personal danger. The court concluded that, on these facts, qualified immunity could not protect the officer.[574]

The Supreme Court reversed.[575] Without deciding whether Officer Mullenix acted unreasonably in violation of the Fourth Amendment, the Court found that it could not conclude that Mullenix violated clearly established law.[576] The Court described the "hazy legal backdrop" of high-speed car chase cases and observed that it could find no case with sufficiently identical facts to "clearly establish" that Officer Mullenix's decision to fire six shots in Leija's vehicle constituted an unreasonable seizure.[577]

Justice Sotomayor, the sole Justice to dissent from the Court's ruling, accused the Court of supporting a "shoot first, think later" culture of policing.[578] She noted that when Officer Mullenix confronted his supervisor after the shooting, his first words were, "How's that for proactive?," referencing an earlier counseling session in which his supervisor had suggested Mullenix was not enterprising enough.[579] Justice Sotomayor continued:

> ['T']he comment seems to me revealing of the culture this Court's decision supports when it calls it reasonable ... to use deadly force for no discernible gain and over a supervisor's express order to "stand by." By sanctioning a "shoot first, think later" approach to policing, the Court renders the protections of the Fourth Amendment hollow.[580]

Mullenix puts the full, unjustifiable absurdity of qualified immunity on display. Officer Mullenix was subjectively motivated to use deadly force not because he thought it was reasonably necessary, but to impress his supervisor. But the Court found this subjective motivation irrelevant. Officer Mullenix took a grossly reckless action that a reasonable officer would not have taken. But the Court could not conclude that his actions were "plainly incompetent." Officer Mullenix killed someone in a display of force that was patently unreasonable, even under *Graham*'s cramped understanding of objective reasonableness. But the Court could not find a factually identical, published court case proving this clear Fourth Amendment violation was "clearly established." And so, the Court reasoned, it could not hold that Mullenix's action was unreasonable.

[574] *Id.*
[575] *Id.* at 19.
[576] *Id.* at 309–11 (discussing the "hazy legal backdrop against which Mullenix acted" but declining to resolve the Fourth Amendment issue because of the existence of a viable qualified immunity claim).
[577] *Id.*
[578] *Id.* at 26 (Sotomayor, J., dissenting).
[579] *Id.* at 25.
[580] *Id.* at 26.

5.7 THE THIN BLUE ROBE

The last time I taught *Mullenix*, an astute student asked, "If a prior case clearly establishing a right is required before a court can find that a right is clearly established, how can there ever be a case establishing that right?" She was more correct than she may have realized. Between 1982, when the *Harlow* decision was released, and 2017, the Supreme Court decided thirty qualified immunity cases involving police officers. Only two of those cases were decided in favor of the plaintiffs; the majority of the twenty-eight victories for police officers rested on the Court's inability to find a "clearly established" right.[581] In these cases, the Court has repeatedly instructed lower courts to define "clearly established" narrowly and has overturned lower-court decisions that failed to find controlling precedent identical to the facts of the case before it. Moreover, of the fifteen qualified immunity appeals the Supreme Court has taken since 2005, twelve have been interventions on behalf of police appealing an adverse decision, and many of these cases did not meet the Court's own criteria for granting certiorari.[582]

In 2017, dissenting from a denial of certiorari in another officer shooting case dismissed on the basis of qualified immunity, Justice Sotomayor described the Court's continued willingness to prioritize an officer's right to use force over a person's right to be free from unnecessary police violence:

> [This decision] continues a disturbing trend regarding the use of this Court's resources. We have not hesitated to summarily reverse courts for wrongly denying officers the protection of qualified immunity in cases involving the use of force. But we rarely intervene where courts wrongly afford officers the benefit of qualified immunity in these same cases. The erroneous grant of summary judgment in qualified-immunity cases imposes no less harm on "society as a whole" than does the erroneous denial of summary judgment in such cases.[583]

As University of Chicago Law School Professor William Baude has observed, all of this activity by the Supreme Court has sent a clear message to lower courts: "because lower courts are somewhat regularly reversed for erring on the side of liability, but almost never reversed for erring on the side of immunity, the current docket signals to lower courts that they should drift toward immunity."[584]

Lower courts have gotten the message. A Reuters analysis found that courts often ignore the question of whether police have exercised excessive force, instead ruling

---

[581]   *See* William Baude, *Is Qualified Immunity Unlawful?*, 106 CALIF. L. REV. 45, 82 (2018); *see also* Joanna C. Schwartz, *The Case Against Qualified Immunity*, 93 NOTRE DAME L. REV. 1797, 1852 n.2 (2018) (citing Baude and noting that two Supreme Court decisions from 2018 "puts the count at thirty-two. Twenty of those decisions have been issued within the past ten years.").

[582]   *Id.*

[583]   *Salazar-Limon v. City of Houston*, 137 S. Ct. 1277, 1282–1283 (2017) (Sotomayor, J., dissenting) (quoting *City & Cty. Of San Francisco v. Sheehan*, 135 S. Ct. 1765, 1774 n.3 (2015)) (citations omitted).

[584]   Baude, *supra* note 581, at 83.

that the law is not clearly established, often based on absurdly fine distinctions. For instance, the Sixth Circuit granted immunity to an officer who shot a fourteen-year-old boy after he dropped a BB gun and raised his hands, rejecting as precedent a case in which an officer shot a man as he lowered a shotgun.[585] The Reuters study identified several similarly thin distinctions:

> [C]ourts have sided with police because of the difference between subduing a woman for walking away from an officer, and subduing a woman for refusing to end a phone call; between shooting at a dog and instead hitting a child, and shooting at a truck and hitting a passenger; and between unleashing a police dog to bite a motionless suspect in a bushy ravine, and unleashing a police dog to bite a compliant suspect in a canal in the woods.[586]

The result is what some call a "closed loop" of stagnant case law: since courts can nearly always find some factual distinction between cases, they can find the law is not clearly established and avoid the constitutional question altogether. As a result, no clearly established precedent exists for the next plaintiff to point to. This "closed loop" is not merely hypothetical. In 2018, the Eleventh Circuit granted qualified immunity to police officers who hog-tied a man and knelt on his back until he lost consciousness and later died.[587] The court acknowledged that it had previously heard a nearly identical case involving hog-tying but had granted immunity because no "clearly established" case law existed to find that use of force so grossly excessive as to fall outside the bounds of immunity.[588] As a result, this earlier case could not provide the required precedent of "clearly established" case law.

It really is turtles all the way down.

5.8 MORE SHIFTING BURDENS

The Supreme Court has also stacked the procedural deck against plaintiffs claiming police brutality. In a move eerily similar to the shifting of burdens in Stand Your Ground jurisdictions, the Supreme Court has shifted the burden of proof for qualified immunity. Most affirmative defenses require the defendant to prove at trial that he is eligible for the defense. But in the qualified immunity context, a police officer need only assert the defense; the plaintiff has the burden to prove the defense does not apply. Moreover, the Court has called for qualified immunity issues to be resolved as early in the litigation as possible, making it significantly less likely that a plaintiff will be able to put her police brutality claims before a jury at trial.

---

[585] Andrew Chung et al., *Supreme Defense*, REUTERS INVESTIGATES: SHIELDED (May 8, 2020), www.reuters.com/investigates/special-report/usa-police-immunity-scotus/.

[586] *Id.*

[587] *Callwood v. Jones*, 727 Fed. Appx. 552 (11th Cir. 2018).

[588] *Id.* at 561. The preceding case is *Lewis v. City of West Palm Beach, Fla.*, 561 F.3d 1288 (2009).

In 2009, the Supreme Court further restricted plaintiffs' ability to prove police brutality claims in court when it held in *Pearson v. Callahan* that courts had the discretion to consider whether qualified immunity applied *before* considering whether a constitutional violation occurred.[589] Thus, a plaintiff who suffered excessive force at the hands of a police officer may never get to present evidence at all unless she can overcome the near insurmountable hurdle of qualified immunity. This subtle shift has two important effects. First, because the only "relevant" evidence in overcoming the qualified immunity defense is the existence of prior controlling precedent, plaintiffs may be denied access to information critical to proving their claims – such as police reports, body camera footage, and internal affairs records – if they cannot first find a perfectly identical prior case to overcome qualified immunity. Second, each subsequent case decided on qualified immunity grounds without even considering whether the police action violated the Fourth Amendment represents one less opportunity to "clearly establish" whether hog-tying an unarmed man, shooting into a vehicle about to be nonlethally disabled, or kneeling on the neck of a handcuffed man for nine minutes violates a constitutional right.

5.9 ABSOLUTE IMMUNITY

By design, qualified immunity provides a broad and generally successful defense to most civil rights claims. As the Court has explained, qualified immunity ensures that only "the plainly incompetent or those who knowingly violate the law" will be found liable for misconduct.[590] Indeed, even when courts find that officers violated the "objective reasonableness" test under *Graham* by using excessive force, they still shield officers from liability if the officer reasonably believed that no "clearly established" right existed at the time.[591] As one scholar observed in describing this two-layered level of officer protection:

> When these two standards [objective reasonableness and qualified immunity] are both operating, a court must first determine whether a defendant's actions are objectively reasonable. Then, assuming that the actions were not objectively reasonable, the court must determine whether it was nonetheless objectively reasonable for the defendant to have believed his actions were objectively reasonable.[592]

As a result of this multilayered system of protection for police abuse, "[q]ualified immunity has moved closer to a system of absolute immunity for most defendants, resulting in a finding of liability for only the most extreme and most shocking misuses of police power."[593]

---

[589]   *Pearson v. Callahan*, 555 U.S. 223, 236–37 (2009).
[590]   *Malley v. Briggs*, 475 U.S. 335, 341 (1986).
[591]   Hassel, *supra* note 553, at 119.
[592]   *Id.* at 125.
[593]   *Id.* at 124; *see also* Nicholas T. Davis & Philip B. Davis, *Qualified Immunity and Excessive Force: A Greater or Lesser Role for Juries?*, 47 N.M. L. REV. 291, 291 (2017) ("In the past thirty-five years the

These egregious results not only flatly contradict basic Fourth Amendment law and the plain text of Section 1983, but they also have no basis in the Framers' original purpose or understanding of how people would enforce their rights under the constitution. When the Bill of Rights was ratified in 1791, the primary mechanism a civilian had for enforcing his or her rights – including vindicating constitutional rights against government officials – was a civil lawsuit in state court.[594] If a constable in 1795 Virginia unlawfully entered a civilian's home and seized evidence of a crime in violation of the Fourth Amendment, that civilian's only recourse was a common-law action for trespass. Police officers enjoyed limited immunity from suit for arrests based on probable cause when the arrestee later turned out to be innocent in fact, but this limited protection did not immunize officers from constitutional violations because the arrests still had to comply with the Fourth Amendment's probable cause requirement.[595]

An early Supreme Court opinion written by Chief Justice John Marshall highlights the lack of immunity for government officials who broke the law. In 1799, the commander of a warship incorrectly seized a ship, thinking it was preparing to violate US law by traveling to a French port. In reality, it was traveling from a French port to the United States. President John Adams sought to protect the commander by claiming the statute could be read to permit seizures of ships going to or from French ports. Chief Justice Marshall disagreed; while he acknowledged that the commander was simply following orders in good faith, that reality did not excuse the commander from his duty to compensate the plaintiffs for his violation of the law. As scholar Sina Kian notes, "[T]his was the original system of constitutional remedies, as envisioned by the framers, and the result was exactly as intended: government, knowing it would be held accountable for any transgressions, was cautious and protective when it came to people's rights."[596]

5.10 CONVICTED MURDERER, NOT LIABLE FOR EXCESSIVE FORCE?

Some hope for reform exists. Calls for legislative reforms to qualified immunity have been raised in the wake of George Floyd's murder. Even before that, in March 2020, the Sixth Circuit Court of Appeals reversed the district court's decision and denied qualified immunity to the five police officers who shot a motionless Wayne Jones twenty-two times.[597] Circuit Judge Henry Franklin Floyd summed up in plain terms

largest roadblock in any viable civil rights case involving excessive force under the Fourth Amendment of the Constitution has been the doctrine of qualified immunity.").

[594]   Sina Kian, *The Path of the Constitution: The Original System of Remedies, How It Changed, and How the Court Responded*, 87 N.Y.U. L. Rev. 132, 138 (2012).

[595]   *Id.*

[596]   Sina Kian, *Opinion: Supreme's Court Key Choice on Police Wrongdoing*, CNN (June 3, 2020), https://www.cnn.com/2020/06/03/opinions/supreme-courts-key-choice-on-police-wrongdoing-kian/index.html.

[597]   *Estate of Jones v. City of Martinsburg, W. Va.*, 961 F.3d 661 (4th Cir. 2020).

the absurd question before the court: "we are asked to decide whether it was clearly established that five officers could not shoot a man 22 times as he lay motionless on the ground."[598] But while this result represents some perverse form of progress, it remains just one case against a tidal wave of qualified immunity grants.

When I discussed the murder of George Floyd in my Criminal Procedure class, my students and I used it as an opportunity to apply *Graham*'s objective reasonableness test to an obvious example of excessive force. Applying the relevant factors articulated by the Court, we noted that Mr. Floyd was suspected of committing the nonviolent, nonserious crime of passing a counterfeit twenty-dollar bill, that he was not actively resisting arrest or attempting to evade arrest by flight because he had been handcuffed and placed on the ground, and that he did not pose an immediate threat to the safety of the four officers surrounding him because he had been secured on the ground by Chauvin. Given these factors, Chauvin's "split-second" decision to press his knee into Mr. Floyd's neck for the next 559 seconds clearly amounted to an unreasonable seizure, because no reasonable officer in that situation would have felt sufficiently threatened to use such lethal force. Or so we hoped.

For good measure, we revisited first-year Criminal Law and noted that Chauvin's conviction for second-degree murder seemed appropriate, because the gruesome video of Mr. Floyd's lynching showed actions taken without obvious premeditation but with the intention to cause serious bodily harm and with extreme indifference to Mr. Floyd's life.

What I did not have the heart to discuss with my students in that emotionally draining class was that, had Chauvin not chosen to plead guilty to violating Mr. Floyd's federal constitutional right to be free from unreasonable seizures, Chauvin might have escaped liability in the civil suit. One hopes something as plainly and violently unlawful as a murder would qualify as a violation of a "clearly established" constitutional right. In researching for this book, however, I scoured United States Supreme Court, Eighth Circuit Court of Appeals, and Minnesota Supreme Court precedent for a case directly analogous to Mr. Floyd's: an officer pressing his knee into the neck of a handcuffed man on the ground for multiple minutes. I found none. At a minimum, absent any clearly established case law and under the Supreme Court's current precedent, it remains a legitimate open question whether Chauvin would have found refuge in the doctrine of qualified immunity. That speaks volumes.

---

[598]   *Id.* at 673.

6

Permanent Fear

Bayard Love and Deena Hayes-Greene of the Racial Equity Institute provide seminars and trainings aimed at creating racially equitable organizations and systems. They provide these trainings to private businesses, nonprofit organizations, academic institutions, and government agencies. Many of their trainings begin with the following anecdote:

> If you have a lake in front of your house and one fish is floating belly-up dead, it makes sense to analyze the fish. What is wrong with it? . . . But if you come out to that same lake and *half* the fish are floating belly-up dead, what should you do? This time you've got to analyze the lake. . . . Now . . . picture five lakes around your house, and in *each and every* lake half the fish are floating belly-up dead! What is it time to do? We say it's time to analyze the groundwater.[599]

This anecdote is an allegory for the racially structured society in which we live. Love and Hayes-Greene ask participants to imagine that the single fish is a lone failing student.[600] Did she study hard enough? Is she getting the support she needs at home? But when that student is not alone, but part of an entire underperforming population segment, the problem is not the student but the school system – the groundwater. When Black Americans are 2.3 times more likely to experience infant death,[601] 2 times more likely to die of diabetes,[602] 1.5 times more likely to be below proficient in reading,[603] 6.5 times more likely to be suspended in K–12,[604] 5.2 times

---

599   BAYARD LOVE & DEENA HAYES-GREENE, THE RACIAL EQUITY INSTITUTE, THE GROUNDWATER APPROACH: BUILDING A PRACTICAL UNDERSTANDING OF STRUCTURAL RACISM 3 (2018) (emphasis in original).

600   *Id.*

601   Office of Minority Health, *Infant Mortality and African Americans*, U.S. DEP'T OF HEALTH & HUM. SVCS. (November 8, 2019), https://www.minorityhealth.hhs.gov/omh/browse.aspx?lvl=4&lvlid=23.

602   Office of Minority Health, *Diabetes and African Americans*, U.S. DEP'T OF HEALTH & HUM. SVCS. (December 19, 2019), https://www.minorityhealth.hhs.gov/omh/browse.aspx?lvl=4&lvlid=18.

603   ANNIE E. CASEY FOUND'N, EARLY READING PROFICIENCY IN THE UNITED STATES 1 (January 2014), https://www.aecf.org/m/resourcedoc/aecf-EarlyReadingProficiency-2014.pdf.

604   Matthew P. Steinberg & Johanna Lacoe, *What Do We Know About School Discipline Reform?*, Education Next (Winter 2017), https://www.educationnext.org/what-do-we-know-about-school-discipline-reform-suspensions-expulsions/.

more likely to be denied a mortgage,[605] 1.7 times less likely to own a home,[606] 2.7 times more likely to be pulled over and 5 times more likely to be searched during a traffic stop,[607] and 7 times more likely to be incarcerated,[608] the problem lies not with millions of individual fish lying belly-up. The problem is society's groundwater.

Chapter 1 explored how America's groundwater became tainted over the course of four centuries, while Chapters 2 through 5 examined how that tainted groundwater expresses itself in the form of racist private policing of Black and White spaces, with the help and support of government actors. This chapter discusses how today's invisible groundwater – pervasive implicit racial bias – drives that racist system of private policing and how, like groundwater, it is not easily purified.

Like groundwater, implicit or unconscious bias is invisible, lying deep within us. Also like groundwater, purifying White America's minds of implicit bias in any meaningful way is nearly impossible in the short term. Like the cleaning of a Superfund site, the cleansing of a nation's racist psyche will take generations of antiracism work. In the meantime, society must acknowledge and confront the permanence of White America's racial fear as a necessary precondition to reforms that reduce the number of unnecessary criminal legal contacts infected by this racial fear and the increased risk of harassment, violence, and death these contacts impose on vulnerable Black Americans.

6.1 UNCONSCIOUS FEAR

Four centuries of carefully cultivated racial fear have had a profound effect on the White psyche. The attitudes this long campaign has bred are enduring and pernicious, and they cannot be expected to change quickly. Racist tropes are so deeply ingrained in America's collective unconscious that no amount of bias awareness alone will rid White people of the epidemic of racial fear.[609]

---

[605] Sarah Mikhitarian, *Black Mortgage Applicants Denied at More Than Twice the Rate of Whites*, ZILLOW RESEARCH (April 19, 2018), https://www.zillow.com/research/black-white-mortgage-denials-19616/.

[606] Troy McMullen, *The "Heartbreaking" Decrease in Black Homeownership*, WASH. POST (February 28, 2019), https://www.washingtonpost.com/news/business/wp/2019/02/28/feature/the-heartbreaking-decrease-in-black-homeownership/.

[607] Radley Balko, *There's Overwhelming Evidence That the Criminal Justice System Is Racist. Here's The Proof.*, Wash. Post (June 10, 2020), https://www.washingtonpost.com/graphics/2020/opinions/systemic-racism-police-evidence-criminal-justice-system/ (citing F.pp, *supra* note 283).

[608] John Gramlich, *Black Imprisonment Rate in the U.S. Has Fallen by a Third Since 2006*, PEW RESEARCH CENTER: FACTTANK (May 6, 2020), https://www.pewresearch.org/fact-tank/2020/05/06/share-of-black-white-hispanic-americans-in-prison-2018-vs-2006/.

[609] Aaron Mak, *What Can Starbucks Accomplish?*, SLATE (April 20, 2018), https://slate.com/technology/2018/04/does-implicit-bias-training-work-starbucks-racial-bias-plan-will-probably-fail.html; *see generally* Brian A. Nosek et al., *Harvesting Implicit Group Attitudes and Beliefs From a Demonstration Web Site*, 6 GROUP DYNAMICS 101 (2002) (discussing results of over 600,000 implicit association test tasks that demonstrate implicit racial preferences).

The most common implicit racial stereotypes include "the cultural stereotype of Blacks, especially young men, as violent, hostile, aggressive, and dangerous."[610] These stereotypes can motivate a private citizen to call 911 or brandish a firearm in response to innocuous behavior. When police arrive, an officer who harbors no conscious racial animosity and who rejects the use of race as a proxy for criminality may nevertheless unintentionally treat individuals differently based on their physical appearance.[611] Thus, Black persons targeted for unwarranted suspicion by fearful civilians face two waves of implicit discrimination: first at the hands of the bias-motivated civilian who makes the complaint, and then at the hands of the officer who responds to the complaint.

A half-century of social psychological research has repeatedly demonstrated that virtually all individuals in the United States harbor implicit, unconscious racial biases conforming to the myth of the "Black bogeyman."[612] These biases – automatic in nature and affecting individuals from all races and classes – link dark-skinned individuals with criminality and light-skinned individuals with innocence.[613] The pervasiveness of the "Black bogeyman" trope is such that "[p]eople possess these unconscious associations even if these associations conflict with their consciously and genuinely held beliefs."[614]

These biases are rooted in the operation of the human brain, which largely proceeds by categorization. Human beings categorize people and objects "to make sense of experience. Too many events occur daily for people to deal successfully with each one on an individual basis; we must categorize in order to cope."[615] Racial categorization, like most categorization processes, occurs automatically, unintentionally, and without conscious awareness.[616] That categorization then invokes the associated fears and biases.

The operation of these implicit biases affects behavior in three ways. First, implicit biases can result in increased scrutiny of certain people based upon their racial appearance.[617] Second, these biases can affect the evaluation of ambiguous behavior, causing identical behavior to be interpreted differently depending upon

[610] L. Song Richardson, *Implicit Racial Bias and the Fourth Amendment*, in THE CONSTITUTION AND THE FUTURE OF CRIMINAL JUSTICE IN AMERICA 59, 60 (John T. Parry & L. Song Richardson eds., 2013); *see also* Correll et al., *supra* note 247, at 1013–15.

[611] Richardson, *supra* note 610, at 75.

[612] Nosek, *supra* note 609.

[613] L. Song Richardson, *Implicit Racial Bias and Racial Anxiety: Implications for Stops and Frisks*, 15 OHIO ST. J. CRIM. L. 73, 75 (2017).

[614] *Id.*

[615] Charles R. Lawrence III, *The Id, the Ego, and Equal Protection: Reckoning with Unconscious Racism*, 39 STAN. L. REV. 317, 337 (1987).

[616] *Id.* at 338; *see also* L. Song Richardson, *Arrest Efficiency and the Fourth Amendment*, 95 MINN. L. REV. 2035, 2042 (2011).

[617] Sophie Trawalter et al., *Attending to Threat: Race-Based Patterns of Selective Attention*, 44 J. EXPERIMENTAL SOC. PSYCHOL. 1322, 1326–27 (2008).

the appearance of the person performing the act.[618] Third, implicit biases can cause individuals to treat members of different racial groups disparately.[619] These biases – known as attentional bias, interpretation bias, and treatment bias – all work together in the civilian weaponization of racial fear.

Attentional: Researchers consistently find that dark-skinned individuals, especially young Black men, capture the attention of people before light-skinned individuals.[620] Scientists "attribute this difference in attention to the fact that people have automatic and rapid threat reactions toward Black men."[621]

Interpretation: Once attention is directed toward dark-skinned individuals, cultural stereotypes of Black men as violent, criminal, and dangerous affect the bystander's interpretation of the witnessed behavior.[622] One study found that individuals of all races "are more ready to identify an ambiguous object as a dangerous weapon when in the hands of a black male than a white male."[623] Another study that asked participants to observe and rate ambiguous physical contact between two people found that participants overwhelmingly rated the contact as deliberate, aggressive, and hostile when at least one of the individuals was Black.[624] "Unconscious racial biases can even influence how people read another's facial expressions, with identical expressions being evaluated as more hostile on a Black face than on a White face."[625]

Treatment: Not surprisingly, bystanders modify their behavior in the presence of a person of color, particularly during an interracial encounter.[626] One study found that, in such encounters, White individuals become increasingly uncomfortable and are more likely to respond defensively.[627] People of color also tend to change their

---

[618] Richardson, *supra* note 613, at 82.

[619] *See* sources cited *supra* notes 610–17.

[620] Trawalter et al., *supra* note 617, at 1327.

[621] Richardson, *supra* note 616, at 2044; *see also* Richardson, *supra* note 610, at 76 ("[T]his attentional bias is correlated not with conscious racial attitudes, but rather, with how strongly the perceiver unconsciously associates Blacks with danger.").

[622] Jules Holroyd, *Implicit Racial Bias and the Anatomy of Institutional Racism*, CTR. CRIME & JUSTICE STUDS., https://www.crimeandjustice.org.uk/publications/cjm/article/implicit-racial-bias-and-anatomy-institutional-racism (last visited January 27, 2019).

[623] *Id.; see also* B. Keith Payne, *Prejudice and Perception: The Role of Automatic and Controlled Processes in Misperceiving a Weapon*, 81 J. PERSONALITY & SOC. PSYCHOL. 181, 187 (2001) (providing results from an experiment testing the effect of racial information on the speed with which participants identified weapons).

[624] H. Andrew Sagar & Janet Ward Schofield, *Racial and Behavioral Cues in Black and White Children's Perceptions of Ambiguously Aggressive Acts*, 39 J. PERSONALITY & SOC. PSYCHOL. 590, 593–96 (1980).

[625] Richardson, *supra* note 610, at 77; *see also* Kurt Hugenberg & Galen V. Bodenhausen, *Facing Prejudice: Implicit Prejudice and the Perception of Facial Threat*, 14 PSYCHOL. SCI. 640, 640–43 (2003) (describing further the effects of racial bias on study participants' interpretation of facial expressions).

[626] *See* Jennifer A. Richeson & J. Nicole Shelton, *Stereotype Threat in Interracial Interactions, in* STEREOTYPE THREAT: THEORY, PROCESS, AND APPLICATION 231, 238 (Michael Inzlicht & Toni Schmader eds., 2012).

[627] *Id.*

behavior during interracial interactions, with their behaviors becoming "more rigid and less warm and friendly than [they] would be in a nonthreatening context."[628] These responses can make each party appear unfriendly and uncomfortable, which has the effect of "confirming" the implicit bias of Black people as hostile and aggressive.[629]

Police officers are not immune to the influence of implicit racial biases on their perceptions. Officers also experience attentional bias, interpretation bias, and treatment bias,[630] and those biases shape their interactions with Black people.

Attentional: In one study, researchers found that unconscious biases "associating Blacks with dangerousness caused officers' attention to be drawn to Black faces over White faces."[631] This study also showed that once an officer's attention was focused on a Black face, that attention was held longer than attention to a White face.[632]

Interpretation: Officers are more likely to interpret Black behavior as aggressive or dangerous. For instance, "the unconscious association between Blacks and crime influences how quickly officers identify weapons. In computer simulations, officers are quicker to determine that individuals are armed when they are Black as opposed to White."[633] Even when no evidence exists to suggest the presence of a weapon, "automatic stereotype activation can cause officers to interpret behavior as aggressive, violent, or suspicious even if identical behavior performed by a White individual would not be so interpreted."[634] The confronted individual may respond in kind, unconsciously fulfilling officers' beliefs that the individual is suspicious and aggressive.[635] Researchers have also observed that officers are more likely to assume a Black individual will view them as racist and illegitimate, increasing the likelihood that the officers will feel unsafe and thus further increasing the likelihood of an unnecessarily violent encounter.[636]

---

[628] Richardson, *supra* note 610, at 79 (alteration in original) (quoting Richeson and Shelton, *supra* note 626, at 238).

[629] *See* Tamara Rice Lave, *Ready, Fire, Aim: How Universities Are Failing the Constitution in Sexual Assault Cases*, 48 ARIZ. ST. L.J. 637, 676 (2016).

[630] *See* Richardson, *supra* note 610, at 74–77.

[631] *Id.* at 76 (citing Jennifer L. Eberhardt et al., *Seeing Black: Race, Crime, and Visual Processing*, 87 J. PERSONALITY & SOC. PSYCHOL. 876, 886–87 (2004)).

[632] *Id.*

[633] *Id.* at 77. Social psychologists explain this reaction as a consequence of automatic racial categorization; it simply "takes less time for the mind to process information that is congruent with racial stereotypes." *Id.* This automatic processing has two troubling effects. First, officers are more likely to act quickly on the incorrect belief that African-Americans are armed and to respond with unnecessary lethal force. *Id.* Second, officers may take longer to correctly identify that a White individual is armed, thus increasing the risk that the weapon will be used before police can respond. *Id.*

[634] Richardson, *supra* note 616, at 2053.

[635] This "stress of racial anxiety is associated with a variety of physiological responses including sweating, increased heart rate, facial twitches, fidgeting, and avoiding eye contact." Richardson, *supra* note 613, at 77 (footnotes omitted).

[636] *See* Phillip Atiba Goff et al., *Illegitimacy Is Dangerous: How Authorities Experience and React to Illegitimacy*, 4 PSYCHOL. 340, 343 (2013).

Treatment: Researchers also find that, when officers automatically focus attention on Black individuals as dangerous and unconsciously interpret their behaviors as hostile, they are more likely to conduct unnecessary stops and frisks triggered not by conscious racial animus but by implicit racial biases.[637] The objective but easily malleable standards of "reasonable suspicion" and "reasonable force" do little to constrain officers from acting on these implicit biases.[638]

In short, social cognition confirms how implicit biases "perpetuate discrimination through covertly influencing who is deemed suspicious, who is stopped and searched, who is deemed a threat, what determinations of 'reasonable force' are made, who is judged to be armed and dangerous, and who gets shot."[639]

6.2 400 YEARS OF HISTORY, ONE DAY OF RETRAINING

Rittenhouse Square is described as one of the "toniest neighborhoods" in Philadelphia. Its trendy restaurants and cocktail bars, high-end stores, and small art galleries make it a hotspot for wealthy out-of-towners and locals alike. Its residents are overwhelmingly white-collar and White.

Situated on the southeast edge of Rittenhouse Square, just below the posh David David Fine Art Gallery, sits a nondescript Starbucks Coffee Shop. Rashon Nelson, Donte Robinson, and Andrew Yaffe agreed to meet at this Starbucks on April 15, 2018, at 4:45 p.m. to discuss a business investment opportunity. Nelson and Robinson, who are Black, arrived at 4:35 p.m. and Nelson asked to use the restroom.[640] When the store manager stated that restrooms were for paying customers only, the two men "left it at that" and waited at a table for Yaffe to arrive.

At 4:37 p.m., the White store manager called 911, stating "I have two gentlemen in my café that are refusing to make a purchase or leave." At 4:41 p.m., six uniformed and armed police officers entered the Starbucks and immediately arrested Nelson and Robinson. Video footage of the incident shows that Nelson and Robinson were the only two Black individuals in the store at the time. Multiple patrons expressed disbelief that an arrest was taking place for something that "literally everyone does." The end of the video shows Yaffe, a Philadelphia-based real estate investment manager, arriving just in time to see his business associates led away in handcuffs.

As discussed in Chapter 2, this type of "Living While Black" injustice has received significant media coverage in recent years. The increased focus on informal racial

---

[637] Richardson, *supra* note 610, at 83 ("They will be stopped and frisked more often than similarly situated Whites, not because they are acting more suspiciously, but because implicit biases will impact how police interpret their ambiguous behaviors.").

[638] *Id.*

[639] Holroyd, *supra* note 622.

[640] This timeline is drawn from Daniel Craig, *It Took Two Minutes for Philly Starbucks Manager to Call Cops on Two Black Men,* Philly Voice (April 19, 2018), https://www.phillyvoice.com/philadelphia-starbucks-rashon-nelson-donte-robinson-black-men-arrested/. The article includes a link to audio of the manager's 911 call.

discrimination is a positive development in the ongoing conversation about race relations in America. It is particularly beneficial for White audiences in racially homogenous communities who may not understand the continued "obsession" over race dialogue. As explained by Robin DiAngelo, author of *White Fragility: Why It's So Hard for White People to Talk About Racism*, the deluge of videos and social media posts about biased 911 calls, racial hoaxes, and unprovoked shootings have made it more difficult to dismiss allegations of profiling. "These incidents have always happened, but white people do not always believe it because it doesn't happen to us. The only real difference we have now is that we are able to record it in a way that makes it undeniable."[641]

This consciousness-raising effort has another consequence: an explosion in the cottage industry of companies promising to retrain people to eliminate their racial biases. A flood of implicit bias retraining programs has appeared over the last ten years, with companies promising not only to make people aware of their biases but to remove them altogether. These programs attempt to make individuals aware of their biases and encourage them to refrain from acting on them.[642] Corporations in the United States began offering these trainings, often characterized as "diversity" trainings, in earnest in 2013.[643] Perhaps most famously, Starbucks closed nearly 8,000 store locations on May 29, 2018, to conduct mandatory racial bias training in response to the experience of Messrs. Nelson and Robinson.[644]

The response to Starbucks's action from implicit bias experts was as surprising as it was uniform: racial bias trainings simply do not work. Many pointed to the fact that these one-size-fits-all solutions are not sufficiently tailored to the unique problems faced in different locations by different people to have any real impact.[645] More fundamentally, though, implicit bias experts expressed grave skepticism that any such program can have a lasting impact on behavior. As Brian Nosek, a University of Virginia psychology professor and cofounder of a nonprofit organization promoting awareness of implicit bias, observed, "I have been studying this since 1996, and I still have implicit bias. . . . We can be sure that training by itself is not going to get rid of implicit bias."[646]

Perhaps most damning was the response of Anthony Greenwald, one of the creators of the Implicit Association Test that helps researchers and individuals

---

[641] P. R. Lockhart, *911 Calls on Black People Were One of 2018's Biggest Stories about Race*, Vox (December 31, 2018), https://www.vox.com/identities/2018/12/31/18159465/living-while-black-racial-profiling-911-police-racism.

[642] Mak, *supra* note 609.

[643] *Id.*

[644] Press Release, Starbucks, Starbucks to Close All Stores Nationwide for Racial-Bias Education on May 29 (April 17, 2018), https://news.starbucks.com/press-releases/starbucks-to-close-stores-nationwide-for-racial-bias-education-may-29.

[645] Mak, *supra* note 609.

[646] *Id.*

identify implicit bias. When asked to comment on Starbucks's training plan, Greenwald said:

> Starbucks would be wise to check out the scientific evidence on implicit bias training. . . . [T]his training has not been shown to be effective, and it can even be counterproductive. It will appear that Starbucks is doing the right thing, but the training is not likely to change anything. The Implicit Association Test is a valuable educational device to allow people to discover their own implicit biases. However, taking the IAT to discover one's own implicit biases does nothing to remove or reduce those implicit biases. Desire to act free of implicit bias is not sufficient to enable action free of implicit bias.[647]

The research supports these perspectives. A wide-ranging study of 800 US corporations that had implemented mandatory racial bias training "ultimately found that the positive effects of diversity training often don't last beyond two days, and may actually entrench biases due to backlash."[648] According to one of the study's authors, "The studies that look out six months to a year tend to be equally likely to show increased bias after the training as they are to show decreased bias."[649]

The limits of these retraining efforts are understandable, given the inherent and automatic nature of implicit bias. Indeed, bias is hardwired into a person's neurological circuitry: "Brain scans reveal that the amygdala, a part of the brain associated with fear, responds more when people view Black male faces as opposed to White male faces."[650] This kind of hard wiring can be almost impossible to undo, particularly when that wiring has been reinforced by a lifetime of perceptions reinforced by centuries of explicit racial bias.

But even if these institutional retraining programs worked, they would solve only one side of the implicit bias equation. The negative treatment people of color receive often causes them to respond in kind, creating a "self-fulfilling prophecy or behavioral confirmation effect."[651] Even when the police officer who interacts with them is not evidently bias-motivated, people of color may automatically respond with apprehension, aggression, or hostility – precisely the types of behaviors officers are trained to view with suspicion.[652] No amount of institutionalized police

[647] Katie Herzog, *Is Starbucks Implementing Flawed Science in Their Anti-Bias Traning?*, The Stranger (April 17, 2018), https://www.thestranger.com/slog/2018/04/17/26052277/is-starbucks-implementing-flawed-science-in-their-anti-bias-training.

[648] Mak, *supra* note 609; *see also* Frank Dobbin & Alexandra Kalev, *Why Diversity Programs Fail*, Harv. Bus. Rev., July–Aug. 2016, at 52–60.

[649] Mak, *supra* note 609. Similar studies have criticized the efficacy of racial bias training programs within police departments. *See* Tom James, *Can Cops Unlearn Their Unconscious Biases?*, Atlantic (December 23, 2017), https://www.theatlantic.com/politics/archive/2017/12/implicit-bias-training-salt-lake/548996/.

[650] Richardson, *supra* note 610, at 76.

[651] *Id.* at 80.

[652] *See* Richardson, *supra* note 616, at 2052 ("This behavioral confirmation effect 'provide[s] a powerful mechanism by which stereotypes and prejudicial behavior are maintained, propagated and justified'

department training can "retrain" the inherent distrust and fear people of color feel and exhibit when confronted by law enforcement.

Institutionalized racial bias trainings also do not alter the unconscious behaviors of the bias-motivated civilians who call police in the first place, at least in most situations. While Starbucks presumably sought to train its employees not to call the police on patrons for "living while Black," the typical civilian does not have the benefit of institutionally mandated sensitivity training when he or she calls 911 to report a suspicious person for sleeping while Black,[653] selling lemonade or water while Black,[654] or eating a sandwich while Black.[655]

The pervasiveness and permanence of racial fear, the limited efficacy of retraining programs in reducing racial fear, and the inability of these programs to address the fear of civilian bystanders all suggest that little can be done to reduce or eliminate racial bias from police interactions. In that sense, this chapter acts as a bridge between the first and second parts of this book. Chapters 1 through 5 identified and highlighted the problems of pervasive private policing of White and Black spaces, driven by racial fear and promoted by government institutions. Chapters 7 and 8 suggest solutions to begin dismantling this system of private violent racial policing. This chapter, by highlighting the unfortunate reality that the fear driving much of this system is ingrained, unconscious, and slow changing, provides context for why the balance of this book offers the solutions it does: solutions that shift away from trying to change the *quality* of police interactions with Black people and toward limiting the *quantity* of such interactions, including most notably those interactions primed by dubious private policing.

since 'the perceiver interprets the target's behavior in line with the expectancy and encodes yet another instance of stereotype-consistent behavior.'" (quoting Mark Chen & John A. Bargh, *Nonconscious Behavioral Confirmation Processes: The Self-Fulfilling Consequences of Automatic Stereotype Activation*, 33 J. EXPERIMENTAL SOC. PSYCHOL. 541, 542 (1997))).

[653] Cleve R. Wootson Jr., *A Black Yale Student Fell Asleep in Her Dorm's Common Room. A White Student Called the Police*, WASH. POST (May 11, 2018), https://www.washingtonpost.com/news/grade-point/wp/2018/05/10/a-black-yale-student-fell-asleep-in-her-dorms-common-room-a-white-student-called-police/.

[654] Drew Costley, *Black Owner of SF Lemonade Stand Has Police Called on Him While Trying to Open His Business*, SF GATE (July 22, 2018), https://www.sfgate.com/bayarea/article/Black-owner-of-SF-lemonade-police-Gourmonade-13094735.php; *Permit Patty: Woman 'Calls Police' on Eight-Year-Old for Selling Water*, BBC (June 25, 2018), https://www.bbc.com/news/newsbeat-44601668.

[655] Breanna Edwards, *#EatingOutWhileBlack: Subway Employee Calls 911 on Black Family Because She Thought They Would Rob Her*, ROOT (July 5, 2018), https://www.theroot.com/eatingoutwhile-Black-subway-employee-calls-911-on-blac-1827358215.

7

Rethinking Maximum Policing

Implicit racial biases are pervasive, permanent, and deadly. The autonomic nervous system responds to these biases automatically, sounding alarm bells when confronted with the targets of these biases, creating ever-present threats to Black bodies occupying public White spaces. The work of implicit bias researchers, diversity and inclusion awareness experts, and antiracism activists to identify and combat these internal messages is laudable and important. It is also generational. Four hundred years of anti-Black messaging cannot be erased in a half-day corporate training. Nor can the ascendance of Black people to positions of power and prestige create a "post-racial" society free of this baggage. Racial progress should be viewed as just that: progress. Not perfection. Incremental change can and does occur. But to claim that such progress has fixed – or in the short term can fix – the problem of weaponized racial fear is wrong and dangerous.

Why begin a chapter on "solutions" to the problems identified in this book with such a pessimistic assessment of the world? For one simple reason: because immediate solutions are needed to protect Black bodies from the violence of private policing in the near term while the long-term work of reprogramming a nation's psyche proceeds alongside them. A steady chorus of police reform advocates focus on improving the quality of interactions between officers and communities of color through improved "procedural justice," as well as funding for community outreach programs and other non-adversarial "community policing" initiatives.[656] These reforms may help generate long-term change, though their record is mixed at best. But to suggest they will protect the young Black boy strolling through a gentrified neighborhood today, at this very moment, ignores the cold, hard reality of ingrained

---

[656] See, e.g., President's Task Force on 21 st Century Policing, Final Report of the President's Task Force on 21 st Century Policing 9–11 (2015), https://d3n8a8pro7vhmx.cloudfront.net/nacole/pages/115/attachments/original/1570474092/President-Barack-Obama-Task-Force-on-21st-Century-Policing-Final-Report-min.pdf?1570474092 (describing "[b]uilding trust and nurturing legitimacy on both sides of the police-citizen divide" as "the foundational principle" for police reform); German Lopez, How to Reform American Police, According to Experts, Vox (June 1, 2020) https://www.vox.com/2020/6/1/21277013/police-reform-policies-systemic-racism-george-floyd (describing suggested reforms from police apologies for historic abuses to bias training to accountability regimes).

racial fear. It is this recognition that leads Mariama Kaba and other police abolitionists to declare, "The only way to diminish police violence is to reduce contact between the police and the public."[657]

Increased societal awareness of racial bias did not prevent Amy Cooper from dialing 911. Implicit bias initiatives did not stop the McMichaels from gunning down Ahmaud Arbery. Antiracism institutes and police sensitivity trainings did not stop Derek Chauvin from murdering George Floyd. Of course, no solution can entirely eliminate these racist acts. But policies aimed solely at improving dialogue when contact is made are doomed to fail those who must answer today for yesterday's sins. The risk that pernicious, largely unchangeable bias will lead to unnecessary use of force by cell phone warriors, civilian vigilantes, and aggressive police officers is simply too great to wait for the promise of a post-racial society.

Attempts to improve the *quality* of civilian and police contacts with Black persons in the White space *might* generate change over time. But in the near term, they will fall short; they will not protect Black lives or Black bodies from White racial fear. Our short-term focus should be on decreasing the *quantity* of contacts with this community. Policies aimed at preventing unnecessary, frivolous, involuntary encounters with the criminal justice system acknowledge the limited efficacy of individual retraining efforts; such efforts can help prevent what far too often becomes an inevitable cycle of escalation within that system. What begins as a meme-worthy but dehumanizing "Living While Black" moment can quickly become an unjustified arrest and leveraged plea bargain that ushers its target into a broken criminal justice system that all but promotes recidivism. A White person's call to the "cost-free protection agency"[658] to enforce the color line can lead to a life-altering use of excessive force that exacerbates community trauma and distrust. Or, as is far too often the case, another dead Black woman or man whose name becomes another rallying cry for change.

Changes aimed at limiting unnecessary contacts come in many forms, including deterring racist 911 abuse in the first place and punishing it when it occurs, increasing dispatcher and police discretion to ignore frivolous 911 calls, mandating alternative, nonpolice responses to emergency situations for which an armed officer is not necessary or helpful, and rethinking how police respond when they are required to react. Many of these proposals derive from the same basic premise: that a fundamental reallocation of police resources is both required and desirable if society is to prevent the continued weaponization of racial fear and the continued abuse of law enforcement by private actors.

---

[657] Mariame Kaba, *Yes, We Mean Literally Abolish the Police*, N.Y. TIMES (June 12, 2020), https://www.nytimes.com/2020/06/12/opinion/sunday/floyd-abolish-defund-police.html.

[658] *See* Aya Gruber, *Why Amy Cooper Felt the Police Were Her Personal "Protection Agency*," SLATE (May 27, 2020), https://slate.com/news-and-politics/2020/05/amy-cooper-white-women-policing.html.

To many, this call to reallocate police resources may sound like "Defund the Police," the controversial catchphrase that dominated the racial justice reform movement in 2020. A more modest and accurate characterization is that these proposals ask society to rethink what I call "maximum policing," a ubiquitous and dangerous approach to policing that calls on officers and departments to pursue, investigate, and arrest as much as resources will allow, and to do it as aggressively and violently as the law will allow. In the maximum policing model, 911 dispatchers send armed officers to every call whether or not criminal activity has been reported. Those officers respond in force, and always with guns. Militarized units respond to medical emergencies and minor disputes with weaponry better suited for the battlefield. The default law enforcement behavior is to conduct invasive stops and frisks, often accompanied by handcuffs, not because the situation demands it but because the law allows it. Maximum policing becomes a tool for racist over-policing when departments engage in proactive, dragnet-style invasions of poor Black neighborhoods. When weaponized by White caller criminals, maximum policing allows the misuse of police to give legitimacy to the private enforcement of the White space.

Rethinking maximum policing calls for a racial fear détente, one that takes the attention of both private actors and police away from enforcing the color line while the difficult work of antiracism retraining takes root.

7.1 THE MIRAGE OF COMMUNITY POLICING

An exploration of failed attempts to improve the quality of police contacts with Black communities is necessary to understand the need to reduce the quantity of police contacts with these communities. That exploration begins with the checkered history of "community policing" in the United States. Community policing refers broadly to an approach to policing that focuses on building collaborative partnerships with community stakeholders with the aim of addressing problems proactively and cooperatively rather than reactively and unilaterally. According to the US Department of Justice Community Oriented Policing Services (COPS) office, "Community policing is a philosophy that promotes organizational strategies that support the systematic use of partnerships and problem-solving techniques to proactively address the immediate conditions that give rise to public safety issues such as crime, social disorder, and fear of crime."[659] In contrast to the reactive policing approaches that preceded it, community policing is proactive,

---

[659]   U.S. DEPARTMENT OF JUSTICE, COMMUNITY ORIENTED POLICING SERVICES (COPS), COMMUNITY POLICING DEFINED 1 (2014), https://cops.usdoj.gov/RIC/Publications/cops-p157-pub.pdf [hereinafter COMMUNITY POLICING DEFINED]. *See also* Bureau of Justice Statistics, *Community Policing*, https://www.bjs.gov/index.cfm?ty=tp&tid=81 ("Community-oriented policing seeks to address the causes of crime and to reduce fear of social disorder through problem-solving strategies and police-community partnerships.").

seeking to prevent crime, eliminate fear, and build trust in the police.[660] The goal of community policing is to create "a collaboration between the police and the community that identifies and solves community problems."[661] Police agencies that follow the community policing model are organized to "infuse community policing ideals throughout the agency" and create a culture that values proactivity, problem solving, and partnership.[662]

Community policing emerged in the 1980s as a response to a number of forces. First, the professionalization of the police in the middle of the twentieth century had produced bureaucratic, inwardly focused organizations with arcane rules, their difference made visible by uniforms and other trappings of militarization.[663] The aggressive tactics used by these forces created resentment in communities, particularly among the young, minority men who were often their target.[664] At the same time, technology fundamentally changed police work; police were increasingly in cars and on radios rather than on the street in the communities they patrolled.[665] All of these factors served to isolate police from the people they ostensibly served.

The civil and political unrest of the 1960s amplified the growing tensions between police and communities. The often brutal police responses to the Civil Rights movement and Vietnam War protests drew severe criticism.[666] Several national commissions, created to investigate the sources of unrest, identified the police as a primary source of tension.[667] In response to these criticisms, police agencies across the country reconsidered their isolated, bureaucratic structures. Community policing emerged from these reexaminations; the model broke into the mainstream of policing by the 1980s.[668] The goal of the new strategy was to improve relations between police and the communities they served, primarily by decentralizing the police organization.[669] The focus of community policing thus was less about reactive law enforcement and more on proactive crime prevention.[670]

---

[660] COMMUNITY POLICING DEFINED, *supra* note 659, at 2, 13.

[661] U.S. DEPARTMENT OF JUSTICE, BUREAU OF JUSTICE ASSISTANCE, UNDERSTANDING COMMUNITY POLICING: A FRAMEWORK FOR ACTION vii (1994), https://www.ncjrs.gov/pdffiles/commp.pdf.

[662] *Id.* at 5.

[663] Gary Potter, *The History of Policing in the United States, Part 5* (July 23, 2013), https://plsonline.eku.edu/insidelook/history-policing-united-states-part-5.

[664] *Id.*

[665] *Id.*

[666] Gary Potter, *The History of Policing in the United States, Part 6* (July 30, 2013), https://plsonline.eku.edu/insidelook/history-policing-united-states-part-6.

[667] *Id.*

[668] *Id.*

[669] *Id. See also* ELAINE B. SHARP, DOES LOCAL GOVERNMENT MATTER? HOW URBAN POLICIES SHAPE CIVIC ENGAGEMENT 77 (2012) ("In its most quintessential form, community policing involves three elements: problem solving, citizen involvement, and decentralization.").

[670] Sharp, *supra* note 669, at 78.

7.2 TOWARD MAXIMUM POLICING

A collaborative, proactive approach to preventing crime that includes broad involvement from non-officer community members sounds empowering and peaceful. Indeed, when successful, community policing advocates claim these policies make the police "an agency of empowerment" in the community.[671] But almost immediately after the broad theoretical adoption of community policing in the early 1980s, a particularly punitive and aggressive form of community policing began taking root in departments across the country: "broken windows" policing.

Broken windows policing, discussed previously in Chapter 2, posited that small outbreaks of disorder – in the form of unmaintained property or unchecked "socially undesirable" behavior – lead to larger outbreaks of disorder, in the form of crime.[672] From this perspective, the best way to prevent serious crime is to punish small infractions, to have police on the street issuing citations for things like broken windows. The criminologists behind the theory suggested that police should shift focus, from solving crimes to literally "clean[ing] up the streets."[673] Of course, implementing this theory requires dramatic increases in police budgets, police street presence, and police contact with the community. Such police omnipresence, even if employed collaboratively and in partnership with community stakeholders, often causes uneasiness within communities traditionally oppressed by government forces.[674]

Broken windows is a kind of community policing. Community policing itself is a broad model premised on increased police contact with communities; that contact can take a range of forms, from true "partnership models" that emphasize working with the community to "aggressive order-maintenance practice," which uses coercive action to enforce order.[675] George Kelling himself envisioned broken windows policing beginning with *residents* identifying their concerns and police acting accordingly.[676] But in the decades since its introduction, the broken windows theory has evolved into a justification for broad, oppressive overpolicing tactics that bear no

---

[671] Madeleine Smith, *The Camden County (NJ) Police Department: An Agency of Empowerment*, DISPATCH (October 2019), https://cops.usdoj.gov/html/dispatch/10-2019/camden.html. *See also* Sarah Holder, *The City That Remade Its Police Department*, BLOOMBERG BUSINESSWEEK (June 4, 2020), https://www.bloomberg.com/news/articles/2020-06-04/how-camden-new-jersey-reformed-its-police-department.

[672] Kelling & Wilson, *supra* note 233.

[673] Shankar Vedantam at al., *How a Theory of Crime and Policing Was Born, and Went Terribly Wrong*, NPR: HIDDEN BRAIN (November 1, 2016), https://www.npr.org/2016/11/01/500104506/broken-windows-policing-and-the-origins-of-stop-and-frisk-and-how-it-went-wrong.

[674] Holder, *supra* note 671. Importantly, it's unclear whether proactive policing – methods such as community policing or broken windows policing – are effective in reducing crime. At least one study shows the opposite. Christopher M. Sullivan & Zachary P. O'Keeffe, *Evidence That Curtailing Proactive Policing Can Reduce Major Crime*, 1 NATURE HUMAN BEHAVIOUR 730 (2017).

[675] Sharp, *supra* note 669, at 81.

[676] Sarah Childress, *The Problem with "Broken Windows" Policing*, PBS: FRONTLINE (June 28, 2016), https://www.pbs.org/wgbh/frontline/article/the-problem-with-broken-windows-policing/.

resemblance to the partnership and empowerment ideals of early community policing advocates.

Perhaps the most notorious example of this evolution is New York City, where Rudy Giuliani was elected mayor in 1993 on a promise to reduce crime in the city by fully implementing broken windows policing in the NYPD.[677] That implementation took the form of an aggressive enforcement strategy, accomplished through significant increases in police department budgets and personnel, that included arresting people and levying heavy fines for minor offenses such as graffiti, turnstile jumping, and panhandling.[678] Giuliani also authorized police chief Bill Bratton to create a computer-driven comparative statistical program called CompStat, which ostensibly allowed officers to map crime geographically and charted officer performance by quantifying criminal apprehensions.[679] Not surprisingly, this system incentivized officers to investigate, contact, and arrest as many people as possible, and to do so in Black and Brown neighborhoods where questionable (and at times, outright manipulated) data pointed to "emerging crime patterns."[680]

This initiative, hailed by Harvard's Kennedy School of Government for its innovation,[681] further evolved under Mayor Michael Bloomberg into an explicit and pervasive "stop and frisk" program that authorized involuntary seizures and searches of individuals on reasonable suspicion of minor "broken windows-style" offenses.[682]

This punitive, maximum policing interpretation of community policing should have come as no surprise. Giving already powerful armed government agents more power and discretion to enter communities and contact as many comparatively powerless civilians as possible was always destined to result in a consolidation of that power. Moreover, America's long history of resolving social disputes punitively and violently foretold the consequences of unleashing armies of armed officers competing with one another to enforce as many minor violations of social order as possible.

The timing of maximum policing's arrival in the early 1980s was no accident either. It arrived as part of a larger American move toward a "punishing

---

[677] Vedantam et al., *supra* note 673.

[678] *Id. See also* Rocco Parascandola et al., *NYPD Chief Bratton Releases Report on Why "Broken Windows" Policing Works*, DAILY NEWS (May 1, 2015), https://www.nydailynews.com/new-york/nyc-crime/nypd-bratton-releases-report-broken-windows-works-article-1.2204978.

[679] Chris Smith, *The Controversial Crime-Fighting Program That Changed Big-City Policing Forever*, N.Y. INTELLIGENCER (March 2018), https://nymag.com/intelligencer/2018/03/the-crime-fighting-program-that-changed-new-york-forever.html.

[680] Ash Center for Democratic Governance and Innovation, Harvard Kennedy School, *CompStat: A Crime Reduction Management Tool*, GOVERNMENT INNOVATORS NETWORK: INNOVATIONS IN AMERICAN GOVERNMENT AWARDS (1996), https://www.innovations.harvard.edu/compstat-crime-reduction-management-tool.

[681] *Id.*

[682] Vedantam et al., *supra* note 673. Kelling and Wilson acknowledged the danger of giving police wide discretion to rein in disorder. *Id.* (quoting Kelling & Wilson, *supra* note 233).

democracy"[683] that supports a "thin safety net, [and] an expansive security state."[684] Erica Meiner traces the roots of this shift to the drive to shrink government, to "get big government off the backs of the working people."[685] Often, Meiner points out, shrinking government meant only shrinking specific parts of the government – typically social safety net programs.[686] Thus, in the forty years since President Reagan's call for "smaller government" first gained traction, social safety net programs, such as housing, food assistance, and unemployment insurance, have shrunk steadily while funding for law enforcement agencies – the Drug Enforcement Agency, the Bureau of Prisons, and Immigration and Customs Enforcement – have grown by 10 percent a year or more.[687] This transition, Meiner argues, has its roots in White supremacy; the creation of the prison-industrial complex relied on an interlocking set of race-based stereotypes, including welfare queens and superpredators.[688] Thus, the "smaller government" regime requires "the maintenance and reinvention of longstanding tropes about race and gender."[689]

Likewise, the single largest problem with broken windows-style maximum policing continues to be a race problem. The central underlying premise in broken windows policing is that social disorder must be snuffed out before it grows into crime. But whose conception of "disorder" matters? Definitions of disorder, and perceptions of what is disorder, are highly freighted – "racially loaded, culturally loaded, politically loaded."[690] One study found that people saw more disorder in Black neighborhoods than in other neighborhoods with the same level of graffiti, litter, and loitering.[691] To the extent broken windows still retains any resident-driven partnership, these private, racist views of disorder drive disproportionate police presence to Black neighborhoods with a charge to "clean them up."

These are not simply the costs of an otherwise effective method of crime reduction and prevention. In fact, very little evidence exists to suggest that broken windows maximum policing actually reduces crime.[692] Broad reductions in violent crime in

---

[683] Erica R. Meiners, *Building an Abolition Democracy; or, The Fight Against Public Fears, Private Benefits, and Prison Expansion, in* CHALLENGING THE PRISON-INDUSTRIAL COMPLEX 15, 19 (Stephen John Hartnett ed., 2011).

[684] Annie Lowrey, *Defund the Police*, THE ATLANTIC (June 5, 2020), https://www.theatlantic.com/ideas/archive/2020/06/defund-police/612682/.

[685] Meiners, *supra* note 683, at 20.

[686] *Id.*

[687] *Id.* In other words, "the United States has an extreme budget commitment ... to law and order, meted out discriminately. It has an equally extreme budget commitment to food support, aid for teenage parents, help for the homeless, child care for working families, safe housing, and so on. It feeds the former and starves the latter." Lowrey, *supra* note 684. Meiners points out that calls for smaller government extend back at least to Reconstruction, but the political and economic context of the 1970s allowed the ideas to enter the mainstream. Meiners, *supra* note 683, at 21–23.

[688] Meiners, *supra* note 683, at 23.

[689] *Id.*

[690] Childress, *supra* note 676 (internal quotation marks omitted).

[691] Vedantam et al., *supra* note 673.

[692] *Id.*; Childress, *supra* note 676.

New York City during the Giuliani and Bloomberg administrations are more commonly and convincingly explained by other sociocultural factors, including growing economic prosperity and a corresponding drop in crime rates across the country. What broken windows policing does do, however, is "strain criminal justice systems, burden impoverished people with fines for minor offenses, and fracture the relationship between police and minorities."[693]

7.3 THE FALSE PROMISE OF PROCEDURAL JUSTICE

Decades of maximum policing, disproportionately in communities of color, has increased already significant feelings of distrust and resentment of police in these communities. These feelings have been further exacerbated by the disproportionately hostile, violent treatment Black and Brown targets receive from officers during involuntary encounters. As discussed in greater detail in Chapter 2, Black targets of police attention report significantly higher levels of disrespectful language from officers, violations of constitutional rights, and unnecessary force, such as the use of handcuffs and chokeholds during peaceful encounters. These procedural inequities have led many police reform advocates to focus their attention on procedural justice, which aims to rework the *process* of policing, to improve the quality of police–civilian interactions without meaningfully changing substantive community policing practices.

The death of George Floyd presents a particularly powerful argument for the failure of such procedural justice reform. In 2015, the Minneapolis Police Department was one of six selected to train in a new kind of policing, one that emphasized racial reconciliation and trust building.[694] A 2018 MPD report characterized the department as "a national leader in procedural justice initiatives."[695] According to longtime police abolitionist Alex S. Vitale, the problem with procedural justice, which has become the dominant approach in police reform, is that it focuses on the processes of justice – making people feel better about their interactions with police – instead of addressing failures of substantive justice.[696]

---

[693] Childress, *supra* note 676.

[694] Zachary Siegel, "*Starve the Beast": A Q&A with Alex S. Vitale on Defunding the Police*, THE NATION (June 4, 2020), https://www.thenation.com/article/society/alex-vitale-defund-police-interview/.

[695] *Id.* (quoting Minneapolis Police Dep't., 2018: *Focusing on Procedural Justice Internally and Externally* (2018), https://www.insidempd.com/wp-content/uploads/2018/07/Focusing-on-Procedural-Justice-Internally-and-Externally-2018-5.pdf).

[696] *Id.* Vitale is the author of *The End of Policing* (2017), which argues that modern policing is a tool not of justice but of social control that does not provide the protection it promises. *See also* Alex S. Vitale, *The Answer to Police Violence Is Not "Reform." It's Defunding. Here's Why*, GUARDIAN (May 31, 2020), https://www.theguardian.com/commentisfree/2020/may/31/the-answer-to-police-violence-is-not-reform-its-defunding-heres-why. For a critique of Vitale's arguments, *see* Matthew Yglesias, *The End of Policing Left Me Convinced We Still Need Policing*, VOX (June 18, 2020), https://www.vox.com/2020/6/18/21293784/alex-vitale-end-of-policing-review.

Substantive justice includes, among other things, reducing the amount of actual contact between police and citizens. Such a reduction can be accomplished in a number of ways, including legalizing or decriminalizing drug possession and other minor "social disorder" offenses and more tightly regulating, through law or policy, the standards by which officers can seize individuals on reasonable suspicion or probable cause. But the single most effective way to reduce unnecessary police contact as a form of substantive justice is to remove police from situations where their limited expertise in crime prevention is not necessary. Decoupling armed police from the enforcement of civil infractions, removing "warrior cops" from noncriminal mental health episodes, and requiring police and dispatchers to ignore clearly frivolous complaints designed to weaponize law enforcement are the types of substantive justice reform that can immediately demilitarize the color line in America – without legislative or constitutional change.

"Budget interventions," as Vitale calls them, are the beginning of that process.[697] While Vitale aligns himself with the abolitionist movement, he "understand[s] abolition as about a process more than an outcome."[698] The focus is not on the end goal of eliminating the police, he says, but on the process of reshaping the institutions involved and their relationships to the communities they are supposed to serve. "What's important," he says, is "creat[ing] a new understanding of what we mean by justice that is not rooted in punishment and revenge, but rooted instead in trying to build people up to restore relationships, to strengthen communities."[699] Similarly, Mariame Kaba calls for abolition of the police in the long term; in the meantime, she argues, "The only way to diminish police violence is to reduce contact between the police and the public."[700] The quickest way to do that, she argues, is to cut police departments in half, in terms of both staffing and budget.[701]

7.4 WHAT DOES "DEFUND THE POLICE" REALLY MEAN?

Cutting police departments in half sounds a lot like "Defunding the Police." And indeed, Kaba clarified her personal position in a June 2020 *New York Times* opinion piece: "Yes, we mean literally abolish the police." This complete abolitionist stance is not new, nor is the actual phrase "Defund the Police," which became a popular rallying cry during the Civil Rights Movement. But the phrase has a range of meanings, supported by different elements of the movement behind it, from literally

[697]   Siegel, *supra* note 694.
[698]   *Id.*
[699]   *Id.*
[700]   Kaba, *supra* note 657. Kaba provides an overview of various investigations of police misconduct in the nation's history, none of which changed police behavior.
[701]   *Id.*

defunding and completely dismantling the police to more modestly reducing police budgets and "unbundling" services currently provided by the police.[702]

At one extreme is the call for completely dismantling the police, which sits as one element of a wider movement, abolition democracy.[703] Supporters of abolition democracy argue that upending fractured police–community relationships requires more than reform, which focuses on correcting extreme dysfunctions without changing the existing system. Rather, punitive, legal approaches to justice should be replaced with "a holistic engagement with the structural conditions that give rise to suffering, as well as the interpersonal dynamics involved in violence."[704] In contrast to current forms of legal justice, which focus on punishment or restitution, abolitionist conceptions of justice seek "accountability and repair" and seek to address structural sources of violence and poverty.[705] These arguments extend not just to law enforcement, but also to punishment; advocates of abolition democracy call for the abolition of prisons as well as police.[706]

Defunding the police, in its mainstream meaning, calls not for eliminating the police force entirely but for reducing its size and power – reducing funding, reducing officer numbers, eliminating militarized weaponry and training, and redirecting funding to social programs that have been shown to reduce poverty and violence. This version of defund the police goes by several names, including Invest/Divest[707]

---

[702] For an overview of the varieties of meanings embedded in "defund the police" with useful links, *see* Matthew Yglesias, *Growing Calls to "Defund the Police," Explained*, Vox (June 3, 2020), https://www.vox.com/2020/6/3/21276824/defund-police-divest-explainer. The *New York Times* provides an overview of more moderate positions, as well as a quick note on current city actions. Dionne Searcy, *What Would Efforts to Defund or Disband Police Departments Really Mean?*, N.Y. Times (June 8, 2020), https://www.nytimes.com/2020/06/08/us/what-does-defund-police-mean.html. *Forbes* also offers a good overview with current links, including the appearance of "defund the police" in presidential politics. Jack Brewster, *The Defund the Police Movement Is Sweeping the Country – Here's What It Really Means*, Forbes (June 10, 2020), https://www.forbes.com/sites/jackbrewster/2020/06/09/the-defund-the-police-movement-is-sweeping-the-country-heres-what-it-really-means/. The *Christian Science Monitor* also offers a useful "explainer." Harry Bruinius, *"Defund the Police": What Does It Really Mean? Three Questions*, Christian Science Monitor (June 16, 2020), https://www.csmonitor.com/USA/Justice/2020/0616/Defund-the-police-What-does-it-really-mean-Three-questions.

[703] *Autostraddle* offers a good overview of current abolitionist thinking with links to resources that address specific questions. Rachel, *Police and Prison Abolition 101: A Syllabus and FAQ*, Autostraddle: Politics + Activism (June 2, 2020), https://www.autostraddle.com/police-and-prison-abolition-101-a-syllabus-and-faq/.

[704] Allegra M. McLeod, *Envisioning Abolitionist Democracy*, Harv. L. Rev. 1613, 1616 (2019).

[705] *Id.*

[706] *See, e.g.*, Meiners, *supra* note 683. Ruth Wilson Gilmore is a leader in the prison abolition movement. A recent *New York Times* profile offers an overview of her thinking along with a brief history of the movement. Rachel Kushner, *Is Prison Necessary? Ruth Wilson Gilmore Might Change Your Mind*, N.Y. Times Mag. (April 17, 2019), https://www.nytimes.com/2019/04/17/magazine/prison-abolition-ruth-wilson-gilmore.html.

[707] *See, e.g.*, Center for Popular Democracy et al., Freedom to Thrive: Reimagining Safety and Security in Our Communities (2019), https://populardemocracy.org/news/publications/freedom-thrive-reimagining-safety-security-our-communities; *see also* Brentin Mock, *The Price of Defunding*

and "unbundle the police."[708] All of these varieties of defund the police start from the premise that police have been tasked to do things that have little or nothing to do with criminal law enforcement, from responding to medical emergencies and triaging mental health crises to addressing homelessness and clearing fender benders.[709] This proliferation of roles for the police both increases their presence in citizens' everyday lives and introduces the "punitive impulse" into situations where it does not belong, criminalizing social issues likehomelessness and medical issues like substance abuse and mental illness.[710] In this version of defund the police, police forces shrink because their jobs shrink; police are involved only in matters related to serious crime. The money that once went to maintaining massive, militarized police forces is redirected to a range of social supports that reduce the structural pressures that lead to violence and provide nonpunitive means to address conflict.

Most activists, when they talk about defunding the police, mean that governments should fund social services and thereby reduce the scope of what police have to do. But whatever activists mean by the phrase, what they communicate to mainstream society is something decidedly different and more radical. Defunding, in rhetoric and in reality, is usually a tool to cripple or eliminate an organization, not reform it. When national Republicans threaten to "Defund NPR" or "Defund Planned Parenthood," they do not intend to redesign the funding mechanisms for public radio or women's health clinics, or find alternate ways to support the work they do. They want to destroy these "bastions of liberalism." When "defund the police" reemerged as a rallying cry for police reform advocates in 2020, the voting public heard "abolish the police."

And that interpretation had an effect at the polls. What was widely expected to be a Democratic landslide in the House of Representatives and a liberal retaking of the Senate never materialized, and surveys showed that the albatross of the phrase "defund the police" hanging around vulnerable Democrats played a role in the outcomes of tight races. When asked if they supported "reducing funding for the police in your community in order to fund an increase in social services for programs like housing and mental health," this initiative polled seventeen points better than "defunding the police." When asked about "redirecting funding for the police department in your local community to support community development pro-grams," the idea outpolled "defund the police" by thirty-one points. When partici-pants were asked about "gradually redirecting police funding toward increasing the number of social workers, drug counselors and mental health experts responsible for responding to non-violent emergencies," that formulation outpolled "defund the

the Police, BLOOMBERG CITYLAB (July 14, 2017), https://www.bloomberg.com/news/articles/2017-07-14/what-it-really-means-to-divest-from-policing.

[708] Derek Thompson, *Unbundle the Police*, ATLANTIC (June 11, 2020), https://www.theatlantic.com/ideas/archive/2020/06/unbundle-police/612913/.

[709] Sarah Jones, *We Are Asking the Police to Do Too Much*, N.Y. INTELLIGENCER (June 2, 2020), https://nymag.com/intelligencer/2020/06/killing-of-george-floyd-shows-our-over-reliance-on-police.html.

[710] *Id.*

police" by 37 percent. Attempts to explain the word "defund" did not help. For example, when any of these more palatable descriptions was combined with the word "defund," support for the proposal cratered. This reality led President Obama to decry the "snazzy" slogan in a post-election interview, claiming that dozens of Democrats potentially lost races over a single word.

Of course, activism and electoral politics do not always, or often, share the same objective. Yale psychology professor and cofounder of the Center for Policing Equity Phillip Atiba Goff said as much, when he asked rhetorically in response to Obama's assessment, "Can we fixate any harder on this absurd narrative that activist language should only serve electoral ends, thereby alienating the folks who made electoral victory possible? 'Yes we can!'" Kaba also responded to Democratic lawmakers' attempts to "repackage" radical police reform as something more modest, noting that activism and politics often do not mix. Moreover, there often is a positive political calculation to be made by staking out less mainstream ground in an attempt to move the acceptable range of mainstream thought closer to your position – to shift the "Overton window," in the words of political theorists. But, at least in this instance, it appears that policies centered on reallocating police resources and retreating from a position of maximum policing already enjoys widespread support.[711] It is the slogan that people detest.

While unbundlers and abolitionists may argue about how best and how radically to reform policing, they share the common belief that reducing unnecessary police contact is a critical step in reducing unnecessary police violence. It also is essential to disarming cell phone warriors and other private policers of the color line who seek to weaponize the maximum policing state and remove all "social disorder" from their White space. Those reforms must account not just for how police proactively seek out contact with civilians, but also for how they react to racist 911 abuse. To accomplish this broad goal, reforms must do three things: (1) deter White caller criminals from picking up the phone; (2) authorize dispatchers and police to ignore 911 abusers; and (3) punish these racist acts as what they are – armed hate crimes.

7.5 PUT THE PHONE DOWN

The first step is to end misuse of the 911 system to enforce the color line.[712] Current tools to accomplish this goal are woefully inadequate. Most jurisdictions impose some form of liability for frivolous misuse of the 911 system.[713] Typically these statutes criminalize behavior such as dialing 911 to make a false report or

---

[711] William Saletan, *"Defund the Police" is a Self-Destructive Slogan*, Slate (November 19, 2020), https://www.msn.com/en-us/news/politics/e2-80-9cdefund-the-police-e2-80-9d-is-a-self-destructive-slogan/ar-BB1b9cuJ.

[712] Much of this section is reprinted with permission from an earlier article I wrote on this subject, published in the Tulane Law Review. *See Fields, supra* note 30.

[713] *See, e.g.*, Christina M. Eastman, *Chapter 89: Rescuing 911?*, 40 McGEORGE L. REV. 486, 490 (2009).

nonemergency request, preventing another person from making a 911 call, or dialing 911 to relay a prerecorded message.[714] But many of these jurisdictions only impose modest fines after multiple documented instances of abuse.[715] Moreover, many states are unable to meaningfully enforce their 911 abuse laws because of the decentralized, regional nature of 911 call centers, lack of information sharing between dispatchers, and lack of knowledge regarding the identities of the callers themselves.[716] As a result, these laws do little to deter frivolous abuse of the system, as demonstrated by the high volume of abusive 911 calls and comparatively few enforcement measures taken in response.[717]

The most common legislation addressing 911 abuse are "false alarm" laws, which punish those who use 911 to report a false alarm.[718] These laws punish only a narrow, specific type of 911 abuse and do nothing to deter the vast majority of nonemergency calls, including racially motivated calls. Other state laws cover a broader range of 911 abuse, but impose heightened, subjective requirements, rendering enforcement virtually impossible. In Massachusetts, "maliciously" calling 911 is a misdemeanor, but the law requires a finding that the caller acted with a specific intent to harm another person.[719] Other states, including California and Tennessee, use unhelpful, broad language that makes it a misdemeanor to call 911 for "any reason other than because of an emergency."[720] Individual Louisiana parishes also prohibit calls without "a legitimate and justified purpose for the presence of police, fire or emergency medical personnel."[721] These statutes help by clearly prohibiting the "broken toilet" 911 call,[722] but are too vague to meaningfully address racially motivated calls.

---

[714]   Veronica Rose, *Information on 9–1–1 Laws* (Off. Leg. Rsch., Research Report 2006-R-0118, 2006), https://www.cga.ct.gov/2006/rpt/2006-R-0118.htm (analyzing 9–1–1 abuse laws in Connecticut, Maine, New Hampshire, New Jersey, and Rhode Island).

[715]   *See, e.g., id.*

[716]   *See* Weaver, *supra* note 270.

[717]   Eastman, *supra* note 713, at 492.

[718]   *See, e.g.,* ALA. CODE § 13A-10-9 (2015) ("A person commits the crime of false reporting to law enforcement authorities if he knowingly makes a false report."); HAW. REV. STAT. § 710-1014.5 (2018) ("A person commits the offense of misuse of 911 emergency telephone service if the person ... [k]nowingly causes a false alarm"); IND. CODE § 35-44.1-2-3(d) (2018) ("A person who ... gives a false report of the commission of a crime ... commits a Class B misdemeanor.").

[719]   MASS. GEN. LAWS. ANN. ch. 269, § 14B (2008); see also PENN. CH. 5.21.020. MASS. GEN. LAWS. ch. 269 § 14B (2018). In particular, subsection A makes it an offense to "willfully and maliciously communicates with a PSAP, or causes a communication to be made to a PSAP, which communication transmits information which the person knows or has reason to know is false and which results in the dispatch of emergency services to a nonexistent emergency."

[720]   CAL. PENAL CODE § 653y(a) (West 2018) ("A person who knowingly allows the use of or who uses the 911 emergency system for any reason other than because of an emergency is guilty of an infraction."); TENN. CODE ANN. § 7-86-316(a) (2018) ("Contacting 911 for some purpose other than to report an emergency ... is a Class C misdemeanor.").

[721]   TANGIPAHOA PARISH, LA., CODE OF ORDINANCES, pt. II, § 16-10 (2018).

[722]   *See supra* text accompanying note 721.

Furthermore, some states only impose liability for the second instance of documented abuse, with fines and jail time increasing with each subsequent violation.[723] But these laws are also unenforceable, because 911 call centers are managed regionally, not by state, and the various call centers within each state do not typically have the infrastructure, resources, or time to share and cross-reference records of frivolous calls.[724] For example, a California caller could make frivolous calls in rapid succession to San Diego, Los Angeles, Sacramento, and Oakland with little chance of facing liability for their "second-time" offense.

Oregon has perhaps the most robust, carefully tailored 911 abuse legislation. Oregon law makes it a misdemeanor to call 911 "for a purpose other than to report a situation that the person reasonably believes requires prompt service in order to preserve human life or property."[725] This connection to immediacy and preservation of life and property helpfully eliminates calls for golfing too slowly or failing to make a purchase in a coffee shop.

This statute provides a useful starting point to address and deter racially motivated 911 calls. Reducing the epidemic of 911 abuse choking the emergency response system requires a more robust, coherent, and enforceable deterrent mechanism. That deterrent and punishment mechanism is even more necessary for racist 911 calls, whose deleterious impacts on human dignity, corrosive effect on community trust, and potentially lethal consequences require a more serious deterrent response.[726]

An increasing chorus of commentators and legislators have argued for zero-tolerance policies that impose harsh criminal penalties or costly civil liability for a single nonemergency call.[727] And states have started to respond, although somewhat haphazardly. A New Jersey lawmaker "proposed legislation to apply a criminal penalty to someone who 'knowingly provides false information to a law enforcement officer with the purpose to implicate another because of race.'"[728] In August 2018, New York State Senator Jesse Hamilton proposed legislation making racially motivated 911 calls a hate crime after a White woman called police on him for "campaigning while black" in her neighborhood.[729]

---

[723] *See, e.g.*, Cal. Penal Code § 653y(a)(1)-(2) ("For a first violation, a written warning shall be issued ... For a second or subsequent violation, a citation may be issued by the public safety entity originally receiving the telephone call.").

[724] *See* Eastman, *supra* note 713, at 493.

[725] Or. Rev. Stat. § 165.570(a) (2017).

[726] *See* Patton & Farley, *supra* note 27 ("Right now, calling 911 on innocent black people is a costless form of indulgence in racialized fear – or worse, racist amusement. But lawsuits and publicity might make callers think twice and decrease the danger of false arrest and death.").

[727] *See id.*

[728] Weaver, *supra* note 270.

[729] Madeleine Thompson, N.Y. *Bill Would Outlaw Racially Biased 911 Calls*, Phila. Trib. (August 21, 2018), http://www.phillytrib.com/news/n-y-bill-would-outlaw-racially-biased-calls/article_8aef8926-c27b-5052-96ad-a0b76341a487.html.

Others have suggested that targeted individuals could use tort law and sue for defamation, malicious prosecution, or intentional infliction of emotional distress, to hold 911 abusers accountable through civil lawsuits.[730] In 2019, Oregon and Washington amended their existing 911 abuse statutes to authorize some civil relief for targets of 911 abuse. In 2020, the San Francisco Board of Supervisors unanimously approved hate crime legislation giving the targets of racist 911 calls the ability to sue the caller. The act gained national notoriety for its name – the Caution Against Racial and Exploitative Non-Emergencies Act, or CAREN Act – a clear nod to the popular meme using the name "Karen" to describe an entitled White woman whose actions, most often using police to target people of color, stem from her privilege. This evocation of a sexist pop-culture meme, which inaccurately singles out women for enforcing the color line and stems largely from tired tropes about nagging and complaining middle-aged women, overshadowed an otherwise robust municipal reform.[731] Supervisor Shamann Walton, who introduced the measure, explained that it was designed to "emphasize that 911 is not a customer service line for some-one's racist behavior."

Other states have since attempted to update their criminal codes to respond to White caller crime. In the wake of the Birdwatching While Black incident and 2020's Summer of Racial Reckoning, the legislatures in New York and California pushed to pass 911 abuse laws that imposed lengthy criminal sentences for race-based frivolous calls. In New York, Governor Andrew Cuomo revived a 2018 bill first introduced by Assemblyman Felix Ortiz that would classify false police reports (including 911 calls) motivated by race, color, nationality, ancestry, gender, religion or religious practice, age, sexual orientation, or disability as hate crimes punishable by one to five years in prison. In California, Assemblymember Rob Bonta introduced a similar bill that would add making a false emergency report motivated by race to the state's hate crimes statute, which already authorizes prison sentences up to ten years. In explaining the purpose of his bill, Bonta told reporters outside the capitol in Sacramento:

> If you are afraid of a Black family barbecuing in a community park, a man dancing and doing his normal exercise routine in a bike lane, or someone who asks you to comply with dog leash laws in a park, and your immediate response is to call the police, the real problem is with your own personal prejudice.

[730]   Patton & Farley, *supra* note 27 ("In some cases, lawsuits could be filed for intentional infliction of emotional distress. Many state and municipal laws protect civil rights better than their federal equivalents; suits could be brought under these laws in some cases, too.").

[731]   Many disagree that the Karen meme is overtly sexist and point to its male counterpart – Ken – as evidence. But there remains a notable lack of "Ken memes" flooding the internet or our popular consciousness. For a thoughtful rebuttal that the Karen meme instead responds to the longstanding myth of White female victimhood and a long history of White female violence against Black people in America, *see* Cady Lang, *How the 'Karen Meme' Confronts the Violent History of White Womanhood*, Time (July 6, 2020), https://time.com/5857023/karen-meme-history-meaning/.

But the noble intent behind these rushed legislative reforms is belied by the numerous normative and practical problems with them. First, neither the New York nor California bills provide specific guidance on the mental state required to make a 911 call legally motivated by race or another protected characteristic. Bonta acknowledged as much, in the same interview in which he introduced the initiative, when he noted that, under the bill's language, proving that someone acted with racial prejudice will be difficult.

Second, both bills promote the same overcriminalizing legislative reaction to a social problem that plagues so much of America's response to social disorder. The United States leads the world in incarceration rates, not only because the War on Drugs provided cover for a "New Jim Crow" focused on the deliberate mass imprisonment of Black people, but because the United States and its several states criminalize more activity than virtually any other country. The immediate response to punish with lengthy prison sentences anyone who abuses 911 arguably creates another problem without solving the original issue. When Representative Ilhan Omar called for federal hate crimes legislation to curb 911 abuse, some scholars derisively referred to this blunt approach as the "Moar Crimez Plz" response to all of society's ills. Indeed, Christian Cooper himself decried as "unnecessary and counterproductive" the arrest of Amy Cooper for calling 911 on him in Central Park.

That is not to say there is no room for criminal sanctions to deter and punish racist 911 abuse. But after-the-fact punishment is a second-best solution to prevention. If the actual desire is to protect Black people trying to exist in public, the rush to cleanse White America's collective guilty conscience by punishing racially fragile White people should be complementary to – and secondary to – legislative and departmental reforms explicitly granting dispatchers and police discretion to ignore these calls in the first place. Only by allowing officers and dispatchers to ignore racist attempts to enforce the color line, or preventing officers from responding to such calls, can the physical and psychological violence of armed response truly be stopped.

Each of these two problems relates to the third, and perhaps most complicated, problem with rushed legislative reform: 911 hate crimes legislation, which promises stiff prison sentences for calling 911 with an easy-to-infer but difficult-to-prove biased mental state, may instead chill lawful and necessary participation in emergency management systems. Calls for civil or criminal liability for abusing emergency responses systems are understandable, but the desire to reduce frivolous, race-based 911 calls must be balanced against the potentially chilling effect that harsh penalties may have on people using 911 for legitimate purposes. While many of the intentional 911 calls described in this book qualify on their face as true "nonemergency" calls, others present closer questions, at least to the untrained civilian eye. The legal system cannot, and should not, expect civilians to become trained experts in criminal behavior, discerning and distinguishing suspicious and innocent conduct from suspicious and possibly criminal conduct, especially when police officers – the trained experts who are expected to make such distinctions – are held only to the preposterously low "reasonable suspicion" standard.[732] A careful balance must be struck between the need to reduce 911 abuse and the weaponization of racial fear on the one hand and the equally compelling need to provide free and open access to emergency response systems on the other.

7.6 SLAPPing Down 911 Abuse[733]

I propose an innovative solution to frivolous 911 calls that borrows from a legal solution to frivolous lawsuits: the anti-SLAPP motion. A "SLAPP suit," short for "strategic litigation against public participation," is a frivolous lawsuit filed not to obtain any actual relief from a court but instead to censor, intimidate, and silence critics by burdening them with the cost of a legal defense until they abandon their criticism or opposition.[734] SLAPP suits take many forms, but classic examples involve multinational corporations engaged in polluting the environment baselessly suing environmental groups that protest their actions[735] or online retailers suing customers who post negative reviews.[736] In both cases, the plaintiff files a frivolous suit to scare away an antagonist engaged in constitutionally protected free speech.

SLAPP suits and 911 abuse may seem nothing alike. But much like the bias-motivated 911 caller who abuses scarce law enforcement resources for improper intimidation purposes, a SLAPP plaintiff abuses scarce judicial resources for improper intimidation purposes. The analogy fits remarkably well for other reasons: SLAPP suits and frivolous 911 calls are similar in (1) the motives of SLAPP plaintiffs and biased 911 callers; (2) the object and effect of SLAPP suits and frivolous 911 calls; (3) the problems in detection of and response to SLAPP suits and frivolous 911 calls; (4) the need to balance competing interests in both cases; and (5) the need for early identification and response mechanisms.

Motives of the Actors: Much like the SLAPP plaintiff that frivolously weaponizes the legal system to intimidate a party presenting a political or business threat, the racially fearful 911 caller frivolously weaponizes law enforcement to intimidate a perceived safety threat. The SLAPP plaintiff ultimately seeks to force its opponent to back down from constitutionally protected activity – freedom of speech – to enlarge the scope of the plaintiff's power and authority. Likewise, the racially fearful

---

[732] *See Terry v. Ohio*, 392 U.S. 1, 30 (1968).

[733] Parts of this section are reprinted with permission from an earlier article I wrote on this subject, published in the Tulane Law Review. *See* Fields, *supra* note 30.

[734] Pub. Participation Project, *What Is a Slapp?*, https://anti-slapp.org/what-is-a-slapp/ (last visited February 6, 2022).

[735] *See, e.g.*, Sarah Aron, *A Win for Advocacy: Court Dismisses SLAPP Suit Against Environmental Activists*, Ctr. for Iynt'l. Env't L. (January 24, 2019), https://www.ciel.org/court-dismisses-slapp-environmental-activists/.

[736] CBS News, *Posting a Negative Review Online Can Get You Sued*, CBS News (July 22, 2019), https://www.cbsnews.com/news/posting-a-negative-review-online-can-get-you-sued/.

911 caller seeks to restrict the alleged suspect's constitutionally protected freedom of movement to reinforce the White dominant role in public places.[737]

The Object and Effect of the Actions: Both SLAPP plaintiffs and racially biased 911 callers seek to intimidate undesired classes of people, to discourage them from public participation and push them back into the shadows. SLAPP suits ultimately work by chilling the right of free expression and free access to government.[738] The first scholars to study SLAPP suits "conservatively estimate that thousands have been sued into silence, and that more thousands who heard of the SLAPPs will never again participate freely and confidently in the public issues and governance of their town, state, or country."[739] This intimidation, and the personal cost and psychological trauma to victims of the SLAPP technique, is itself a matter of concern, as is anything that deters citizens from participating in or accessing the resources of government; "more fundamentally, the use of wealth to dominate access to government is deeply subversive. All of these factors together make the SLAPP suit a dangerously corrupting influence in our society."[740]

Likewise, thousands of people of color have been unfairly targeted into compliance and thousands more who hear about the devastating effects of unwarranted police confrontation withdraw from official government actors, distrusting any interaction with law enforcement or other government agents, even when their help is needed.[741] This targeting occurs because those in the dominant White social caste fearfully seek to intimidate undesired classes of people from lawfully participating in White public spaces. And fundamentally, they use their societal wealth – the presumption of law-abidingness afforded them by their privilege – to dominate access to public space in a way that is deeply subversive.

Detection and Response: Similar problems of detection and response exist in each context as well. One of the primary difficulties in addressing SLAPP litigation is that plaintiffs do not overtly admit the frivolousness of their case or the sinister motivations behind the suit.[742] Creating anti-SLAPP legislation is therefore incredibly difficult, as legislators must derive a way to allow early termination of SLAPP suits without

---

[737] *See* Anderson, *supra* note 19, at 10–11.

[738] Alexandra Dylan Lowe, *The Price of Speaking Out*, A.B.A. J. (September 1996), at 48–49 (quoting attorney Mark A. Chertok, who successfully defeated a high-profile SLAPP litigation against environmental groups, as saying, "These things work . . . Citizens see a million-dollar lawsuit and they just want to go run and hide.").

[739] George W. Pring & Penelope Canan, *SLAPPs: Getting Sued for Speaking Out*, at 3 (1996).

[740] Jerome I. Braun, *Increasing SLAPP Protection: Unburdening the Right of Petition in California*, 32 U.C. Davis L. Rev. 965, 972 (1999).

[741] *See* Matthew Desmond & Andrew V. Papachristos, *Why Don't You Just Call the Cops?*, N.Y. Times (September 30, 2016), https://www.nytimes.com/2016/10/01/opinion/why-dont-you-just-call-the-cops.html (describing the chilling effect media attention on police violence has on communities of color, spurring refusal to engage law enforcement, even to seek help).

[742] *See* Braun, *supra* note 740, at 973 ("Because SLAPP suits masquerade as legitimate tort actions, there is no obvious way to identify them from court dockets.").

improperly denying legitimate litigants their day in court. Likewise, the typical 911 abuser does not usually express his racial antipathy to the dispatcher or otherwise articulate his underlying racist motivations in complaining about the lawful conduct of people of color. Indeed, the nature of pervasive implicit bias is such that callers themselves may not be consciously aware of the race-based motives behind their fearful calls. Thus, it becomes nearly impossible to craft a remedy that deters and punishes racist behavior without deterring or unfairly punishing genuine emergency calls.

Competing Interests: The balance between opposing fundamental interests in the SLAPP and 911 contexts is also instructive. The most common criticism of anti-SLAPP laws comes from those who believe there should be no barriers to the right to petition the court for redress. This right of access to the courts is absolutely fundamental to the concept of justice in a free and democratic society.[743] The SLAPP penalty circumscribes this fundamental liberty by providing an early penalty to claimants who seek judicial redress.

On the other hand, the problem anti-SLAPP legislation seeks to address also implicates fundamental constitutional freedoms: free speech and access to courts. Courts and legislatures have recognized the need to address intimidation-oriented litigation designed for the sole purpose of curtailing a citizen's fundamental right to speak freely about matters of public importance.[744] Moreover, the SLAPP suit itself represents a threat to access to justice, as these frivolous suits clog court dockets and delay or deny access to legitimate litigants with genuine needs.

The comparison to frivolous 911 calls is unmistakable. Imposing any liability for misusing the emergency response system threatens to deny access to the critical, often life-saving police and medical apparatuses charged with keeping the citizenry safe. Unlike anti-SLAPP concerns, however, there exists no general constitutional right to police protection.[745] While state police forces are charged with protecting the public and most departments across the country are required as a matter of policy to respond to all 911 calls, a "fundamental principle [of American law is] that a government and its agents are under no general duty to provide public services, such as police protection, to any particular individual citizen."[746]

But like frivolous SLAPP suits, frivolous 911 calls both affect fundamental constitutional guarantees and delay relief to legitimate 911 callers. Marshaling armed officers to restrain individuals engaged in innocent conduct restricts the

---

[743] Carol Rice Andrews, *A Right of Access to Court Under the Petition Clause of the First Amendment: Defining the Right*, 60 Ohio St. L.J. 557, 557 (1999).

[744] Aaron Smith, Note, *SLAPP Fight*, 68 Ala. L. Rev. 303, 305 (2016) (citing cases and anti-SLAPP legislation).

[745] *Warren v. District of Columbia*, 444 A.2d 1, 10 (D.C. 1981) (en banc).

[746] *Id.* at 3; *see also DeShaney v. Winnebago Cty. Dep't of Soc. Servs.*, 489 U.S. 189, 196–97 (1989) (holding that no duty arises from the "special relationship" between police and civilians and concluding that constitutional duties of care and protection only exist as to certain individuals, such as incarcerated persons, involuntarily committed mental patients, and others restrained against their will and unable to protect themselves).

fundamental freedom of movement for victims of these calls. In the racially fearful context, constitutional equal protection becomes a concern when state actors are involved. Moreover, frivolous 911 calls threaten the safety of civilians in genuine need of protection because they delay response to legitimate, time-sensitive calls and thus unfairly and unnecessarily put citizens at risk.

Early Detection and Deterrence: The importance of effective deterrent mechanisms is evident in both contexts as well. "The importance of effective anti-SLAPP laws is highlighted by the lack of protections available through other common law and statutory solutions to the problem of SLAPPs."[747] While defendants may pursue sanctions under Rule 11 of the Federal Rules of Civil Procedure or a state analogue, such sanctions are rarely granted and "do not save a SLAPP defendant from the burden of extensive court proceedings."[748] Likewise, targets of racially biased 911 calls theoretically can access after-the-fact civil remedies, but these avenues for relief do little to protect them from the risk of degradation, arrest, or violent and potentially lethal confrontations in the first place.

Despite the difficulty of finding the right balance between deterring frivolous suits and protecting access to the courts, a majority of states have attempted to strike that balance in anti-SLAPP legislation.[749] The exact contours of each state's laws differ, but the broad mechanisms remain the same. Anti-SLAPP laws "focus on the swift and efficient dismissal of frivolous lawsuits against protected activity and emphasize subjecting the SLAPPed party to as little time in court as possible. These statutes thus force plaintiffs to take a harder look at litigation by both deterring meritless claims and hastening their resolution."[750] A special motion to strike is a central feature of anti-SLAPP legislation, allowing a defendant to defeat a lawsuit if he can "show that the claim is based on an action involving public participation, petitioning, or free speech covered by the statute."[751]

Just as states have enacted legislation to give courts tools to eliminate the threat to SLAPP defendants at the outset of litigation and not merely through after-the-fact remedies, states should also enact legislation to reduce or eliminate the threat to targets of race-based 911 calls on the front end. Here, a major difference exists between a frivolous lawsuit and a frivolous 911 call. Courts lack the discretion to turn away a frivolous lawsuit at the door. Dispatchers and officers do – or at least should – have that discretion. Thus, rather than merely focusing on post-

---

[747] Benjamin Ernst, *Fighting SLAPPs in Federal Court: Erie, The Rules Enabling Act, and the Application of State Anti-SLAPP Laws in Federal Diversity Actions*, 56 B.C. L. Rev. 1181, 1186 (2015).

[748] *Id.* at 1186–87. The same is true for civil countersuits bringing malicious prosecution or abuse of process claims. These tort remedies may ultimately provide relief, but only when a defendant has already been forced to litigate a time-consuming and expensive lawsuit. *Id.*

[749] *See, e.g., Davis v. Cox*, 351 P.3d 862, 865 (Wash. 2015).

[750] Ernst, *supra* note 747, at 1187 (footnote omitted).

[751] *Id.* at 1188.

incident punishment for wasting law enforcement resources, "[p]erhaps the best way to deal with erroneous calls is for regular officers not to respond."[752]

This focus on pre-incident deterrence, and the anti-SLAPP legislative experience, guides the annotated model legislation I have drafted and included at the end of this chapter. This model legislation, which I call the "911 Abuse Act" and which is under consideration for sponsorship in the North Carolina General Assembly, strikes a delicate balance between protecting the rights of civilians to call 911 for true emergencies and deterring and punishing all forms of 911 abuse. Among other things, it singles out for greater sanction a more narrowly and specifically defined form of racially motivated 911 abuse, grants express discretion to dispatchers and officers not to respond to clearly frivolous calls, and establishes a statewide 911 recordkeeping call system to interface with nationwide call centers.

7.7 TRUE PARTNERSHIP

Carefully tailored legislation aimed at curbing 911 abuse, coupled with departmental changes authorizing discretion in responding to frivolous calls, can significantly reduce unnecessary racially fearful contacts along the color line. But a wide range of 911 calls report activity that resides somewhere between "Barbecuing While Black" and armed home invasion. For many, if not most, of these calls, a rational reallocation of police resources can and does promote a racial fear détente. When "Defund the Police" means redirection of resources to communities that need it rather than complete abolition of all law enforcement infrastructure, the results are not only popular, but effective.

For decades, "community-led safety initiatives" around the country have redirected police funding to infrastructure and services addressing community needs and relying on nonpolice emergency responders trained to deal with particular situations.[753] These programs dispatch social workers and mental health counselors to address people in crisis, with the goal of helping mentally ill, housing-insecure, and other marginalized or troubled people access needed resources rather than simply removing them from the street and into a jail cell.[754] Trained unarmed "conflict interrupters" replace aggressive police tactics with measured responses to defuse tense situations before they erupt into deadly violence.[755] These and other initiatives replace police with unarmed responders wherever possible, reducing unnecessary contact with the criminal justice

---

[752] Couper, *supra* note 293.

[753] Cassidy Johncox, *Policing Alternative: What a Community-Led Public Safety System Might Look Like*, ClickOn Detroit (June 9, 2020), https://www.clickondetroit.com/news/national/2020/06/09/policing-alternative-what-a-community-led-public-safety-system-might-look-like/.

[754] *Id.*

[755] *Id.*

system for endangered populations and reducing the likelihood of unnecessary violence.

These programs highlight that a very small number of 911 calls require the kind of intervention police are trained to provide.[756] A key element of these programs is that they "place communities at the center" of efforts to reduce crime and address critical needs.[757] Community-led initiatives are supported by investment in community-level public safety strategies and organizations, creating "targeted interventions that meet the priorities that communities identify for themselves."[758] The result often is stronger communities with a greater capacity to address the problems beyond the expertise of police, such as mental illness and homelessness.[759]

Some results suggest that community-led programs that reduce the level of policing in communities may reduce costs[760] as well as crime.[761]

The most successful and long-running such community-led safety initiative is called CAHOOTS, for Crisis Assistance Helping Out on the Streets.[762] First piloted in Eugene, Oregon, in 1989, CAHOOTS has become a mainstay of the community over the past thirty years. The program is a cooperation between the Eugene police department and the White Bird Clinic, a community medical clinic and volunteer network. Under the program, police dispatchers redirect calls about homelessness, mental illness, or substance abuse to White Bird, which sends a medic and an unarmed crisis worker – usually a mental health professional – to assess the situation. Every worker receives hundreds of hours of training in crisis counseling, de-escalation, conflict resolution, and medical skills, and response personnel have the resources to connect people to social services, transport them to the hospital, or provide other needed support. Nearby Springfield, Oregon, has also joined the program. In 2019, White Bird responded to nearly 20 percent of police calls in both cities and required police assistance less than 1 percent of the time. The

---

[756] One study found that 80 percent of 911 calls concern nonviolent offenses; a *New York Times* study estimated that officers spend as little as 4 percent of their time dealing with violent crime. Sarah Holder & Kara Harris, *Where Calling the Police Isn't the Only Option*, BLOOMBERG (September 3, 2020), https://www.bloomberg.com/news /articles/2020–09–03/alternative-policing-models-emerge-in-u-s-cities.

[757] LEAH SAKALA ET AL., URBAN INSTITUTE, PUBLIC INVESTMENT IN COMMUNITY-DRIVEN SAFETY INITIATIVES: LANDSCAPE STUDY AND KEY CONSIDERATIONS 2 (November 2018), https://www.urban.org/sites/default/ files/publication/99262/public_investment_in_community-driven_safety_initiatives_1.pdf.

[758] *Id.* at 3.

[759] *Id.* at 3–4.

[760] For instance, the longest-running program, CAHOOTS in Eugene, Oregon, responds to about 17 percent of calls to police and saves the city about $8.5 million each year. Anna V. Smith, *There's Already an Alternative to Calling the Police*, MOTHER JONES (June 13, 2020), https://www .motherjones.com/environment/2020/06/theres-already-an-alternative-to-calling-the-police/.

[761] A study of several years of data from the New York Police Department found that reports of major crimes decreased during periods when proactive policing was reduced. Christopher M. Sullivan & Zachary P. O'Keeffe, *Evidence That Curtailing Proactive Policing Can Reduce Major Crime*, 1 NATURE HUMAN BEHAVIOR 730 (2017), https://www.nature.com/articles/s41562-017-0211-5.

[762] Holder & Harris, *supra* note 756; Smith, *supra* note 760.

program has saved the cities an estimated $22 million in police and hospital costs, in part because many of the homeless, mentally ill, or drug-addicted people CAHOOTS helps would otherwise end up in emergency rooms. Recognizing this success, Senator Ron Wyden has proposed a bill that would provide a 95 percent Medicaid match to any state, city, or county that creates a similar program.[763]

Indeed, CAHOOTS has inspired several similar programs. For example, in Portland, Oregon, the "Portland Street Response,"[764] patterned after CAHOOTS, is conceptualized as "a third branch of our city's first responder system, joining fire and police."[765] Like CAHOOTS, the program, which piloted in Spring 2020, responds to appropriate 911 calls with a medic and a crisis worker. In June 2020, the Portland City Council provided $4.8 million to expand the program.[766] Similarly, Denver, Colorado, piloted a six-month program modeled after CAHOOTS, Support Team Assisted Response (STAR), beginning in June 2020.[767] STAR service sends a van with a paramedic and mental health clinician to respond to nonviolent incidents, such as those associated with drug overdoses, mental illness, and public intoxication. The service has also conducted welfare checks and helped connect people to service providers. And like CAHOOTS, the service takes calls diverted from the city's 911 lines. After the six-month pilot, which is limited to the downtown area, the city unveiled plans to roll out the service throughout the city.

In Oakland, California, community leaders took an even more proactive approach in 2013, with Oakland Unite,[768] which uses funds from commercial real estate taxes and parking surcharges to fund violence prevention programs that provide skill-building, crisis response, and community asset-building services. The program has resulted in lower arrest rates among clients of participating organizations, while reducing recidivism rates by offering life coaching and education programs. Oakland added a CAHOOTS-like program in 2020. The program, called Mobile

---

[763] Molly Harbarger, *Eugene's Alternative to Policing, CAHOOTS, Would Go National Under Bill to Provide Medicaid Funding for Similar Programs Nationwide*, THE OREGONIAN (August 5, 2020), https://www.oregonlive.com/politics/2020/08/eugenes-alternative-to-policing-would-go-national-under-bill-to-provide-medicaid-funding-for-similar-programs-nationwide.html.

[764] STREET ROOTS, PORTLAND STREET RESPONSE: A PLAN FOR THE FUTURE OF CRISIS AND DISORDER INTERVENTION IN PUBLIC SPACES (April 2, 2019), https://portlandstreetresponse.org/wp-content/uploads/2019/04/Portland-Street-Response-%C2%A9-Street-Roots.pdf.

[765] Kaia Sand, *We Did It!*, PORTLAND STREET RESPONSE (November 21, 2019), https://portlandstreetresponse.org/we-did-it.

[766] Everton Bailey Jr., *Portland Approves Budget with Millions in Cuts to Police, but Short of Public Demand for $50 Million Reduction*, THE OREGONIAN (June 18, 2020), https://www.oregonlive.com/portland/2020/06/portland-passes-budget-with-millions-in-cuts-to-police-spending-but-short-of-public-demand-for-50-million-reduction.html.

[767] Press Release, Denver Justice Project, DJP Helps Launch Alternative Public Health Emergency Response Pilot in Denver (June 8, 2020), http://www.denverjusticeproject.org/2020/06/08/press-release-alternative-public-health-emergency-response-pilot-launches-in-denver/. DASHR is a participating organization.

[768] SAKALA ET AL., *supra* note 757, at 32–33.

Assistance Community Responders of Oakland (MACRO),[769] authorizes credentialed local nonprofits to provide services and referrals in response to 911 calls; dispatchers redirect appropriate calls to the program.[770]

These and similar reform initiatives seek to reduce crime, but their primary objective is to reduce the type of unnecessary aggressive police response that needlessly escalates a noncriminal matter into a violent, potentially lethal criminal encounter. Implicit in their objectives is a recognition that the vast majority of 911 calls report neither criminal behavior nor true emergencies. While these programs are not specifically aimed at curbing White caller crime or other fear- or hate-based 911 abuse, they certainly can help demilitarize the private policing of the color line. Sending an unarmed conflict interrupter to respond to someone sleeping peacefully in a dormitory common room or dancing while wearing a ski mask may still be unnecessary, but at least it reduces the risk of a violent encounter with criminal justice. And when coupled with legislation specifically targeting, deterring, and punishing clearly frivolous Living While Black 911 abuse, it makes possible a retreat from the violent enforcement of Black and White spaces.

7.8 911 ABUSE ACT

Finally, I propose model legislation aimed at deterring and punishing frivolous, racist 911 abuse. This legislation strikes a balance between deterring illegitimate uses of emergency response systems while continuing to encourage citizens to call 911 when necessary. It also narrowly limits the availability of carceral responses to 911 abuse, in recognition that one ought not reform the "maximum policing state" by blindly criminalizing more acts.

Title: This Act shall be called the "911 Abuse Act" ("Act").[771]

Definitions: The following terms shall have the following definitions for purposes of this Act:

> "Dispatcher" shall mean any individual answering a phone call placed through the 911 or other emergency response system.
> "Officer" shall mean any police officer or other law enforcement personnel.
> "Caller" shall mean any individual placing a phone call through the 911 or other emergency response system.

---

[769] Holder & Harris, *supra* note 756; Haaziq Madyun, *Oakland Considers Policing Model Involving Civilians Responding to Specific 911 Calls*, KRON4 (June 8, 2020), https://www.kron4.com/news/bay-area/oakland-considers-policing-model-involving-civilians-responding-to-specific-911-calls/.

[770] Supporters of the program point to the reliance on 911 calls as a strength, arguing the system will work better if it integrates with the emergency reporting channels people already know. However, some believe the 911 approach will not work in Oakland, which has a much larger Black population than Eugene, because Black communities are reluctant to call 911 for any reason. *Id.*

[771] Model legislation reprinted with permission from the Tulane Law Review.

"'Target' shall mean any individual against whom a complaint is made through a 911 or other emergency response system call.

"Abuse" or "Abusive"[772] shall mean the misuse of the 911 or other emergency response system by i) making a false alarm report; ii) reporting false information; iii) reporting exaggerated information; iv) making a report other than to report a situation that the person reasonably believes requires prompt service to preserve human life or property; v) intentionally calling and hanging up; vi) intentionally remaining on the line to prevent Dispatchers from handling other calls; or vii) intentionally or knowingly making a report for the sole purpose of implicating a person or persons in criminal activity on the basis of their race or ethnicity.[773]

Purpose: The purpose of this Act shall be to deter and minimize the abusive misuse of 911 and other emergency response call systems, including but not limited to abusive misuse of 911 for racially biased purposes. This Act is not designed to address, deter, minimize, or punish "unintentional" misuses of 911 and other emergency response systems, including phantom wireless calls, misdials, and accidental hang-ups.

Penalty: Any person who abuses the 911 service as defined herein or otherwise makes a call to 911 for a purpose other than to report a situation that the person reasonably believes requires prompt service to preserve human life or property[774] commits a misdemeanor of the first degree, punishable by a fine of no more than $10,000 and a term of imprisonment not to exceed six months. Any person who is convicted of a second offense under this Act shall be guilty of a class three felony, punishable by a fine of no more than $25,000 and a term of imprisonment not to exceed one year. Any person who is convicted of a third or subsequent offense under this Act shall be guilty of a class one felony, punishable by a fine of no more than $50,000 and a term of imprisonment not to exceed two years.[775]

Enhanced Penalty for Racially Motivated Abuse: Any person who abuses the 911 or other emergency response system with the intention to and for the purpose of harassing, intimidating, causing unwarranted police contact with, or otherwise targeting an individual on the basis of that Target's race or ethnicity shall face enhanced penalties as follows:[776]

---

[772] This statute is narrowly tailored to address intentional 911 abuse calls, not unintentional 911 misuse calls.

[773] This definition deters most abusive conduct by not imposing a specific intent requirement. It also makes a normative statement about the seriousness of racially motivated abuse by singling it out and requiring specific intent for this kind of conduct. Enhanced penalties for this intentional conduct follow.

[774] By borrowing from the precise language in Oregon's 911 abuse statute, the statute makes clear what constitutes a "nonemergency" and narrowly circumscribes the legitimate uses of the 911 system.

[775] Imposing penalties for first-time offenders solves the enforcement problems faced by California and other states that impose fines for multiple offenses but cannot meaningfully track multiple instances of misconduct. *See* Carl Takei, *How Police Can Stop Being Weaponized by Bias-Motivated 911 Calls*, ACLU (June 18, 2018), https://www.aclu.org/blog/racial-justicerace-and-criminal-justice/how-police-ca-stop-being-weaponized-bias-motivated.

[776] The statute makes a normative statement that racially biased 911 abuse is a more serious and morally blameworthy act that engenders greater harm to the target and to society and deserves greater punishment.

(a) First Offense: Class Three Felony, punishable by a fine of no more than $25,000 and a term of imprisonment not to exceed one year.

(b) Second and All Subsequent Offenses: Class One Felony, punishable by a fine of no more than $50,000 and a term of imprisonment not to exceed two years.

Dispatcher Discretion: Notwithstanding any conflicting departmental or administrative policy, Dispatchers shall have discretion to decline to assign an Officer to respond to a 911 call if the Dispatcher reasonably believes that the Caller is committing an Abuse of the 911 system as defined under this Act. The Dispatcher shall, if required, articulate facts with reasonable specificity indicating why the Dispatcher believed the Caller was committing an abuse of the 911 system.[777]

If, in the exercise of this discretion, the Dispatcher reasonably believes the Caller is abusing the 911 system but decides to assign an Officer to respond to the call, the Dispatcher shall describe to the Officer, with reasonable specificity, the facts and circumstances giving rise to the Dispatcher's belief that the call amounts to an abuse of the 911 system.[778]

911 Call Abuse Recordkeeping: Any Dispatcher who reasonably believes a Caller is abusing the 911 system shall log the call in the Statewide 911 Abuse Database (defined herein) and shall record all reasonably pertinent information, including the identity and phone number of the Caller, the substance and nature of the call, and the facts indicating an abuse of the 911 system.

Statewide 911 Abuse Database: The State shall create, fund, and maintain a statewide, centralized 911 database for the purpose of collecting and cross-referencing 911 abuse call logs at emergency response regional centers throughout the State. This database shall be used for the purpose of enforcing the provisions of this Act and maintaining statistical data regarding 911 abuse in the State.[779]

Officer Discretion: Officers and their departments are encouraged to use or authorize the use of discretion when responding to 911 calls the Officer reasonably believes to constitute an Abuse under this Act, including without limitation, declining to respond to the call, sending unarmed law enforcement personnel to respond to the call, or responding to the call for purposes

---

[777] This discretion is critical to front-end prevention of unwarranted police contact, something not available to judges in the SLAPP context. The statute also protects against negligent or bias-motivated Dispatchers by imposing a requirement that Dispatchers articulate facts to justify why they declined to respond to a particular complaint.

[778] This provision specifically addresses situations like the one in Tamir Rice's case, where the Caller stated the gun was "probably fake" and that Tamir was "probably a juvenile," but the Dispatcher failed to communicate those statements to the Officers. *See* Takei, *supra* note 775.

[779] These two provisions address the enforcement and recordkeeping problems demonstrated by California's system. *See* Eastman, *supra* note 713.

of investigating the 911 abuse.[780] When an Officer becomes aware of facts giving rise to probable cause for 911 abuse, the Officer shall respond to and investigate the 911 abuse.[781]

Civil Remedies: This Act is not intended to create any new cause of action under civil law, or to increase or decrease the availability of any civil remedy otherwise available to a Target for any harm resulting from an abusive 911 call, except as follows:

(a) A conviction for 911 Abuse under this Act shall conclusively satisfy any causation element under any civil tort.

(b) A conviction for 911 Abuse under this Act shall presumptively satisfy any harm element under any civil tort, provided that Officers are dispatched to the call, respond to the call, and make contact with the Target.[782]

(c) For purposes of any conviction for 911 Abuse under this Act qualifying for an "Enhanced Penalty for Racially Motivated Abuse," a defense of qualified immunity from civil or criminal liability shall only be available to a Dispatcher who assigns an Officer to respond to the call, or to an Officer who responds to the call, if the Dispatcher or Officer identifies specific and articulable facts demonstrating that the Dispatcher or Officer objectively reasonably believed that the call did not constitute an Abuse under this Act.[783]

---

[780] This provision recognizes the need to afford officers and departments flexibility to develop their own policies regarding how to deescalate responses to frivolous 911 calls. The use of "encourage" in this context may be disputed, but a state-mandated policy preventing any officer discretion in responding to a possibly frivolous 911 call unnecessarily limits the discretion of expert law enforcement agencies. Other provisions in the model statute address the need for officers to exercise discretion and the limits of that discretion.

[781] This provision addresses the underenforcement of frivolous 911 abuse, by requiring Officers to treat it as seriously as other crimes.

[782] This provision recognizes the inherent psychological harm to the Target of being confronted by a police officer responding to a frivolous criminal complaint.

[783] This provision narrows unduly broad qualified immunity protections by requiring a clear and articulable statement of why, in the face of a clearly frivolous, racially motivated 911 call, Dispatchers and Officers allowed the weaponization of racial fear.

8

Resisting a "Shoot First, Think Later" Culture

When I began writing this chapter in my office in Raleigh, North Carolina, news broke that an unarmed Black man named Andrew Brown, Jr. had been fatally shot by police officers two hours east in Elizabeth City. Initial reports indicated that multiple officers had attempted to serve search and arrest warrants, found Brown sitting in his car, and seconds later fired fourteen rounds into the car, killing Brown with a bullet to the back of the head. Rumors swirled, with Brown family attorneys calling the homicide an "execution" in a press conference shortly after being shown a short clip of police body camera footage.[784] But as protests spread throughout North Carolina, the truth remained elusive because Pasquotank County District Attorney Andrew Womble sought a court order to shield any footage from public view. Judge Jeff Foster obliged.[785]

Four agonizing weeks later, District Attorney Womble held a press conference in which he exonerated all five officers on scene that day, including the three officers who fired at Brown. Reading from prepared remarks, Womble explained over the course of twenty minutes that the officers personally felt their lives were in danger and acted "consistent with their training," particularly given that "[t]he law does not require officers in a tense and dangerous situation to wait" for a suspect to produce a deadly weapon "to act to stop the suspect."[786] Womble concluded that the officers acted reasonably in killing Brown.

Womble then played for the assembled press a forty-four second clip excerpted from nineteen minutes of body camera footage. The clip showed five White officers in body armor and holding assault weapons in the back of a pickup truck that sped at high speed over a curb and onto Brown's front yard, screeching to a halt feet from

---

[784] Adeel Hassan, *What We Know About the Killing of Andrew Brown Jr. in North Carolina*, N.Y. TIMES (May 18, 2021), https://www.nytimes.com/2021/04/28/us/andrew-brown-jr-shooting-north-carolina.html.

[785] Laura Lee & Jordan Wilkie, *Update: NC Judge Denies Petition to Immediately Release Body Camera Footage in Andrew Brown Jr. Case*, CAROLINA PUB. PRESS (April 28, 2021), https://carolinapublicpress .org/44948/will-body-camera-footage-be-released-in-andrew-brown-jr-case/.

[786] Rev.com, *Pasquotank District Attorney Press Conference Transcript: Fatal Police Shooting of Andrew Brown Jr. "Justified"* (May 18, 2021), https://www.rev.com/blog/transcripts/pasquotank-district-attorney-press-conference-transcript-fatal-police-shooting-of-andrew-brown-jr-justified.

Brown's car. The five officers jump out screaming, guns drawn and pointed directly at Brown, sitting alone and motionless in his car. Brown responds to this show of deadly force by slowly backing his car away from officers, turning the vehicle left away from the officers, and slowly accelerating his car away from the officers toward an empty street. At that point – and only at that point – do shots ring out. Fourteen in total. One to the back of Brown's head as he faced directly away from any officer threat.[787]

After viewing this footage, the first nine questions from the press attempted in various ways to get at this one simple unknown: Why did the officers shoot a fleeing suspect who no longer posed a threat to them, and why were those actions deemed justified?[788] The ensuing hourlong press conference took on a surreal quality, with a noticeably combative and defiant Womble acting more like a personal defense attorney for the officers than the truth-seeking, impartial public servant he was elected to be. Rather than directly answer questions, Womble repeatedly challenged reporters, confrontationally asking whether reporters had ever feared for their lives or what they would have done in a similar situation, ignoring the fact that reporters are not trained law enforcement officers.[789] Multiple times he refused requests to show the video again or make it available to the public or the press (I and the rest of the public only saw the video because someone in the room recorded it on a cell phone the one time it played). At one point, Womble claimed the officers were justified because it was "possible" that the car "could have been a deadly weapon" and "could have posed an imminent threat" to the officers, going so far to say "I don't care what direction you're going, forward, backward, sideways. I don't care if you're stationary, and neither do our courts and our case law."[790] In other words, in Womble's eyes, officers are justified shooting and killing suspects sitting motionless in cars because it is conceivable that at some point the car could pose a threat.

When I had the opportunity to discuss this shooting and Womble's decision on television in the days that followed, I was heartened that my fellow panelists – ranging from the Mecklenburg County (Charlotte) Sheriff and Wake County (Raleigh) District Attorney to a prominent social justice advocate, fellow law professor, and the President of the North Carolina NAACP – all agreed that Womble's statements were inappropriate, factually suspect based on the short snippet of footage released, and legally inaccurate.[791] Of course, that universal condemnation changed nothing in one very real sense. As the District Attorney and final decision-maker on whether to

[787] *Id.; see also* CNN, *Police Release Body Cam Video from Andrew Brown Shooting* (May 18, 2021), https://www.youtube.com/watch?v=jw-ofgWwXQU.

[788] Rev.com, *supra* note 786.

[789] *Id.*

[790] *Id.*

[791] Capital Tonight, *Reaction to DA's Decision Not to Charge Officers in Andrew Brown Death* (May 18, 2021), https://spectrumlocalnews.com/nc/charlotte/capital-tonight/2021/05/18/reaction-to-da-s-decision-not-to-charge-officers-in-andrew-brown-death; WRAL, *On the Record May 22, 2021: A Year Since the Death of George Floyd* (May 22, 2021), https://www.wral.com/on-the-record-may-22-2021-a-year-of-action-since-the-death-of-george-floyd/19691017/.

bring criminal charges against the officers, Womble's verdict effectively ended any prospect for accountability. The five officers involved were internally disciplined by their department and are now back on patrol.[792] During one interview, Professor Irving Joyner of North Carolina Central University School of Law reminded viewers that federal civil rights lawsuits could still be filed under Section 1983 by Brown's family, but his dejected demeanor in providing this insight accurately reflected the reality of such suits: they can be filed, but they will likely never be successful.[793] And they will never bring back Andrew Brown, Jr.

This tragedy encapsulates so many facets of a fundamentally broken system and cultural attitude toward violence, private and public policing, race relations, and accountability in America today. Elizabeth City and Pasquotank County reflect many local jurisdictions in this country: a poor, Black, largely marginalized metropolitan area surrounded, governed, and policed by the more politically powerful White, rural county wherein the Sheriff and his deputies hold tangible and intangible clout dating back centuries.[794] The District Attorney, himself an elected official sworn to fight crime hand in hand daily with the very police officers on whom he was asked to pass judgment, served as the sole, unreviewable arbiter of justice with no external impartial review by an independent prosecutor.

And while the District Attorney incorrectly claimed that officers can shoot to kill on nothing more than the conceivable possibility of a future threat, in a larger sense he accurately reflected upon the flexible, amorphous, and officer-friendly use-of-force standards articulated by the Supreme Court. The Fourth Amendment does not require deadly force to be necessary, nor does it categorically prohibit shooting a fleeing suspect in the back of the head. Instead, the Fourth Amendment only requires a showing that, *from the officer's perspective*, owing to the *officer's training and experience*, taking into account how *tense, uncertain, and rapidly evolving* a situation can be, but not accounting for any context other than *the exact moment force is used*, the officer's actions were *reasonable*. Such a test gives enormous latitude to launder and justify murder as reasonable policing even under circumstances as egregious as these, if a willing district attorney is so inclined. And even if a civil rights investigation tries to fill in the gap, as an ongoing federal Department of Justice investigation is attempting to do in the Brown case,[795] qualified immunity almost certainly will protect the officers from accountability.

[792] Yanqi Xu, *Pasquotank Sheriff's Deputies Who Shot Andrew Brown Jr. to be Disciplined, But Not Charged*, NC POLICY WATCH (May 18, 2021), http://pulse.ncpolicywatch.org/2021/05/18/pasquotank-sheriffs-deputies-who-shot-andrew-brown-jr-disciplined-but-not-charged/#sthash.FtogaCyW.7eJh5Daa.dpbs.

[793] WRAL, *supra* note 791.

[794] Tim Pulliam, *A Mostly Black City. A Mostly White County. Some Say Andrew Brown Jr.'s Shooting Deepened a Racial Divide*, ABC11 (May 4, 2021), https://abc11.com/andrew-brown-jr-video-funeral-pasquotank-county/10580164/.

[795] Tucker Higgins, *FBI Opens Civil Rights Probe into Killing of Andrew Brown Jr. in North Carolina*, CNBC (April 27, 2021), https://www.cnbc.com/2021/04/27/andrew-brown-jr-fbi-opens-civil-rights-probe-into-police-shooting.html.

And what of those contextual facts the Supreme Court forbids us to consider? What of the fact that the officers were serving warrants for a nonviolent drug offense, warrants backed only by a third-hand confidential informant's statement? Or that the response to this allegation of nonviolent activity was a SWAT-style assault onto a man's property, a truck in rural North Carolina barreling headlong toward a motionless Black man in a car, five White men jumping out of the back and shouting while pointing assault rifles at him? What of the fact that this overzealous (to put it mildly) police response escalated the encounter, creating the very conditions necessary for a fatal shooting? The law, in its current iteration, finds these factors irrelevant. But are they? Is this the best we can expect from those sworn to protect and serve?

This episode also informs on contemporary attitudes about private policing in the name of self-defense. Womble himself appealed to the private fears of reporters in his press conference, suggesting that as private citizens they would be justified in shooting and killing an unarmed Black man based on nothing more than the possibility that he could at some point pose an imminent threat. This kind of "shoot first, think later" culture, described by Justice Sotomayor in the context of policing, permeates private life as well and increasingly finds sanctuary in relaxed self-defense standards and Stand Your Ground laws turning Black and White neighborhood borders into private battlefields in the name of personal protection.

This final chapter reflects upon all of these systemic issues that work in concert to foster a shoot first, think later culture, and offers proposals for reform that may appear as radical departures from current law and policy but which find broad popular support across demographic lines throughout the country. Beginning with reforms to address private use of lethal force and ending with reforms to police practices and accountability, this chapter highlights some new and existing proposals that could work together to redefine Black and White citizens' relationship with police and each other.

8.1 RETURNING TO THE ENGLISH COMMON LAW MODEL OF SELF-DEFENSE

District Attorney Womble's shocking suggestion that reporters would shoot an unarmed man in the back of the head in self-defense if given the opportunity, and be legally justified in doing so, did not occur in a vacuum. Self-defense as a form of lawful private violence has been a bedrock principle of Anglo-American criminal law for at least seven centuries. But only in the last three decades has a concerted legislative effort been made to expand the boundaries of permissible self-defense far beyond what one might consider necessary violence. This governmental permission to shoot first and think later has only exacerbated tensions and raised the stakes in the battle to police Black and White spaces in America, with disastrous results.

American common law developed from and remains largely influenced by English common law. That fact is true in criminal law, including in the common law development of the affirmative claim of self-defense. At both English and early American common law, a person was only justified in using self-defense if that person had an honest and reasonable belief that they faced an imminent threat of unlawful force, that the force was necessary to repel the threat, that the force used was proportional to the threatened force, and the person using self-defense was not the initial aggressor.[796] These elements existed to narrowly define the parameters within which the law would recognize private use of deadly force, and at least in England, were applied narrowly.[797]

One major divergence appeared in early American common law, however. In England, force was never *necessary* outside the home if there existed a completely safe avenue of retreat wherein the person could simply escape harm without inflicting it. But this "duty to retreat" was broadly rejected by early American courts, and today thirty-nine states do not require any attempt to retreat before using deadly force.[798] Legal scholars and sociologists have explained this divergence as connected to the masculine frontiersman ethos of not backing down permeating early American settler life. Whether or not this is accurate, some evidence for this theory exists in court cases themselves. In 1876, the Ohio Supreme Court in *Erwin v. State* defended its rejection of the duty to retreat rule by articulating the "true man" doctrine: "a true man who is without fault is not obliged to fly from an assailant."[799] Opining on *Erwin v. State* eighty years later, the New Jersey Supreme Court summed up this true man doctrine succinctly: "the manly thing is to hold one's ground and hence society should not demand what smacks of cowardice."[800] Proponents of a no duty to retreat rule also promote its deterrent effect on criminals; as one Oklahoma state legislator asserted in defense of the doctrine, "it's going to give crooks second thoughts about carjackings and things like that. They're going to get a face full of lead."[801]

This approach to self-defense, allowing private citizens lawfully to shoot and kill when not necessary to do so, contradicts a fundamental premise of a civilized, ordered society: the notion that free women and men can and should resolve their disagreements peaceably when at all possible. Permitting the intentional killing of one private citizen by another when such killing is avoidable no more protects the sanctity of life than finding it reasonable for officers to shoot and kill a nonviolent

---

[796]   Cynthia Lee & Angela P. Harris, CRIMINAL LAW: CASES AND MATERIALS 605 (4th ed. 2019).

[797]   Richard Maxwell Brown, NO DUTY TO RETREAT: VIOLENCE AND VALUES IN AMERICAN HISTORY AND SOCIETY 3–4 (1994).

[798]   *Id.; see also* Joshua Dressler, UNDERSTANDING CRIMINAL LAW § 17.05 (6th ed. 2012).

[799]   29 Ohio St. 186, 199 (1876).

[800]   *State v. Abbott*, 36 N.J. 63, 74 (1961).

[801]   Associated Press, *Deadly Force Campaign Is Gaining National Support*, Deseret News (May 25, 2006), https://www.deseret.com/2006/5/25/19955165/deadly-force-campaign-is-gaining-national-support.

suspect driving away from them. Whether the no duty to retreat rule emanated from a macho frontiersman mentality or reflects toxic masculinity run amok, at the end of the day, is not nearly as relevant as the actual tangible consequences of relaxing self-defense standards to allow such killings. Homicide rates in states with relaxed self-defense standards continue to rise and are rising faster in states with broad Stand Your Ground protections.[802] Rather than act as a deterrent against criminal behavior, these relaxed standards risk creating open season anytime two or more individuals have a disagreement.

Moreover, as with any relaxed, amorphous, or flexible standards governing the use of force in the face of a perceived threat, broad self-defense protections disproportionately benefit White shooters against Black victims and penalize Black shooters against White victims. As discussed in detail in Chapter 5, numerous studies have found that White defendants claiming self-defense against perceived Black perpetrators are as much as ten times more likely to be acquitted than Black defendants claiming self-defense against perceived perpetrators of any race.[803] And Black defendants claiming self-defense against White aggressors have virtually no chance of acquittal, foreclosing for one marginalized group the ability to benefit from these expanded protections.[804]

These disproportionate findings are exacerbated in Stand Your Ground jurisdictions, where necessity is not the only self-defense element under attack. As discussed in Chapter 5, legislatures in Texas, Florida, and elsewhere have taken cues from the NRA and other gun lobbying groups and authorized private civilians to stand their ground and shoot to kill even when faced with a nondeadly threat, even if the threat is not imminent, and even if the threat is only to property.[805] Expanding the once-narrow concept of "self-defense" to this degree not only untethers lawful deadly force from all historical or moral understanding, but it provides yet another opportunity for the Trayvon Martins and Ahmaud Arberys of the world to face the deadly consequences of a racially fearful society.

These findings are not surprising, as they simply reflect the logical product of a White polity ingrained with fear of the "violent" or "criminal" tendencies of Black persons and the legal cover to shoot and kill when threatened even if not necessary. Those White shooters claiming self-defense against Black aggressors just as easily can be White jurors placing themselves in the defendant's shoes and finding – implicitly or explicitly, consciously or unconsciously – that a reasonable person would have pulled the trigger. And so it is with any societal system, legal or otherwise, imbued with discretion, flexibility, and "reasonableness" value judgments. Those judgments will always, structurally, systemically, and disproportionately, benefit the White dominant class over the Black marginalized class. That reality does not mean all discretion must

---

[802] *See generally supra* Chapter 5.

[803] *Id.*

[804] *Id.*

[805] *Id.*

be removed from the law; that is neither possible nor preferable. But when the stakes are as high as life and death, that discretion ought to be significantly curtailed to prevent as much unnecessary, unjust, and unequal bloodshed as possible. The English common law recognized as much; America should do the same. States should listen to the dire warnings of the ABA, criminal justice professionals, and social justice advocates who have shown for nearly a decade that Stand Your Ground laws and no duty to retreat rules make communities less safe, increase homicide and crime rates, put officers at greater risk of injury or death, and work to further harm and marginalized Black communities. These laws must be repealed.

8.2 REDEFINING REASONABLE USE OF POLICE FORCE

Just as private self-defense standards need recalibration to prevent unjustified, racially fearful vigilantism masked as lawful protection, so too do police use of force standards. As discussed throughout this book, the formless "objective reasonableness" standard articulated in *Graham* affords too much deference to police officers, refuses to consider the entire context surrounding a deadly police encounter, relies too much on the subjective, implicitly race-biased judgments of all involved, does not require deadly force to be used as a last resort, and results in too many unnecessary deaths being deemed justified. Just as with private self-defense standards, police use of force standards eschew any requirement of *necessity* in favor of what merely is *reasonable*, a value judgment that both diminishes the value of human life and disproportionately results in the deaths of Black people.

Meaningful changes to these Fourth Amendment standards in the judiciary are unlikely in the near term, given the current composition of the Supreme Court.[806] However, significant headway is being made at the legislative level, with important reform proposals offered by George Washington Law School Professor Cynthia Lee and the police reform organization Campaign Zero.

In 2018, Professor Lee wrote a law review article proposing model legislation to raise the standard for objectively reasonable use of deadly force by requiring three elements: (1) a reasonable belief that deadly force was immediately necessary; (2) the officer's actions were reasonable under the totality of the circumstances; and (3) the officer exhausted all other reasonably available options prior to using deadly force.[807] In

---

[806] Andrew Chung & Lawrence Hurley, *Analysis: U.S. Supreme Court nominee Barrett often rules for police in excessive force cases*, Reuters (October 25, 2020), https://www.reuters.com/article/us-usa-court-barrett-police-analysis/analysis-u-s-supreme-court-nominee-barrett-often-rules-for-police-in-excessive-force-cases-idUSKBN27A0C1; Osagie K. Obasogie, *The Bad-Apple Myth of Policing*, The Atlantic (August 2, 2019), https://www.theatlantic.com/politics/archive/2019/08/how-courts-judge-police-use-force/594832/.

[807] NPR, *Law Professor's Research Raises Bar for Police Use of Force* (May 23, 2021), https://www.npr.org/2021/05/23/999634385/law-professors-research-raises-bar-for-police-use-of-force; Cynthia Lee, *Reforming the Law on Police Use of Deadly Force: De-Escalation, Pre-Seizure Conduct, and Imperfect Self-Defense*, 2018 U. ILL. L. REV. 629, 674 (2018).

Professor Lee's own words, "just like the law of self-defense that applies to civilians, the new legislation that applies to police officers requires necessity, immediacy, and proportionality with an overlay of reasonableness."[808]

To the untrained eye, these reforms may seem modest, perhaps even redundant. They are anything but. First, Professor Lee's proposal requires a showing that the officer believed deadly force was actually *necessary* and not simply *reasonable* based on some unspecified potential future threat. Second, the language of Professor Lee's model legislation makes clear that the "totality of the circumstances" includes all context prior to the use of deadly force.[809] This includes the violent or nonviolent nature of the suspect's offense, any previous attempts by the officer to de-escalate the situation, and whether the officer himself took aggressive actions to escalate the situation. Third, by requiring officers to exhaust all reasonably available options, Professor Lee has injected a rough parallel to the English duty to retreat. While of course the officer will not actually retreat from an encounter with a suspect, Professor Lee's proposal requires the officer to first seek all other available avenues before using deadly force – in a sense, officers must retreat from deadly force if there exists a safe and available alternative option. Professor Lee's model legislation has been adopted, in whole or in part, by the District of Columbia, the State of Connecticut, and the Commonwealth of Virginia.[810]

Likewise, Campaign Zero has authored a model use of force policy for implementation not as legislation but as part of police department manuals.[811] Many of the same general principles guide this use of force policy, including requiring the exhaustion of all reasonable alternatives to deadly force, using the minimum amount of force necessary to apprehend a suspect, and using de-escalation techniques where possible. This policy takes on more granular issues as well, including banning chokeholds, strangleholds, and hog-tying, requiring officers to carry less lethal weapons, and requiring officers to intervene to stop officers using excessive force.[812]

One can imagine how the Andrew Brown, Jr. investigation might have unfolded differently under such a standard. It would have been far more difficult for District Attorney Womble to articulate why the officers reasonably believed it was necessary to shoot Mr. Brown in the back of the head as his car drove away from officers. Womble also would have been forced to account for the significant escalation exacerbated by the officers' own conduct, including serving as the overzealous "initial aggressor" in serving nonviolent drug warrants. Womble also would have been required to consider the other available alternatives officers did not exhaust before fatally shooting at Mr. Brown fourteen times, including pursuing the fleeing

---

[808]   NPR, *supra* note 807.

[809]   Lee, *supra* note 493.

[810]   NPR, *supra* note 493.

[811]   Campaign Zero, *Limit Use of Force*, https://www.joincampaignzero.org/force.

[812]   *Id.*

suspect on foot or by car, radioing for backup, or at a minimum, shooting out Mr. Brown's tires.

These proposals, and others like them, have traditionally met with stiff resistance from police unions and lobbies. For example, the International Association of Chiefs of Police authored a "Use of Force Position Paper" harshly criticizing two California state bills that would have justified the use of deadly force by police officers "only when the officer reasonably believes, based on the totality of the circumstances, that such force is necessary."[813] In flatly "oppos[ing] any effort to alter the *Graham v. Connor* standard," the IACP claimed that introducing a necessity component unfairly requires officers to be "perfect" in tense, split-second encounters.[814] Similar concerns have been voiced by Lexipol, a law enforcement agency consulting firm, which compared such legislation to a requirement that sports referees make absolutely perfect calls on the field every time with no benefit of instant replay.[815]

But these claims are not true. In neither Professor Lee's nor Campaign Zero's proposals does there exist a requirement that officers be factually correct. For example, if a violent crime suspect points what looks like a handgun directly at an officer but it later turns out to be a water gun, an officer's deadly response in such situation would not have been actually necessary; in other words, the officer would have been factually incorrect in his assessment of the need for deadly force. But under both proposals the officer's actions likely would be deemed justified, because the officer would have reasonably believed deadly force was immediately necessary to prevent being shot, and the circumstances suggest there would have been no other reasonable alternative (assuming the officer did not know the gun was fake or other known facts negating the immediacy of the threat). Contrary to IACP or Lexipol's claims, these reform proposals only require a reasonable belief that deadly force is necessary, not that officers make perfect judgments in all circumstances.

IACP also advanced a common criticism of raising the reasonableness standard, asserting that "[a]nother cost of the 'necessary' standard will be officer hesitation, resulting in potential injury or death of law enforcement personnel and harm to the community or others nearby."[816] Limited data on restrictive use of force policies tells a different story. Campaign Zero and the Use of Force Project reviewed police department use of force policies in the 100 largest US cities and found that more restrictive use of force policies correlated significantly with fewer assaults on officers. For departments with zero to one restrictive use of force policy in place, an average of 18 percent of officers were physically assaulted by suspects. That number dropped

---

[813] Intl. Assoc. of Chiefs of Police, *Use of Force Position Paper*, https://www.theiacp.org/sites/default/files/2019-05/Use%20of%20Force%20Task%20Force%20Recommendations_Final%20Draft.pdf.

[814] *Id.*

[815] Michael Ranalli, *Police Use of Force: The Need for the Objective Reasonableness Standard*, Lexipol (March 24, 2017), https://www.lexipol.com/resources/blog/police-use-of-force-need-objective-reasonableness-standard/.

[816] IACP, *supra* note 813.

to 16 percent for departments with two to three policies and to 9 percent for departments that had implemented four or more restrictive use of force policies.[817] The results were even more dramatic for officers killed in the line of duty. Departments implementing zero or one restrictive policy average .12 officer deaths per 1,000 officers, a number that dropped over 90 percent to .01 per 1,000 officers for departments implementing three or more restrictive use of force policies.[818]

This data also showed that crime rates remained relatively stable across all 100 departments, regardless of the use of force policy.[819] This finding is important for two reasons. First, it counters the narrative that restricting an officer's ability to use force will simply lead to increased crime as criminals will feel emboldened. Second, it demonstrates that declines in officer assaults and deaths are actually attributable to changes in use of force policies rather than the relative crime rates of the jurisdictions. For example, if a department implementing more restrictive use of force policies also happened to be policing a jurisdiction with far lower crime rates, the lower rate of officer injury and death might be coincidental. That appears not to be the case. Instead, and contrary to the assertions of IACP and other policy lobbying groups, restricting use of force beyond the minimum guardrails placed by the Supreme Court actually keeps officers safer.

8.3 REWIRING THE POLICE RELATIONSHIP TO FORCE

Jurisprudential and legislative changes to police use of force standards are important. But despite these initial successes championed by Professor Lee and others, they also remain longshots, at least at the federal level. Current United States Supreme Court composition does not provide much hope for reform advocates looking for tightened Fourth Amendment use of force requirements. And while Congress has debated the George Floyd Justice in Policing Act, a comprehensive reform bill promising to end qualified immunity, ban chokeholds and no-knock warrants, end racial profiling, limit military equipment in law enforcement, and investigate police misconduct, the prospect for any meaningful portion of this bill becoming law in a sharply divided legislature remains as murky as any number of failed comprehensive reform efforts of the last three decades.[820] State and local efforts to enact similar reforms appear more promising, but remain more uneven and halting.

Thankfully, police departments need not rely on dictates from Congress or the Supreme Court to reframe their own approach to the use of force on America's streets. In fact, more and more police departments are taking the initiative themselves to prioritize de-escalation, reimagine force as a last resort option and not

[817]   Police Use of Force Project, http://useofforceproject.org/#project.
[818]   *Id.*
[819]   *Id.*
[820]   House Committee on the Judiciary, *Justice in Policing Act*, https://judiciary.house.gov/issues/issue/?IssueID=14924.

merely a reasonable choice among many alternatives, and in the process protect both their officers and the citizens their serve.

Much of this reform effort began with the nonprofit Police Executive Research Forum (PERF), a policy organization started by Chuck Wexler to answer a simple question: "Why can police in the UK arrest people without shooting them?"[821] The answer, according to Wexler, is "about training, not just policy."[822] In 2016, PERF developed the ICAT training, standing for Integrating Communications, Assessment, and Tactics. This training challenges many of the notions undergirding both police training and Supreme Court opinions, including "[t]he notion that cops have to [always] make split-second decisions" and that deadly force should be permitted anytime it might be "reasonable" to do so.[823] ICAT trains officers in de-escalation techniques designed to increase communication among officers and between officers and suspects, promoting the idea that deadly force is not appropriate unless absolutely necessary, even if it may otherwise be lawful. Since 2016, more than 600 police agencies have attended ICAT training sessions, with many departments integrating the training into their use of force manuals. Other agencies teach similar techniques, but neither PERF nor these other agencies have reached more than a fraction of the 18,000 police agencies across the country.[824]

Early anecdotal returns are promising, as evidenced by two departments plagued with high profile problems: Camden, New Jersey and Louisville, Kentucky. For decades, the Camden Police Department was "considered among the most dangerous in the country, beset with high murder rates and claims of excessive force."[825] In 2013, the department was disbanded and became a countywide operation. De-escalation became a central tenet of the reorganized agency, which stressed "patience and talking to suspects rather than using aggressive takedowns."[826] In 2019, the Camden County Police Department collaborated with New York University School of Law's Policing Project on an updated use of force manual that garnered the support of the unlikeliest of bedfellows: the ACLU of New Jersey and the local Fraternal Order of Police lodge. These changes have yielded tangible returns, as the number of excessive force complaints dropped from sixty-five in 2014 to only three in 2020. During that same six-year period, officers fatally shot three suspects, all of which were deemed justified.[827]

One example of the training in action, recounted in the American Bar Association's ABA Journal, highlights the policy in action. On September 14, 2020, Camden police approached a rape suspect on a street holding a knife. The officers yelled for the suspect to drop his knife, but the suspect instead began approaching

---

[821] Kevin Davis, *Defusing Deadly Force*, ABA JOURNAL (June–July 2021).
[822] *Id.*
[823] *Id.*
[824] *Id.*
[825] *Id.*
[826] *Id.*
[827] *Id.*

officers slowly and stating "I'll stab you."[828] Under *Graham v. Connor* and its progeny, police likely would have been "justified" in shooting and killing the suspect at this point. Instead, the officers' captain on the radio reminded them to keep a safe five to ten foot distance for as long as possible while they tried to talk the suspect down. After several more minutes of fruitless discussions with the suspect, one officer pulled her Taser and fired a single shot, neutralizing but not seriously injuring him. As Camden County Captain Gabriel Rodriguez explained, the law might have allowed his officers to kill the suspect, but a more sensible and morally justifiable policy is one that reflects not the maximum power potential of police but the "sanctity of life."[829]

Critics of these policies, including many officers, worry that they are "gonna kill cops because you're teaching them to hesitate."[830] And surprisingly, there remains little comprehensive data about the effects of these programs on a national scale. But the Louisville Police Department, beset with scandal involving the killing of Breonna Taylor following the execution of a no-knock warrant, has reported promising results. Since the implementation of de-escalation training and updating its use of force manual, "officers had 20% fewer incidents involving use of force, 26% fewer injuries to citizens, and 36% fewer injuries to officers."[831] Thus, contrary to the perception that these techniques will put officers in greater danger, there is at least some evidence that de-escalation protects both officer and civilian.

8.4 TRUE ACCOUNTABILITY

Departmental changes to use of force policies represent steps in the right direction. But with 1,127 individuals killed by police in 2020, over half of whom either were unarmed, suspected of a nonviolent crime, or suspected of no crime at all, the reality remains that hundreds of officer-involved shootings every year will require significant investigation into potential criminal or civil liability.[832] For far too long, compromised prosecutors, deferential judges and juries, and the doctrine of qualified immunity have all but foreclosed the prospect of any real accountability for police brutality. That must change and must become a pillar of any attempt at rebuilding trust with police departments, alongside community engagement. Only by empowering independent prosecutors to investigate police misconduct, critically examining police incident reports, and dismantling qualified immunity's stranglehold on justice can true accountability, and true trust, begin to take place.

[828] *Id.*
[829] *Id.*
[830] *Id.*
[831] *Id.*
[832] *Id.*

8.5 EMPOWERING THE INDEPENDENT PROSECUTOR

Local prosecutors must, and should, work closely with their jurisdiction's police officers to conduct their business. Although officers respond to alleged criminal activity without prosecutors and prosecutors conduct investigations independently from police, they necessarily work together as a team and depend on each other in carrying out their respective duties. Among other things, prosecutors depend on police officers to properly document arrests and gather sufficient evidence to sustain a conviction, often asking them to testify at trial to present that evidence. In turn, officers rely on prosecutors to carry out the justice of convicting those whom they have arrested. This close working relationship creates potential conflicts of interest when prosecutors are asked to investigate and prosecute the very same officers on whom prosecutors rely for witnesses and evidence. In addition, over 80 percent of all local prosecutors in the United States are elected, and "they not only work closely with police to investigate and punish crimes, but also often depend on police union endorsements to win and keep their jobs. Thus, local prosecutors are heavily influenced not to make decisions that would anger those unions."[833]

Andrew Womble is only the latest in a long line of prosecutors whose conduct in investigating a police shooting left many questioning the independence of the investigation. In 2014, St. Louis County prosecuting attorney Robert McCullough was tasked with investigating Darren Wilson, the Ferguson, Missouri police officer who fatally shot unarmed teenager Michael Brown. McCullough's use of the grand jury responsible for hearing the evidence against Wilson and recommending whether or not to bring charges raised many eyebrows. While grand juries are typically used as a "forum in which prosecutors present their best evidence for a criminal prosecution … and advise a specific charge," McCullough presented significant evidence on Wilson's behalf, "an approach virtually without precedent in the law of Missouri or anywhere else."[834] In fact, McCullough presented Wilson's detailed account of his encounter with Brown, unchallenged, leaving jurors to take the account at face value. When the grand jury failed to return an indictment and the transcript of the proceedings was released, Harvard Criminal Justice Institute director Ronald S. Sullivan, Jr. remarked that it was "the most unusual marshaling of a grand jury's resources I've seen in my 25 years as a lawyer and scholar."[835]

That same year, then-District Attorney Daniel Donovan received harsh criticism for failing to secure a grand jury indictment in the death of Eric Garner, an unarmed Black man selling cigarettes on a street corner who was choked to death by police officers despite not resisting arrest and repeatedly exclaiming, "I can't breathe!" The

---

[833] Kami Chavis Simmons, *Increasing Police Accountability: Restoring Trust and Legitimacy Through the Appointment of Independent Prosecutors*, 49 Wash. U. J. L. & Pol'y. 137 (2015).

[834] David Zucchino, *Prosecutor's Grand Jury Strategy in Ferguson Case Adds to Controversy*, LA Times (November 25, 2014), https://www.latimes.com/nation/la-na-ferguson-da-analysis-20141126-story.html.

[835] *Id.*

grand jury proceedings remained sealed, but many observers were "wary" of Donovan's careful and cautious public approach to the case as he planned what later that year would become a successful run for Congress.[836]

These and other high-profile cases of questionable prosecutorial conduct led members of Congress to propose the Police Training and Independent Review Act of 2015, which among other things, would have provided funding to appoint independent special prosecutors to investigate cases of federal officer-involved shootings.[837] The act never passed, but it represented a step in the right direction toward true, independent investigation of police misconduct.

State and local governments should go further. Recognizing the inherent conflicts of interest local prosecutors have when investigating their own officers, states should establish a permanent Special Prosecutor's Office that is authorized to investigate and prosecute all cases where police kill or seriously injure a civilian and cases where a civilian alleges serious criminal misconduct against a police officer. This Special Prosecutor's Office should utilize independent investigators from across the state, civil servants who are chosen at random to minimize political influence or conflicts of interest. All findings should be reported to the public. While such an office remains theoretically susceptible to the influence of the politicians who appoint the Special Prosecutor, these attorneys will lack the inherent close contacts with the officers they investigate.[838]

8.6 BEYOND POLICE SELF-REPORTING

Independent criminal investigations into police misconduct are important not only because of the inherently compromised positions in which these investigations place sitting district attorneys. They are also critical to incentivize digging deeper than the on-the-record accounts of the officers themselves, which are often incomplete, inaccurate, and even self-serving or false. Perhaps not surprisingly, police self-reporting on fatal shootings often sanitize reality and present facts in a light most favorable to the officers and their decisions to use deadly force. How do we know? By comparing official police incident reports to civilian cell phone footage capturing the same incident. The difference between the officer written narratives and the reality captured on video can be so shocking that they leave one with a single inescapable conclusion: that police can and sometimes do mislead in self-reporting to protect themselves.

Take, for example, the initial Minneapolis police incident report and press release regarding George Floyd's fatal encounter with Derek Chauvin and his three

[836] Alexander Burns, *Daniel Donovan Gets a Wary Welcome to Congress After Eric Garner Case*, NY Times (May 22, 2015), https://www.nytimes.com/2015/05/23/nyregion/daniel-donovan-gets-a-wary-welcome-to-congress-after-eric-garner-case.html.

[837] Congress.gov, *H.R. 2302 – Police Training and Independent Review Act of 2015*, https://www.congress.gov/bill/114th-congress/house-bill/2302/text.

[838] *See* Campaign Zero, *Independent Investigations and Prosecutions*, https://www.joincampaignzero.org/investigations.

colleagues. The press release, titled "Man Dies After Medical Incident During Police Interaction," described officers' interaction with Floyd as follows:

> Two officers arrived and located the suspect, a male believed to be in his 40s, in his car. He was ordered to step from his car. After he got out, he physically resisted officers. Officers were able to get the suspect into handcuffs and noted he appeared to be suffering medical distress. Officers called for an ambulance. He was transported to Hennepin County Medical Center by ambulance where he died a short time later.

The release further claimed that at no time were weapons of any type used by anyone involved in this incident.[839]

In light of the video footage the whole world has witnessed, as well as Chauvin's conviction, "that original press release is worth revisiting to understand the ways that police statements can hide the truth with a mix of passive language, blatant omissions, and mangled sense of timing."[840] This woefully incomplete description of Floyd's murder suggests a physically assaultive suspect, officers acting with restraint to handcuff him without using weapons while responding compassionately and promptly to the suspect's medical issue, and then the suspect dying as an unfortunate result of this medical issue completely independent of any police action.

What a farce. So much of this statement is untrue, incomplete, and misleading, that one shudders to think what might have happened – or not happened – had civilians not recorded the incident on their cell phones and had the Cup Foods convenience store security camera not been pointed in just the right position to capture what really happened. A line-by-line analysis of this statement confirms that Minneapolis officers responsible for Floyd's death deliberately covered up a murder.

"He was ordered to step from his car. After he got out, he physically resisted officers." This statement is simply untrue. Cell phone footage taken by a driver in the car behind Floyd's clearly shows Officer J. Alexander Krueng confronting Floyd in the driver's seat of his car, gun drawn, then physically yanking Floyd from the car and immediately placing him in handcuffs. There was no physical resistance after Floyd stepped from the car, because Floyd was dragged from his car and placed in handcuffs and controlled by Officer Kreung simultaneously.[841] But this statement is critical to presenting a narrative of a suspect ignoring police directives and physically assaulting officers, because both factors help portray an out of control situation justifying police use of force.

[839] *Investigative Update on Critical Incident* (May 26, 2020), https://web.archive.org/web/20210331182901/ https://www.insidempd.com/2020/05/26/man-dies-after-medical-incident-during-police-interaction/.

[840] Eric Levenson, *How Minneapolis Police First Described the Murder of George Floyd, and What We Know Now*, CNN (April 21, 2021), https://www.cnn.com/2021/04/21/us/minneapolis-police-george-floyd-death/index.html.

[841] Evan Hill, Ainara Tiefenthaler, Christiaan Triebert, Drew Jordan, Haley Willis, & Robin Stein, *How George Floyd Was Killed in Police Custody*, NY Times (May 31, 2020), https://www.nytimes.com/video/us/100000007159353/george-floyd-arrest-death-video.html.

"Officers were able to get the suspect into handcuffs and noted he appeared to be suffering medical distress." So much is left unsaid in this single sentence. But the words that are chosen are just as important. The use of passive voice – "were able to get the suspect into handcuffs" – works to minimize the active violence used by officers to force Floyd into handcuffs and pin him to the ground and provoke Floyd's initial pleas that he could not breathe. Likewise, the phrase "appeared to be suffering medical distress" utilizes the passive voice to imply that Floyd simply had a condition that was happening, not that officers actively restricted his airways causing him not to breathe. But of course so much is left unsaid as well. The police report fails to mention that Floyd was handcuffed less than one minute into the encounter and remained handcuffed and under control for the next twenty minutes while officers investigated. It fails to mention that Officer Kreung got Floyd into the back of the squad car, only to have Chauvin appear on the other side of the vehicle, drag Floyd out of the car, and force him face down onto the pavement. It fails to mention that Chauvin kept his knee on Floyd's neck for nine minutes and nineteen seconds until Floyd lay motionless.[842] And of course, it fails to mention that the "medical distress" suffered by Floyd was his inability to breathe – articulated clearly and repeatedly by Floyd – specifically because of Chauvin's knee. None of what happened on the other side of that police car, including Chauvin's involvement, would have come to light if not for two other civilians standing by capturing the fateful video on their cellphones.

"He was transported to Hennepin County Medical Center by ambulance where he died a short time later." This is a lie. Floyd died under Chauvin's neck, a fact of which the officers were aware at least by the time the ambulance arrived and detected no pulse or other signs of life.[843] But this ending is important to transfer any causal blame from police and imply that Floyd had an unrelated medical incident, police promptly called for medical assistance, and unfortunately that medical assistance could not prevent Floyd's death.

"At no time were weapons of any type used by anyone involved in this incident." This statement is technically true only insofar as traditional weapons – firearms, knives, tasers, etc. – are concerned. But again, it omits known critical details, including the use of a knee for nearly ten minutes as a weapon against the suspect. And lest one think the inclusion of a knee as a weapon is a stretch, it bears remembering that officers have justified shooting and killing suspects in other circumstances because they faced imminent threats of death from stationary vehicles, dogs, and fists.

This shameful police self-reporting of George Floyd's murder further confirms the necessity of a full and impartial independent investigation of any potential criminal police misconduct by a special prosecutor who has no connection to the

---

[842]   *Id.*

[843]   BBC News, *Derek Chauvin Trial: Paramedics Say Floyd Had No Pulse When They Arrived* (April 2, 2021), https://www.bbc.com/news/world-us-canada-56606418.

officers involved and thus no inherent reason to trust or defer to the statements made by the officers. While appointing an independent investigator may not solve the systemic problem of giving the benefit of the doubt to officer statements and testimony based solely on their status as officers, the Floyd incident report ought to give all players in the criminal justice system – prosecutors, judges, and juries – pause before affording such automatic deference.

The lethal dangers of police self-reporting extend beyond Minneapolis. Indeed, on March 29, 2021, during the middle of Derek Chauvin's murder trial, the world heard about the shooting of unarmed thirteen-year-old Adam Toledo by Chicago police officer Eric Stillman. The police incident report stated that an adult between the ages of "18 and 25" presented an "imminent threat of battery with [a] weapon" and "used force likely to cause death or great bodily harm" with a "semi-auto pistol."[844] The report also noted that the suspect "did not follow verbal direction" and "fled," which forced police to fire their weapons at him to "overcome resistance or aggression." The Chicago Police Department initially described the incident in a tweet as an "armed confrontation." Based on this self-reporting, on April 10, 2021, Cook County Assistant State Attorney James Murphy alleged in court that the suspect was armed when the officer shot him in self-defense.[845]

However, on April 15, 2021, when police watchdog agency Civilian Office of Police Accountability secured and released bodycam footage of the incident, an entirely different story unfolded. The footage shows a young boy, Adam Toledo, standing unarmed in an alleyway with a recently discarded handgun on the ground. Officer Stillman rushes to Adam and screams "show me your fucking hands," and Adam immediately thrusts his empty hands into the air in compliance. 838 milliseconds (about five-sixths of a second) after Stillman shouted his demand, Stillman shot and killed Adam.[846]

For approximately three weeks after the footage came to light, Mr. Murphy was placed on administrative leave for misleading the court about whether Adam was armed at the time he was shot. On April 19, 2021, Cook County State's Attorney Kim Foxx acknowledged the lack of transparency from Officer Stillman's incident report, observing that "This is about the expectation of law enforcement to be forthright and transparent. There is no sacrificial lamb here. This is about making sure we get it right and when we don't get it right, owning it and doing what we need to do to make

[844] Chicago Police Dept. Original Case Incident Report, https://www.chicagocopa.org/wp-content/uploads/2021/04/Original-Case-Report_REDACTED.pdf; Charles Davis, *Inconsistencies between New Video of Chicago Police Shooting 13-year-old Adam Toledo and the Police Reports*, Business Insider (April 15, 2021), https://www.businessinsider.com/police-report-falsely-states-13-year-old-adam-toledo-adult-2021-4.

[845] *Id.*; Grace Hauck, *Evolution of a City's Account of a Killing: How Chicago's Narrative Changed in the Fatal Police Shooting of Adam Toledo*, USA Today (April 17, 2021), https://www.usatoday.com/story/news/nation/2021/04/16/adam-toledo-police-shooting-how-chicagos-narrative-changed/7260911002/.

[846] Brendan O'Brien, *Chicago Releases Graphic Video of Police Shooting 13-Year-Old*, Reuters (April 15, 2021), https://www.reuters.com/world/us/chicago-release-video-police-shooting-13-year-old-boy-2021-04-15/.

sure that it doesn't happen again."[847] That same day, it was reported that Stillman had been listed as a victim on an initial police incident report, a tactic explained by law-enforcement expert Tom Nolan as a "long-used and hackneyed police trope" to recast "the focus of culpability and blame onto the actual victim of the police deadly-force incident, i.e., the person who the police killed."[848]

On May 5, 2021, it was announced that Mr. Murphy had resumed his role and was no longer on leave. Officer Stillman faced no charges and is back on duty.[849]

8.7 ENDING QUALIFIED IMMUNITY – ALL OF IT

The Supreme Court's expansion of its judicially created doctrine of qualified immunity has shielded virtually all police misconduct from civil liability, no matter how egregious. Lacking the ability to find prior published cases with identical facts, litigants challenging police misconduct under Section 1983 almost always fail to pass the insurmountable hurdle that the officer violated a "clearly established" constitutional right. The farcical nature of this doctrine has led to federal, state, and local legislation across the country seeking to reform or abolish qualified immunity for police officers. The version of the George Floyd Justice in Policing Act that passed in the House of Representatives on March 3, 2021, expressly abolished qualified immunity for police officers in federal civil rights cases.[850] This marked an important symbolic moment in the fight for police accountability, even if that version of the bill is unlikely to pass a sharply divided Senate.

But these reform efforts miss another "more debilitating doctrinal limitation on civil rights claims: the rule that provides all but complete liability protection for municipal governments that employ the police officers who engage in misconduct."[851] While existing qualified immunity reforms focus on limiting or abolishing protections for individual police officers, none of them yet address the fact that local governments remain largely untouchable in Section 1983 lawsuits. In

---

[847] Fran Spielman, *Foxx Says She Should Have Known What Prosecutor Would Say in Court about Police Shooting of Adam Toledo*, Chicago Sun Times (April 22, 2021), https://chicago.suntimes.com/fran-spielman-show/2021/4/22/22397865/kim-foxx-toledo-chicago-police-shooting-adam-toledo-prosecutor-murphy-roman-gun-hearing.

[848] Lauren Frias, *The Police Officer Who Fatally Shot 13-Year-Old Adam Toledo Was Listed As a Victim on an Incident Report: One Law-Enforcement Expert Said it's "an Old Cop Trick Meant to Muddy the Murky Waters,"* Yahoo! News (April 19, 2021), https://news.yahoo.com/police-officer-fatally-shot-13–031838189.html%3Fguce_referrer=aHR0cHM6Ly93d3cuZ29vZ2xlLmNvbvbS8&guce_referrer_sig=AQAAAJpvvo-HXGDrF.lt1-_b1kyXwoYH8KGjGtTzmF.nIpHM-VudUh1yoRqZ7aj1qcvg4cg4j7-90-nIIoM SQMZkCvSIYVCiaqxRBXOMRU5kmfAO_8yqzvALWbv-WaBzAIkvdbBWorsOUOiBVBm NZta9MoGtFHqGQsnCtAVbXhdo3KirjF&guccounter=2.

[849] Erik Ortiz, *Illinois Prosecutor Kim Foxx Admits "Breakdown in Communication" in Adam Toledo Case*, NBC News (May 5, 2021), https://www.nbcnews.com/news/us-news/top-illinois-prosecutor-kim-foxx-admits-breakdown-communication-adam-toledo-n1266395.

[850] *See* House Committee on the Judiciary, *supra* note 820.

[851] Mark C. Niles, *Here's a More Important Reform Than Ending Qualified Immunity*, Lawfare (May 18, 2021), https://www.lawfareblog.com/heres-more-important-reform-ending-qualified-immunity.

Monell v. Department of Social Services of the City of New York, female employees of New York City alleged they were forced by the city to take medical leave because of their pregnancies.[852] Writing for the majority, Justice William Brennan held that municipalities could be sued for Section 1983 claims, but sharply limited the circumstances under which they could face liability for monetary damages in such claims. Brennan concluded that Section 1983 exposed local governments to liability only "where, as here, the action that is alleged to be unconstitutional implements or executes a policy statement, ordinance, regulation, or decision officially adopted and promulgated by the body's officers."[853] In doing so, Brennan expressly rejected the private tort law doctrine of vicarious liability, which holds employers liable for the actions of their employees. In other words, even if a rogue police officer could be held liable for using excessive force in violation of the Constitution, the government employing that officer could not be held liable unless the government had an express policy officially endorsing such force. Suffice it to say, that is an unlikely situation.

This near absolute immunity for local governments has two devastating real-world consequences. First, for the individual litigants seeking to vindicate their rights, there exists the real possibility that any monetary judgment will go unsatisfied as the only defendant required to pay for damages is an individual police officer and not a government entity. Second, and more broadly, without any risk of liability for police misconduct, local governments "have no incentive to address systematic cultures and procedures that habitually result in police misconduct, or to discipline or dismiss officers who commit repeated violations."[854] Instead, local governments have shown a willingness to employ a "reactionary approach to police misconduct," compensating individual victims of police brutality in the small handful of cases with overwhelming evidence of misconduct while largely ignoring the opportunity to take proactive measures to positively reform police departments and prevent misconduct in the future.[855]

Thus, any effort to reform or end qualified immunity should also include imposing vicarious liability for local governments that employ rogue government officials, including police officers. Exposing local municipalities to liability for the actions of their officers would provide a strong incentive that has long been lacking: to take better care to prepare their officers, to implement better training programs before sending officers out in the government's name, to closely monitor the actions of their departments, and to promptly respond to any misconduct as it arises. This approach would shift the focus of governments from reacting to harm already caused by bad policing to proactively preventing it in the first place. And it would better align the objectives of all reform advocates – to reduce structural, systematic violence and

[852] 436 U.S. 658 (1978).
[853] *Id.* at 690.
[854] Niles, *supra* note 851.
[855] *Id.*

inequities in policing – with a tangible solution to meet that objective. While Congress and state governments may implement legislation regulating use of force and mandating stricter de-escalation techniques, at the end of the day "there is no better entity than a local government to spread the costs required for training and maintaining an effective but benign police force," to respond to the unique needs of its individual municipality, and to create the necessary conditions to foster a better and more productive police–community relationship.[856]

8.8 A COMPREHENSIVE APPROACH OF CARROTS AND STICKS

Retreating from this country's culture of shoot first violent response will take more than the implementation of new laws or policies. Intergenerational shifts in attitudes towards guns and violence, in perceived racial biases, and in the foundational approach society takes to policing, are needed for systemic reform. But as this chapter outlines, a series of carrots and sticks designed to persuade and compel both private and public actors to seek nonviolent de-escalation when possible is a necessary start in that direction. Legislatures, courts, and public agencies have played an unfortunate role in weaponizing society's racial fear, and they can play an equally important role in shepherding a societal shift away from this weaponization. Over time, as increased promotion of the "sanctity of life" in policing and private conduct becomes ingrained in the fabric of law and policy, one hopes these shifts can and will create larger incentives and shifts in society at large, and de-escalation will become a hallmark of informal social control in White and Black spaces in America, and all the spaces in between.

[856]   *Id.*

Epilogue

"Send Her Back"

In July 2019, four newly elected Congresswomen – Ilhan Omar, Alexandria Ocasio-Cortez, Ayanna Pressley, and Rashida Talib – held a press conference to challenge what they viewed as inadequate humanitarian aid proposals from Democratic House Speaker Nancy Pelosi. In doing so, these four women of color – all US citizens, three native born – criticized the long history of racism affecting the roots of the US justice system. In response, the President of the United States told these four US citizens, all duly elected members of Congress, to "go back" to the countries "from which they came":

> So interesting to see "Progressive" Democrat Congresswomen, who originally came from countries whose governments are a complete and total catastrophe, the worst, most, corrupt and inept anywhere in the world, now viciously telling the people of the United States, the greatest and most powerful Nation on earth, how our government is to be run. Why don't they go back and help fix the totally broken and crime infested places from which they came. Then come back and show us how it is done.[857]

When he repeated the claim at a campaign rally later that month, he basked and smiled as the crowd chanted, "Send Her Back! Send Her Back! Send Her Back!"[858]

When Donald Trump told these women to "go back" where they came from, he invoked a centuries-old racist trope aimed at eliminating legitimate existence for the "other" in American life. That "other" has often been defined by the dominant social caste as anyone not White, not natively born in America, or not Protestant. But more

---

[857] Donald Trump's tweets are no longer available on Twitter. This tweet was widely publicized. *See*, *e.g.*, Katie Rogers & Nicholas Fandos, *Trump Tells Congresswomen to "Go Back" to the Countries They Came From*, N.Y. TIMES (July 14, 2019), https://www.nytimes.com/2019/07/14/us/politics/trump-twitter-squad-congress.html; Allan Smith, *Trump Says Congresswomen of Color Should "Go Back" and Fix the Places They "Originally Came From,"* NBC NEWS (July 14, 2019), https://www.nbcnews.com/politics/donald-trump/trump-says-progressive-congresswomen-should-go-back-where-they-came-n1029676.

[858] Rebecca Morin, " *Send Her Back" Chants Erupt as Trump Criticizes Ilhan Omar at North Carolina Rally*, USA TODAY (July 17, 2019), https://www.usatoday.com/story/news/politics/elections/2019/07/17/send-her-back-chants-erupt-donald-trump-criticizes-ilhan-omar/1763602001/.

than any other subordinated group in American history, the admonition to "go back" has been reserved for Black Americans. More than any fearful attack on a Black person's legitimacy in a White space, the charge to "go back where you came from" or "Go Back to Africa" seeks to delegitimize Black existence in America in its entirety. Or framed alternatively, to render all of America a White space.

Of course, US citizens cannot be "sent back" anywhere, especially citizens born in Cincinnati, the Bronx, and Detroit. But the offensiveness of this claim takes on a special level of absurdity for Congresswoman Pressley. Ayanna Pressley was born in Cincinnati, Ohio.[859] Her family has lived in the United States for generations – indeed, probably longer than the nation has existed, because Pressley is the descendant of slaves.[860] Her ancestors were stolen from their homes and brought to America forcibly to build the very country its president claimed Pressley needed to leave. People of African descent "were dragged to this land 400 years ago."[861] This "greatest and most powerful Nation on earth" owes its economic fortunes to the centuries of free labor it exploited, a head start akin to national affirmative action. Yet Black Americans' "claim to full citizenry has always been dubious at best and conditional at worst."[862]

But Trump's nakedly racist, sexist, xenophobic rant communicates another message as well: that political space is a White space. Unlike the physical spaces of gentrifying neighborhoods or Ivy League campuses, the political space (and indeed all spaces of social power) is a metaphorical space historically reserved for White people, ceded to "others" only after bloody conflict. A Civil War to emancipate enslaved Black persons and win Black men the right to vote. A Civil Rights movement emblematized by a battered and bleeding John Lewis on the Edmund Pettus Bridge, marching to stop Black voter suppression and win true enfranchisement for all Black citizens. Daily racist invective hurled at all politicians of color, particularly women of color. That the "Insulter in Chief" would reserve this particular slur for four women of color was no accident. Nor was it a surprise, coming from the man who began his political career by baselessly challenging the legitimacy of the first Black man to occupy the White House.

This recognition that the struggle over Black and White spaces extends beyond the street and into the corridors of political power is critical to understanding the issues and solutions discussed throughout this book. Incremental changes can be made at the margins within police departments and 911 call centers. But only sweeping legislative change, backed by true voter enfranchisement, can bring about the racial détente needed to protect Black bodies in public White spaces.

[859] *Meet Ayanna*, U.S. CONGRESSWOMAN AYANNA PRESSLEY, https://pressley.house.gov/about (last visited March 1, 2021).

[860] Kamilah A. Pickett & Suad Abdul Khabeer, *The Long History of Black Americans Being Told to "Go Back,"* AL JAZEERA (July 24, 2019), https://www.aljazeera.com/opinions/2019/7/24/the-long-history-of-black-americans-being-told-to-go-back/.

[861] *Id.*

[862] *Id.*

The reforms advocated within these pages – reallocating police resources, deterring and punishing 911 abuse, reining in self-defense claims, heightening reasonable police use of force requirements, and ending qualified immunity – enjoy broad public support. But these changes elude us because voter suppression tactics deny marginalized communities full voter enfranchisement, because too few Americans equate voting with activism, and because too many people of color are denied meaningful opportunities to occupy the political White space.

"GO BACK TO AFRICA"

"Go back to where you came from" has deep roots in the American psyche. The specific words have changed over time, but the sentiment has been part of the nation's intellectual and emotional history since its beginnings. As historian Michael Cornfield explained, "the idea that we don't have any more room for people, or those people don't look like us, this is a long, ugly strain in American history."[863] The sentiment survives to this day. In the aftermath of Trump's tweet to members of the "Squad," the *New York Times* asked readers to share their own stories of being told to "go back." The request elicited responses from some 16,000 readers – people of varied national and ethnic origins, both natural-born citizens and immigrants.[864]

At least in part, the persistence of anti-immigrant sentiment is a result of tensions persisting from the nation's founding. In the earliest years of the new union, as it struggled to fashion a new kind of political structure, some of the core questions concerned the nature of citizenship: What does it mean to be a citizen of a union rather than the subject of a king? And who is eligible to be such a citizen?[865] Often, at least in popular sentiment, the question appears to have been answered in the negative: by identifying who *doesn't* belong here. That trend can be seen in various admonitions to go away or stay away, addressed to – or hurled at – successive waves of immigrants, from the French "Jacobins and vagabonds" targeted by the Alien and

---

[863] Quoted in Colin Dwyer & Andrew Limbong, *"Go Back Where You Came From": The Long Rhetorical Roots of Trump's Racist Tweet*, NPR: History, July 15, 2019, https://www.npr.org/2019/07/15/741827580/go-back-where-you-came-from-the-long-rhetorical-roots-of-trump-s-racist-tweets. In the same article, Jennifer Wingard, a scholar of rhetoric, argues that the specific phrasing of the sentiment is not really significant: "They carry these sentiments that we have seen over centuries, but then they get repurposed for the current moment – and a phrase like that . . . becomes almost like a shorthand for anti-immigrant sentiment. . . . You know, 'go back where you came from' is the same as 'go back to your own country' is the same as 'you are not allowed here' is the same as 'no immigrants allowed.' Yet it carries all of this historical shorthand with it."

[864] Lara Takenaga & Aidan Gardiner, *16,000 Readers Shared Their Experiences of Being Told to "Go Back." Here Are Their Stories*, New York Times (July 19, 2019), www.nytimes.com/2019/07/19/reader-center/trump-go-back-stories.html.

[865] Douglas Bradburn discusses the evolution of these questions and the struggle with the meaning of citizenship in the early republic in *The Citizenship Revolution: Politics & the Creation of the American Union, 1774–1804* (2009).

Sedition Acts of 1798,[866] to later Chinese, Irish, and Italian arrivals. (For all the horrific treatment to which Native Americans have been subjected, they were largely spared this one insult, though their demands that European colonizers return stolen land and go back to where they came from went ignored.)

The phrase in its current form became more explicitly directed at Black people in the period around the Civil Rights Era. Indeed, it features prominently in two iconic photographs of the era. In a 1963 photograph of young male students protesting school integration in Birmingham, Alabama, a protestor holds a sign reading "Go back to Africa Negroes." In another photograph, taken in Little Rock, Arkansas, on September 4, 1957, a White girl (later identified as Hazel Bryan) screams at Elizabeth Eckford, one of the Little Rock Nine seeking to desegregate Arkansas's schools, as Elizabeth makes her way to Little Rock Central High School on the first day of school. Bryan reportedly screamed, "Go home, n–! Go back to Africa!"[867]

"Go back where you came from" may resonate most strongly with the Civil Rights Era, but the idea of sending Black people back to Africa – back where they came from – has an even longer life in American thought, before and after the Revolution, as anti-immigrant sentiment. It has, in fact, "been an undercurrent of American racial politics for almost as long as there have been blacks in the United States."[868] Indeed, by some accounts, the idea predates the United States itself, dating back as far as 1714.[869] In an 1811 letter, Thomas Jefferson praised the idea of deporting free Blacks to Africa as "the most desirable measure which could be adopted for gradually drawing off this part of our population most advantageously for themselves as well as for us."[870]

Deportation offered an attractive solution to a complex challenge for the slave-owning economy. Free Blacks (both emancipated slaves and free Blacks who had immigrated to the United States of their own will) presented real problems. They

---

[866]   James Bayard, quoted in Carol Berkin, *A Sovereign People: The Crises of the 1790s and the Birth of American Nationalism* 203 (2017).

[867]   The story was widely reported, appearing in newspapers even decades later; it often led stories on the anniversaries of the desegregation effort. *See, for instance,* Erin Blakemore, *The Story Behind the Famous Little Rock Nine "Scream Image,"* HISTORY.COM (September 3, 2018), www.history.com/news/the-story-behind-the-famous-little-rock-nine-scream-image. Bryan later regretted her actions and sought out Eckford to apologize to her; the two became friends for a while, but they ultimately found they could not overcome the racial tensions permeating their relationship. A number of sources tell their story. *See, e.g.,* David Margolick, *Elizabeth Eckford and Hazel Bryan: The Story Behind the Photograph that Shamed America,* TELEGRAPH (October 9, 2011), www.telegraph.co.uk/news/worldnews/northamerica/8813134/Elizabeth-Eckford-and-Hazel-Bryan-the-story-behind-the-photograph-that-shamed-America.html.

[868]   Michael S. Rosenwald & Cleve R. Wootson Jr., *Send Her Back!: Trump, Ilhan Omar & the Complicated History of Back to Africa,* WASH. POST (July 20, 2019), www.washingtonpost.com/history/2019/07/20/send-her-back-trump-ilhan-omar-complicated-history-back-africa/.

[869]   *Id.* The article references Henry Noble Sherwood, *The Formation of the American Colonization Society,* 2 J. NEGRO HIST. 209 (1917), www.jstor.org/stable/2713765?seq=3#metadata_info_tab_contents, which provides a catalog of deportation efforts and the motivations underlying them.

[870]   Letter, Thomas Jefferson to John Lynch, January 21, 1811. Available at National Archives, *Founders Online,* founders.archives.gov/documents/Jefferson/03-03-02-0243.

complicated the enforcement of Slave Codes and inflated an already threateningly large population. States navigated this challenge in a variety of ways. Many states required freed slaves to leave the state immediately; Arkansas ultimately expelled all of its free Blacks.[871] Tennessee, fearful of masses of free Blacks even outside its borders, went even further: freed slaves were not only required to leave the state, but were deported to Africa, all expenses paid.[872] The Tennessee Colonization Society, founded in 1829, transported 870 ex-slaves to Africa by 1866.[873]

Even by 1854, deportation to Africa was an old idea. In fact, enough slaves had been deported, generally by charity societies, to form a new, independent nation on the west coast of Africa. Liberia, established by the American Colonization Society (ACS) in 1822, became an independent nation in 1847.[874] The ACS sent more than 13,000 emigrants to Liberia before the end of the Civil War, some of them with the support of state funds from Virginia, New Jersey, Maryland, and Massachusetts.[875] Given that Tennessee's law specified "the western coast of Africa" as the destination for its freed slaves,[876] those deportees were likely also headed to Liberia.

The motivations for deportation were not all nefarious. Many people believed that returning slaves to Africa would be best for all concerned. The Union Humane Society, for instance, recommended deportation as necessary for "the amelioration of the Negro race," arguing for the need for "the removal of the Negroes beyond the pale of the white man."[877] Many supporters of deportation felt similarly, arguing that Blacks would never receive justice in the United States and would be happier building their own society in Africa.[878] Even some Blacks believed return to Africa the best solution. One of the early advocates for returning freed slaves to Africa was Paul Cuffee, a Quaker of mixed Black and Native American descent.[879] Marcus Garvey and some other twentieth-century activists attempted to take up the argument of the eighteenth- and nineteenth-century colonizers, with limited success.

---

[871] Lawrence M. Friedman & Grant M. Hayden, American Law: An Introduction 269 (3d ed., 2017).

[872] 1st Sess., 30th G. A., p. 121. The law provided that slaves freed by the courts must be transported to "the western coast of Africa"; transport and supplies for six months were to be furnished by the state. *Slave Laws of Tennessee*, Genealogy Trails, genealogytrails.com/tenn/slavelaws.html (last visited March 1, 2021).

[873] Anita S. Goodstein, *Slavery*, Tenn. Encyclopedia (March 1, 2018), tennesseeencyclopedia.net/entries/slavery/.

[874] Library of Congress, *Colonization*, Exhibition: The African-American Mosaic, www.loc.gov/exhibits/african/afam002.html (last visited March 1, 2021).

[875] *Id.*

[876] Goodstein, *supra* note 873.

[877] Sherwood, *supra* note 869, at 211.

[878] Library of Congress, *supra* note 874.

[879] Library of Congress, *Beginnings of the American Colonization Society*, Exhibition: The African-American Mosaic, www.loc.gov/exhibits/african/afam002.html#obj0 ("Cuffee ... gained support from the British government, free black leaders in the United States, and members of Congress for a plan to take emigrants to the British colony of Sierra Leone. ... In 1816, at his own expense, Captain Cuffee took thirty-eight American blacks to Freetown, Sierra Leone, but his death in 1817 ended further ventures. However, Cuffee had reached a large audience with his pro-colonization arguments and laid the groundwork for later organizations such as the American Colonization Society.")

In all cases, however, the "back to Africa" charge, whether it originated with states anxious to reduce Black populations or solve the "Negro problem" or with Black activists themselves, ignored several base realities. First among them, perhaps, is the diversity of Africa itself and of the Black people who came from that continent. Second, Africa did not represent a home land, in any tangible way, for Black descendants of slaves brought to the United States by force. And finally, "colonizers" (in most cases, simple deportees) sent to Liberia faced brutal conditions for which they were ill-prepared and ill-equipped.

Black people, then, face the charge to "go back where you came from" from a very different place than other "immigrants." Many Black people do not even know "where they came from"; their ancestors were abducted from homelands, their histories erased by generations of slavery. Many immigrants were pushed to come to the United States by economic or political conditions; many Black people, if not most, were brought here forcibly. And, ironically, given the early beginnings of slavery on the North American continent, many Black people have roots in this nation predating those of the people who would banish them elsewhere.

CONDITIONAL CITIZENSHIP

Today's version of "go back where you came from" often has less to do with a literal deportation desire than it does an exodus from legitimate social life. Indeed, "part of what is behind Trump's ... racist quip is the reality that when people yell at someone, 'go back where you came from,' they are not necessarily talking about a physical location, but their place in society."[880] In the generations since Emancipation, Black Americans have been reminded in countless openly hostile ways that they do not belong here, wherever "here" may be. "Sundown towns" had legal or social codes prohibiting Black presence after dark;[881] as recently as 1956, 184 towns had signs at their borders which read, "N—, don't let the sun go down on you in [town name]."[882] These towns were not limited to the South; while they were more common in states bordering the Confederacy, they existed throughout the north and as far west as Oregon.[883] Today, these signs and direct statements that "we don't like your kind around here" have given way to passive-aggressive questioning of a Black person's legitimacy in public space: "Where are you *really* from?"; "You must be new here?"; "Do you have a permit?"; "Do you live in this building?"

The ascension of outspoken Black women like Ayanna Pressley and Ilhan Omar to positions of power creates both a "problem" and a "danger" for the racially fearful.

---

[880]   Pickett & Khabeer, *supra* note 861.
[881]   Margalynne J. Armstrong, *Are We Nearing the End of Impunity for Taking Black Lives?*, 56 SANTA CLARA L. REV. 721, 746–50 (2016); ANDREA S. BYLES, RACE, PLACE, AND SUBURBAN POLICING: TOO CLOSE FOR COMFORT 20, 23–24 (2015). Boyles traces the legacy of sundown towns in pervasive neighborhood-level segregation.
[882]   Armstrong, *supra* note 881, at 747.
[883]   *Id.* at 746.

Claiming that these women have no right to speak about America's problems but can only opine about their "home countries" is yet more barely disguised code for their conditional status as out-of-place quasi-citizens. For Omar, these issues are particularly heightened; her intersectional identity as a Black, Muslim refugee "amplifies the mix of anti-Black racism and xenophobia" so central to the cultural movement defined by the Trump administration.[884] That this racially divisive message was communicated during a heated primary election season and sustained through the 2020 presidential election merely reflected an age-old strategy to rally a certain base around fearful, racist tropes. The only innovation on Trump's part was that "he [had] foregone dog whistles in favour of foghorns."[885] This conditional citizenship extends historically to all marginalized "others" who find themselves newly in positions of political power. As women, as Black and Brown women, as Muslim women, they do not really belong and therefore have no right to criticize the United States. They "should just feel lucky to be here." That continued marginalization is reflected further by the willful ignorance of White politicians occupying their privileged positions of power, as freshman Missouri Representative Cori Bush experienced in her first day on Capitol Hill. Bush, the first Black Congresswoman in Missouri's history, wore a mask bearing the name "Breonna Taylor," the Black emergency medical technician who was shot eight times and killed by Louisville, Kentucky, police during a botched drug raid, while she slept in her apartment. Her killing prompted months of nationwide protests, including violent protests after a grand jury returned just a single indictment of the officers involved, for negligently damaging a neighbor's walls (by shooting through them). According to Bush, several legislative colleagues – all White Republican men – called her Breonna, apparently thinking that was her name.[886]

WHITE POLITICAL SPACE

Few examples of policing Black people's legitimacy in White spaces are as poignant or as achingly obvious as that of the forty-fourth president. It is no coincidence that the presidency of the first Black man in history was dogged by allegations of otherness and illegitimacy. Unsubstantiated conspiracy theories that Barack Obama was born in Kenya and thus ineligible to serve as president swirled throughout both his terms. Unhinged chants of "where is his birth certificate?" prompted Obama to engage the embarrassing charade in 2011 by releasing a long-form birth certificate proving his birth in Hawaii.[887] Riding the coattails of this racist conspiracy

[884] Pickett & Khabeer, *supra* note 861.
[885] *Id.*
[886] Kirsten West Savali, *Republicans Confuse Congresswoman-Elect Cori Bush for Breonna Taylor*, ESSENCE (November 13, 2020), https://www.essence.com/news/republicans-cori-bush-breonna-taylor-mask/.
[887] *See* Dan Pfeiffer, *President Obama's Long Form Birth Certificate*, THE WHITE HOUSE (April 27, 2011), https://obamawhitehouse.archives.gov/blog/2011/04/27/president-obamas-long-form-birth-certificate.

theory, political unknown Orly Taitz received 372,000 votes in her 2010 campaign for California Secretary of State as a single-issue candidate.[888] The issue? "Barack Obama is a Muslim from Kenya who is ineligible to be President of the United States."

Nor is it any coincidence that the person who immediately succeeded President Obama to the White House was the very same person whose political career was launched by the birther movement. A failed businessman with no previous political experience fed the narrative for five years leading up to his own run for the presidency, with tweets aimed directly at delegitimizing and othering the only Black person to ever occupy the ultimate White space:

> "I have no idea if this is bad for him or not, but perhaps it would be – that where it says 'religion,' it might have 'Muslim.' And if you're a Muslim, you don't change your religion, by the way." (March 30, 2011)

> "[If] he wasn't born in this country, which is a real possibility . . . then he has pulled one of the great cons in the history of politics." (April 7, 2011)

> "A lot of people do not think it was an authentic certificate." (May 29, 2012)

> "An 'extremely credible source' has called my office and told me that @BarackObama's birth certificate is a fraud." (August 6, 2012)[889]

And even when Trump entertained the idea that Obama "was perhaps born in this country," he attacked the intelligence of the former *Harvard Law Review* Editor-in-Chief as an unjust recipient of affirmative action: "perhaps . . . he said he was born in Kenya because if you say you were born in Kenya, you got aid and you got into colleges."[890] Whether Trump ever believed this nonsense is beside the point. Its purpose, however, was clear: to feed the White supremacist desire to keep powerful Black people in positions of illegitimacy and weakness. In the physical White neighborhood and the metaphorical White political space, the fearful desire to police the out-of-place "other" remains as strong as ever.

Indeed, as this book was headed to print, the fear animating vitriol aimed at prominent Black figures found its way into discussions about the judiciary. When Supreme Court Justice Stephen Breyer announced his retirement in January 2022, attention turned to President Biden's campaign promise to appoint the first Black woman to the Court. Many critics decried the "identity politics" of such a promise, with some exclaiming that Biden's refusal to consider all qualified candidates inevitably will lead to the appointment of a "lesser black woman" to the bench. Of

---

[888]   *Orly Taitz*, Ballotpedia, https://ballotpedia.org/Orly_Taitz.
[889]   Donald Trump's tweets are no longer available on twitter. These examples are gleaned from a CNN story. Gregory Krieg, *14 of Trump's Most Outrageous "Birther" Claims – Half from After 2011*, CNN Politics (September 16, 2016), https://www.cnn.com/2016/09/09/politics/donald-trump-birther/index.html.
[890]   *Id.*

course, most of these critics failed to acknowledge the "identity politics" driving two centuries' worth of Supreme Court picks, wherein "White" and "male" were all but express prerequisites for the job. 108 of the Court's 115 justices have been White men, and only two justices – Thurgood Marshall and Clarence Thomas – have been Black.

FULL CIRCLE: CAMPAIGNING WHILE BLACK

Shelia Stubbs made history in November 2018 when she became the first Black person to represent Wisconsin's 77th District, which spans both the poorest and wealthiest areas in Madison. Weeks before her victory, though, a police officer approached Stubbs while she was canvassing in her district. The officer was responding to an unidentified man's complaint that Stubbs, who was with her seventy-one-year-old mother and eight-year-old daughter, might be in the neighborhood buying drugs.[891] According to the police report, the man called police on August 7 to complain about a "suspicious vehicle," with Stubbs' daughter and mother inside "waiting for drugs at the local drug house."[892] While Stubbs acknowledged having a cordial and uneventful encounter with the officer in the predominantly White neighborhood, she told reporters, "When you specifically target people of color and call the police, sometimes there's different outcomes."[893] Later, she commented, "I belong where I choose to go. You don't have to like me. You don't even have to respect me. But I have a right to be places."[894]

Aspiring Black politicians are not the only ones singled out for suspicion of invading the White political space; incumbents are equally at risk. Earlier in 2018, incumbent Oregon state legislator Janelle Bynum was forced to defend her presence in a neighborhood after someone called 911. Representative Bynum, a member of the Oregon State House of Representatives, had been knocking on doors and talking to residents for two hours when a county deputy pulled up to her.[895] The deputy explained that someone in the neighborhood called 911 because Bynum appeared to be "casing" the neighborhood, presumably for criminal purposes. Like Stubbs, Representative Bynum thanked the deputy for

[891] Jessie Opoien, *Constituent Called 911, Suspecting Drug Deal, on Dane County Supervisor Shelia Stubbs While She Canvassed for Assembly Seat*, CAP. TIMES (September 19, 2018), https://madison.com/ct/news/local/govt-and-politics/election-matters/constituent-called-911-suspecting-drug-deal-on-dane-county-supervisor-shelia-stubbs-while-she-canvassed/article_65a7dcea-52e0-5ad0-acea-135d10c3defo.html.
[892] *Id.*
[893] *Id.*
[894] Maria Perez, *Constituent Calls Police on Black Candidate Canvassing, Suspected Drug Deal*, NEWSWEEK (September 19, 2018), https://www.newsweek.com/police-called-black-candidate-votes-sheila-stubbs-1129332.
[895] Associated Press, *Black Oregon Lawmaker Says Police Were Called as She Knocked on Doors*, NBC NEWS (July 5, 2018), https://www.nbcnews.com/news/nbcblk/black-oregon-lawmaker-says-police-were-called-she-knocked-doors-n888916.

his courteous behavior but noted that, "when people do things like this, it can be dangerous for people like me."[896]

Less than a month after Representative Stubbs's "campaigning while black" encounter, Broward County Florida Teachers Union Secretary and Lauderdale Lakes City Commission candidate Roosevelt McClary was confronted by half a dozen deputies in unmarked cars, police dogs, and a police helicopter when a White homeowner called police to report the Black canvasser.[897] Video of the encounter captured by McClary showed police officers demanding that McClary sit down on the sidewalk and growing visibly agitated when McClary claimed he was the target of racial discrimination.[898] When McClary demanded to know what evidence existed to justify his detention – in other words, when he exercised his constitutional rights – the encounter turned visibly less cordial.

This aggressive, agitated response to a lawful, constitutionally protected request again reflects the conditional nature of Black citizenship. Not only are Black politicians viewed more skeptically when conducting the on-the-ground work necessary to win elected office, but they are treated less fairly when they defend those actions. When Black citizens object to unnecessary or unlawful police practices, when they assert their constitutional rights, when they call out clear discrimination, they are more likely to be treated disrespectfully, forcefully, violently in return. They are more likely to be handcuffed. To be choked out. To be arrested for "disorderly conduct." Much like Representatives Pressley and Omar are expected to stay silent and feel lucky to be where they are, the Roosevelt McClarys of the world should comply unquestioningly and feel lucky to be alive.

New York State Representative Jesse Hamilton used his political power to challenge this paradigm in 2018, shortly after also being stopped for campaigning while Black.[899] Senator Hamilton was campaigning in Crown Heights, Brooklyn, a rapidly gentrifying neighborhood. A woman who Hamilton said didn't agree with his criticism of President Trump called 911 when Hamilton refused to leave the public street corner. Shortly after being contacted and released by the officers who

---

[896] Cristina Cabrera, *Woman Calls Cops on Black State Rep. Canvassing in Neighborhood*, TPM LIVEWIRE (July 4, 2018), https://talkingpointsmemo.com/livewire/cops-janelle-bynum-black-representative-oregon-campaigning.

[897] Nigel Roberts, *Campaigning While Black: Political Candidate Says He Was Racially Profiled*, NEWS ONE (September 16, 2018), https://newsone.com/3826767/black-candidate-racial-profile-campaigning-florida/; David Smiley, *This Candidate Was Campaigning Door-to-Door. Then the Police Helicopter Came*, MIAMI HERALD (September 14, 2018), https://www.miamiherald.com/news/local/community/broward/article218362015.html.

[898] Video is available at StanceGrounded (@_SJPEACE_), TWITTER (September 19, 2018, 4:31 pm), https://twitter.com/_sjpeace_/status/1042511496658472967.

[899] Kathleen Culliton, *Trump Supporter Calls Cops on Campaigning State Senator*, PATCH (August 10, 2018), patch.com/new-york/prospectheights/trump-supporter-calls-cops-campaigning-state-senator-video; Kathleen Culliton, *Calling 911 On Black People May Be Hate Crime Under Proposed Law*, PATCH (August 15, 2018), patch.com/new-york/prospectheights/calling-911-black-people-may-be-hate-crime-under-proposed-law.

responded to the call, Hamilton introduced legislation to punish people for making racially motivated police reports. According to Hamilton, "It's already a crime to make a false report, we just want to enhance it to send a message that you can't just look at someone going about their ordinary life and call 911."[900]

VOTING IS ACTIVISM

In many ways, the Summer of Racial Reckoning began when George Floyd was murdered on Memorial Day 2020 and ended on July 17 with the passing of civil rights icon and US Representative John Lewis. Congressman Lewis was among the first group of Freedom Riders for racial equality in 1961, the Chairman of the Student Nonviolent Coordinating Committee, a leading member of the Civil Rights Movement, a close confidant of Dr. King, and, at twenty-three, the youngest speaker at the March on Washington.[901] He was arrested dozens of times for his nonviolent, peaceful protests for racial justice and equality, getting into what he famously called "good trouble."

But he is perhaps best known and remembered for leading the brave group of 600 marchers across the Edmund Pettus Bridge in Selma, Alabama, en route to the state capitol to demand that Governor George Wallace put an end to Black voter suppression. Throughout Alabama and the Jim Crow South, Black voter registration applicants were subjected to poll taxes, "moral character" tests, and absurd and impossible literacy tests specifically designed to disenfranchise Black voters.[902] When Lewis and the other marchers reached the end of the bridge, Alabama State Troopers ordered them to disperse. When the marchers stopped to pray, the police discharged tear gas and mounted troopers charged the group, beating them with nightsticks.[903] Lewis's skull was fractured, and he bore scars on his head from "Bloody Sunday" for the rest of his life.

When the video of the incident hit the airwaves, the nation was shocked, and a reluctant President Johnson was spurred into action. By the time Martin Luther King Jr. returned to Edmund Pettus Bridge with 25,000 marchers six weeks later, President Johnson had publicly announced support for what would become the Voting Rights Act of 1965.[904] The Act, widely considered the most effective piece of civil rights legislation ever passed in the United States, secured for racial minorities

---

[900] Madeleine Thompson, *She Called Cops When He Was Campaigning While Black; He Filed a Bill to Criminalize Racially Biased 911 Calls*, CNN (August 20, 2018), https://www.cnn.com/2018/08/20/us/911-call-bill-trnd/index.html.

[901] *See* Katherine Q. Seelye, *John Lewis, Towering Figure of Civil Rights Era, Dies at 80*, N.Y. TIMES (July 17, 2020), https://www.nytimes.com/2020/07/17/us/john-lewis-dead.html; *John Lewis*, BIOGRAPHY (January 12, 2021), https://www.biography.com/political-figure/john-lewis.

[902] Erin Blakemore, *How the U.S. Voting Rights Act Was Won – and Why It's Under Fire Today*, NAT'L GEOGRAPHIC (August 6, 2020), https://www.nationalgeographic.com/history/article/history-voting-rights-act/.

[903] *Id.*

[904] *Id.*

the right to vote protected by the Fourteenth and Fifteenth Amendments.[905] Among other things, it required jurisdictions with a history of racial voter suppression to seek preclearance from the federal Department of Justice for any proposed changes to voting laws or policies.[906]

John Lewis's death in 2020 reminded a nation in the midst of widespread protests seeking an end to the types of racial injustice described in this book that activism is more than marching. It is more than shouting. It is more than sloganeering. It is voting. It is voting as a way to enact meaningful change, such as an end to qualified immunity for murderers. An end to a practice of racially focused stop-and-frisk tactics. And the appointment of judges and justices committed to racial justice and the protection of individual liberties from police interference originally envisioned by the Founders. But it is also voting as a responsibility, for the John Lewises and so many others who gave so much to win that full franchise.

That franchise is at risk, as occupiers of the White political space work to deny Black entrance. The disproportionate impacts of mass incarceration have disenfranchised millions of Black voters in states that deny felons the right to vote, even after they have paid their debt to society. And even in states like Florida, where voters overwhelmingly approved a constitutional amendment to abolish this form of voter suppression, legislatures have erected insurmountable obstacles to re-enfranchisement, such as requiring former felons to pay back thousands of dollars in exorbitant court costs, with interest. Partisan gerrymandering efforts in states like Wisconsin and North Carolina have become so sophisticated that individual voters are targeted for unprincipled redistricting to dilute the votes of "undesirable" citizens, all while the United States Supreme Court sits idly by. And in 2016, Donald Trump's presidential campaign used illegally mined data from Facebook to target 3.5 million Black voters in what it called a "deterrence" group – voters the campaign wanted to keep out of polling places.[907] The campaign targeted false ads at these Black voters to convince them to stay home and supported local jurisdiction efforts to close polling places in predominantly Black communities.[908]

This attempt to wrestle the White political space from Black Americans led many former Obama administration officials, including former Attorney General Eric Holder, to focus their efforts on significant voting reforms, including automatic voter registration and the end of gerrymandering. It is also why NBA players, led by LeBron James and others, threatened to boycott the rest of the 2020 season unless the league enacted meaningful racial justice and equity reforms, starting with

---

[905]   U.S. Dep't of Justice, *The Voting Rights Act of 1965*, HISTORY OF FEDERAL VOTING RIGHTS LAWS (July 28, 2017), https://www.justice.gov/crt/history-federal-voting-rights-laws.

[906]   *Id.*

[907]   Veronica Stracqualursi, *Trump Campaign Microtargeted Black Americans Disproportionally to "Deter" Them from Voting in 2016 Election, Channel 4 Reports*, CNN POLITICS (September 29, 2020), https://www.cnn.com/2020/09/29/politics/trump-2016-campaign-voter-deterrence/index.html.

[908]   *Id.*

opening arenas up to serve as polling places on Election Day.[909] And it is why Barack Obama invoked the old Jim Crow "jelly bean test" when eulogizing John Lewis in July 2020: "We may no longer have to guess the number of jelly beans in a jar in order to cast a ballot. But even as we sit here, there are those in power doing their darndest to discourage people from voting – by closing polling locations, and targeting minorities and students with restrictive ID laws, and attacking our voting rights with surgical precision."[910]

The absurdity of Birdwatching While Black, Barbecuing While Black, and Sleeping While Black should anger us. The tragic murders of Ahmaud Arbery, Breonna Taylor, and George Floyd should shock us. The acquiescence of politicians and judges should motivate us to demand change. And the memory of these lost souls, and of fighters like John Lewis, should obligate us. Obligate us to shout, to march, to occupy. To organize, to advocate, to agitate. And when the time comes, to vote. 2020's Summer of Racial Reckoning can become a catalyst, a turning point in this nation's racial history. Whether it will is up to us.

[909] Shanna McCarriston, *NBA Boycott: LeBron James, Other Stars React to Players' Decision Not to Take Court for Playoff Games*, CBS SPORTS (August 27, 2020), https://www.cbssports.com/nba/news/nba-boycott-lebron-james-other-stars-react-to-players-decision-not-to-take-court-for-playoff-games/. The league and teams have given players much of what they asked for, including offering arenas as polling places; the effort is ongoing. Randi Richardson, "*Up the Ante*": *What Players, NBA Are Doing for Racial Justice*, NBC NEWS (December 29, 2020), https://www.nbcnews.com/news/nbcblk/ante-what-players-nba-are-doing-racial-justice-n1252471.

[910] Minyvonne Burke & Doha Madani, *Obama Gives Passionate Eulogy as John Lewis Honored at Funeral in MLK's Atlanta Church*, NBC NEWS (July 30, 2020), https://www.nbcnews.com/news/us-news/john-lewis-funeral-set-mlk-s-church-atlanta-obama-give-n1235302.

Index

accountability mechanisms, for use of force, 172
Adams, John, 123
Adams v. Williams, 82
Adrine, Ronald B., 53
Alabama v. White, 64, 82
American Legislative Executive Council (ALEC), 95–96
Anderson, Elijah, 3, 24–25
anonymous callers, into 911 call system, under Fourth Amendment, 64, 80–84
antiracism, 6–7, 126, 136. *See also* racism
Arbery, Ahmaud, 3–4, 8, 94–95, 135
Armour, Jody David, 75, 100
Ashcroft v. al-Kidd, 117
attentional bias, 128–30
    among police, 128

Baude, William, 120
"BBQing While Black," 36
Beach, Lindsey, 113
Berry, William, 106–7
better-safe-than-sorry racism, 49–54
bias. *See* implicit bias; racial bias
Biden, Joe, 100
Bilbao, Theodore, 29
birdwatching
    "Birdwatching While Black," 2
    Cooper, C., and, 1–2
        as outsider, race as factor for, 2–3
    as "White space," 3
Birth of a Nation, 18
Birtherism, 27, 187–89
Bivins v. Six Unnamed Agents of Federal Bureau of Narcotics, 115–16
The Black and Brown Faces in America's Wild Places (Edmonson), 2–3
Black bogeyman myth, 21–22
    implicit bias and, 127

Black brute myth
    eugenics and, 18–19
    Mandingo trope, 18
    in popular culture, 18
    social science and, manipulation of, 18–19
Black Codes of Reconstruction, 15–16
    criminal law influenced by, 18
Black Lives Matter movement, 10
"Black spaces"
    enforcement of, 6
    after Fair Housing Act, 11
    gentrification of, 41–44
    policing of, 113
    "White spaces" and, boundaries between, 26
"Black tax," 2
Blake, Jacob, 112
Bland, Sandra, 50
Bonta, Rob, 148
Boutwell, Allen, 28–29
Braasch, Sarah, 46–47
Bratton, Bill, 139
Brennan, William (Justice), 179
Broken Windows theory
    community policing and, 138–39
    critique of, 48
    historical development of, 47–48
    maximum policing and, 138–39
    in New York City, 139
        under Bloomberg, 139
        under Giuliani, 139
    911 call system and, 47–49
    quality of life policing, 47–48
    racial fears and, 47–49
    racism and, 140–41
Brooks, Rayshard, 78
Brown, Andrew, Jr., 161–63, 168–69
Brown, Michael, 50, 112, 173
Bryan, Hazel, 184

Printed in the United States
by Baker & Taylor Publisher Services